Top the IELTS

Opening the Gates
to Top QS-Ranked Universities

Also Published by World Scientific Publishing Co.

Published

Top the TOEFL: Unlocking the Secrets of Ivy League Students
    by Kaiwen Leong & Elaine Leong

Top the IELTS
Opening the Gates to Top QS-Ranked Universities

Dr. Kaiwen Leong
Nanyang Technological University, Singapore

Elaine Leong

NEW JERSEY • LONDON • SINGAPORE • BEIJING • SHANGHAI • HONG KONG • TAIPEI • CHENNAI • TOKYO

Published by

WS Education, an imprint of
World Scientific Publishing Co. Pte. Ltd.
5 Toh Tuck Link, Singapore 596224
USA office: 27 Warren Street, Suite 401-402, Hackensack, NJ 07601
UK office: 57 Shelton Street, Covent Garden, London WC2H 9HE

Library of Congress Cataloging-in-Publication Data
Leong, Kaiwen, 1981– author.
  Top the IELTS : Opening the Gates to Top QS-Ranked Universities / Kaiwen Leong (Nanyang Technological University, Singapore) ; Elaine Leong (Citibank Malaysia, Malaysia).
    pages cm
  ISBN 978-9814689694 (hbk. : alk. paper) -- ISBN 978-9814689700 (pbk. : alk. paper)
  1. Test of English as a Foreign language--Evaluation. 2. English language--Study and teaching--Foreign speakers. 3. English language--Ability testing. I. Leong, Elaine, author. II. Title.
  PE1128.L4533 2016
  428.0076--dc23
                                                                 2015025653

British Library Cataloguing-in-Publication Data
A catalogue record for this book is available from the British Library.

Copyright © 2016 by World Scientific Publishing Co. Pte. Ltd.

All rights reserved. This book, or parts thereof, may not be reproduced in any form or by any means, electronic or mechanical, including photocopying, recording or any information storage and retrieval system now known or to be invented, without written permission from the publisher.

For photocopying of material in this volume, please pay a copying fee through the Copyright Clearance Center, Inc., 222 Rosewood Drive, Danvers, MA 01923, USA. In this case permission to photocopy is not required from the publisher.

In-house Editor: Qi Xiao

Typeset by Stallion Press
Email: enquiries@stallionpress.com

Contents

About the Authors	vii
Top the IELTS	ix
Structure	xi

The Academic Reading Section — 1
Introduction — 2
   1. Speed Reading — 6
   2. Scanning and Matching — 39
   3. Two-Layer Processing — 71
   4. Thinking in Synonyms — 83
   5. True, False or Not Given — 93

Academic Reading Practice Examinations — 105
   Practice Examination 1 — 106
   Practice Examination 2 — 119
   Practice Examination 3 — 133
   Practice Examination 4 — 147
   Practice Examination 5 — 159

The Academic Writing Section — 173
Introduction — 174
   1(a). Drawing a Blueprint — 177
   1(b). Introductions — 199
   1(c). Connecting Paragraphs — 213
   1(d). Concise Conclusions — 253

   2. Tone: Formal Writing — 257
   3(a). Data Analysis Skills: Analytic Vocabulary — 273
   3(b). Data Analysis Skills: Generating Insights — 289
   4(a). Argumentative Skills: Forming a Viewpoint — 301
   4(b). Argumentative Skills: Countering Arguments — 307

Academic Writing Practice Examinations — 317
Practice Examination 1 — 318
   Model Essays for Practice Examination 1 — 319

Contents

Practice Examination 2 — 321
    Model Essays for Practice Examination 2 — 322
Practice Examination 3 — 325
    Model Essays for Practice Examination 3 — 326
Practice Examination 4 — 329
    Model Essays for Practice Examination 4 — 330
Practice Examination 5 — 333
    Model Essays for Practice Examination 5 — 334

Appendix — References for Reading Passages — 337

About the Authors

Kaiwen Leong

Dr. Kaiwen Leong graduated from Boston and Princeton Universities with degrees in Economics and Mathematics. He has a Bachelor of Arts (Economics and Mathematics), a Master of Arts (Economics) and a Master of Arts (Mathematics) from Boston University. From Princeton University, he obtained yet another Master of Arts (Economics) as well as a PhD in Economics. Dr. Leong is also a member of several of the most prestigious American academic societies, including Phi Beta Kappa.

However, beneath Dr. Leong's string of shining successes was a journey of immense challenge. Dr. Leong was kicked out of Junior College four times.

When Dr. Leong began studies at Boston University, he faced yet another challenge. He could not speak nor write English well. But within a short period of time, Dr. Leong developed creative strategies of his own to go from a failing high school dropout who could hardly write an English essay to an Ivy League PhD holder in Economics. Some of these experiences are documented in his bestselling biography *Singapore's Lost Son*, and include improving listening skills, academic writing and speaking. His efforts culminated in being successfully published in academic journals spanning from economics to mathematics and physics.

At Princeton University, Dr. Leong applied the techniques that he had used to overcome life challenges to impart knowledge to his students. In 2010 and 2011, he was awarded the Princeton University Towbes Prize for "Outstanding Teaching."

Today, Dr. Leong is an Assistant Professor of Economics at Nanyang Technological University and an Associate Faculty Member at the Singapore Institute of Management. He is also the co-author of numerous bestselling books, including *Singapore's Lost Son* (Marshall Cavendish Business), *The Ultimate Banker* (Aktive Learning), *The Big Money Books Series* (Marshall Cavendish International) and *Intermediate Economic Theory* (McGraw Hill Education).

Elaine Leong

Elaine Leong graduated *magna cum laude* from Princeton University with a Bachelor's degree in Politics and a Certificate in Creative Writing. She entered

About the Authors

Princeton as a Shelby Davis International Scholar, and was once again conferred a similar honor as Princeton's "Exemplary Davis Scholar." Prior to Princeton, she attended the United World College in Wales.

Elaine has an extensive range of writing experience. She is a three-time recipient of Princeton's award for outstanding work in creative writing. Her creative writing thesis was supervised by literary critic, author, and Pulitzer Prize finalist Edmund White. She has given public readings of her work at Princeton University's Lewis Center for the Arts. She also served as a Fellow at Princeton's Writing Center, where she helped fellow Princeton students improve essays and writing skills. She has published six books with Marshall Cavendish International.

Top the IELTS

Thousands of students take the International English Language Testing System (IELTS) each year, and thousands of students also *retake* the IELTS each year in the hopes of improving their scores.

From our experience, there are three types of test-takers.

The first type hopes that the prior experience of sitting for the IELTS would somehow lend a magical boost. This type of student relies on the notion that IELTS skills are gained by test experience and time alone. They also believe that perhaps they were unlucky the first time, and that they might be luckier the second time round.

The second type relies on rote memorization. Many students who find the English language to be challenging and who do not truly understand it often fall back on pure memorization. They pick up a dictionary and start memorizing words, measuring success by the number of new words they are able to learn each day. Some even go as far as to memorize essays, so that on the day of the IELTS, they can write out model essays word for word without having to generate new content on their own.

Both, unfortunately, are mistaken. Taking a standardized test is not the same as learning how to walk. For some, the strategies and skills required do not come naturally. Many end up applying the same old strategies over and over again, only to face repeated failure. Neither does taking standardized tests rely on luck. Sure, you may have fallen sick on the test date itself, resulting in poor score. But to expect that you can strike the lottery and inexplicably become extra fluent on the test date is akin to expecting cash to start raining down from the sky.

The student who relies on memorization will also find that this method cannot bring them far. After reading numerous practice essays that students have written for the IELTS, we have noted that students often use words in inappropriate contexts. For example, instead of saying that they are "thirsty for knowledge," they used terms such as "glutton for knowledge," which carries negative connotations. These students also often struggle with the reading component, where memorization is of little use since the passages differ with each administration of the IELTS. Memorization may be helpful when it comes to vocabulary questions, but it is ineffective when tackling inferential or categorization questions.

Through this guidebook, we want to nurture a *third* type of student, and that is the student who applies strategies that are tailored specifically to the IELTS. Why? The IELTS is a specific test that tests for specific skills. Knowing what you need to do — and more importantly, *how* to do it — will bring you much further.

Thus, we have developed tried-and-tested strategies for each section of the IELTS. Each strategy comes with exercises that can help you understand how the skills can be applied in the test itself, and also help you gauge whether you have mastered the tactic. We would like to thank Lin Li, previously of the East China University of Political Science and Law in China, for assistance in testing and verifying the strategies as well as exercises in this publication. She is currently pursuing a master's degree at Durham University, United Kingdom.

Structure

This book is designed to systematically tackle problems that most students face, and it follows the structure of our TOEFL guidebook, *Top the TOEFL*. The practice questions are broken down such that students take on questions on a scale of increasing difficulty. Further, students are taught a range of strategies that can be applied during the examination itself.

Each section follows the format below to ensure that students can grasp the content easily:

i. **Simple Steps** — The steps that students need to take for each strategy is boiled down into **Simple Steps**. When reviewing the material, students only need to look at the **Simple Steps** to refresh their memory. This will also serve as "handholds" for students who have trouble reading lengthy English text.

ii. **Elaboration with Examples** — The strategy is then explained in greater detail, and most importantly with examples to illustrate each point. Based on experience teaching hundreds of students English as a second language, a common technique that helps students learn much better is to show concrete examples. More importantly, we show both the correct and incorrect application of the strategies so that students can clearly understand what is "right" and what is "wrong."

iii. **IELTS Trainer** — Lastly, to make sure that students truly understand the material that they have just read, each chapter concludes with progressive exercises. Like a personal trainer at the gym, the **IELTS Trainer** gradually increases the exercises' level of difficulty by dividing them according to **Simple Steps** so that students will know where they stand and where they need to improve. If the student is able to complete all the exercises, this will also provide them with a boost of confidence that they need for the IELTS.

The Academic Reading Section

Introduction

There are 40 questions in the academic reading section, and each correct answer is worth 1 point. You will receive an overall mark out of 40, and this is then translated into a band (1–9) based on a table that is calculated internally. This table may change with each round of tests that is administered, so there is no hard and fast rule, but in general, the points roughly convert as follows:

Score	Band
1	1
2–3	2
4–9	3
10–15	4
16–22	5
23–28	6
29–35	7
36–38	8
39–40	9

The academic reading section may seem daunting, especially given the long and seemingly complicated passages that accompany the questions. In total, you will be given 3 passages, which will add up to between 2,000 and 2,750 words, making that an average of about 660 to 910 words per passage. There is no specific formula for word count, but the passages do get more complex as they progress, meaning that the third passage you encounter will be the most challenging of them all. These passages will also be written in an academic style but will not assume any prior knowledge, and the reader should be able to understand.

Given the facts above, we are here to simplify things for you. In effect, we can condense the 40 questions that you will face into four main categories:

(1) True, False or Not Given?

The IELTS places a twist on the usual just "true or false" type question by adding a third option: "not given." The purpose is to test whether you truly understand the question and by reducing the chances of people getting the question correct out of luck. The percentage chance of selecting the right answer, as it were, is about 33 percent compared to the typical 50 percent.

You will be given a list of statements and asked whether:

a) The statement agrees with the claims of the writer
b) The statement contradicts the claims of the writer
c) It is impossible to say what the writer thinks about this

(2) Multiple Choice Questions (MCQ)

The MCQ is a way of testing your comprehension of questions as well as the passage. In this section, pretty much any type of question can appear, even one that is similar to a "true or false," classification or sentence-completion-type question.

However, regardless of the question-type, the MCQ tests your level of comprehension on two levels:

a) Primary — Can you use direct information from the passage to answer questions?

Examples of Primary questions are as follows:

- What are the main chemical components of chlorine?
- Which licenses must you hold if you want to become a pilot in the United Kingdom?
- Who succeeded the throne after the death of King Henry the VII?

As you can see from the examples above, Primary questions often have a clear-cut answer that can be found directly within the passage. You don't have to do any additional thinking or analysis to arrive at the answer.

b) Secondary — Can you process a piece of direct information, and correctly apply it to answer the question?

Examples of Secondary questions are as follows:

- Which of the following phrases best describes the main aim of Reading Passage 2?
- In the United Kingdom, people probably care more about the weather because

- "Modern" art can be described as …
- In the passage above, the general view of biofuel is …

There are no hard and fast rules about what constitute Secondary questions, but essentially there is typically some ambiguity involved which requires further thought and processing.

It also depends on the answer options provided. Some questions may provide answer options that are very similar to each other. Alternatively, the answer options may not use the same words that were used in the text. For example, instead of "food rations" the answer option may say "food supplies." To answer the question correctly, the student must do an additional layer of processing and understand that "food supplies" bears the same meaning as "food rations."

(3) Classification

In a classification question, you may be given three categories, followed by several answer options. You are supposed to match the answer options to the categories accurately. An example is as follows:

Classify the following as typical of
A. British policy
B. American policy
C. French policy

Write the correct letter, **A, B or C**, in the boxes on your answer sheet:

1. Welcoming talented immigrants and offering these immigrants citizenship
2. Providing free day-care services for working mothers
3. Providing subsidized university tuition fees for European students
4. Requiring employers to provide medical insurance for employees
5. Providing critical language scholarship programs

Classification questions are essentially a test of how quickly you are able to scan the text for the categories given, and subsequently understand each category well enough to provide accurate classifications.

Another type of classification question involves assigning each paragraph the correct heading from a list of given headings. For example, if there are nine paragraphs, you will receive a list of possible headings. This tests your ability to comprehend the text, even if only in general terms.

(4) Subjective Questions

Subjective questions do appear in the IELTS, although you are restricted to providing no more than two or three words for each answer (the word limit will be stated upfront).

These can come in two forms:

a)   Sentence Completion

For this type of question, you will be given a series of statements with certain parts blanked out. You are expected to fill in these blanks by using words from the passage.

b)   Open-Ended Questions

You may be asked a series of open-ended questions about the passage, which are similar to the MCQs, except you do not have any answer options. This is purely to test your comprehension, as complete sentences are not needed.

Despite the four broad categories of questions above, there exist in fact general strategies that can be used to tackle them.

Overview of This Section

We will first cover the universal strategies that can be used for each category, namely how to read quickly and still maintain a high level of comprehension. This is important regardless of which type of question you answer, because the IELTS will inevitably require you to read 2,000–2,750 words in a limited amount of time.

Subsequently, we will introduce some category-specific techniques that you can apply on top of the universal strategies. Combined, these will help you answer questions more accurately.

Specifically, we will cover the following:

1. Speed Reading
2. Scanning and Matching
3. Two-Layer Processing
4. Thinking in Synonyms
5. True, False or Not Given?

1 Speed Reading

Speed reading is an essential skill that every student must have, regardless of the test you are taking. For the IELTS, speed reading is a necessity for the academic reading section, where you will have to digest long and complex articles in a short amount of time.

Many students do not speed read an article before jumping into the questions. Different techniques may work better for different people, but on the whole, jumping straight into the questions may not be a good idea for several reasons:
 a) Attempting a question without understanding the passage at all may cause misinterpretation
 b) By referring to the passage that you do not know at all for an answer, you may become not know where to start

This chapter teaches you how to speed read, specifically in the context of the IELTS. How do you understand the general idea of an article in a short amount of time? How do you pick up the essential points needed to answer the questions correctly? It is the precursor to the next chapter on "Scanning and Matching" — before you can scan and match effectively, you have to roughly know where to look. "Speed Reading" helps you do precisely that.

Simple Steps

1. Read the first line of each paragraph; skip words that you do not know
2. Circle concepts or key nouns, and underline definitions or elaboration
3. Roughly categorize each paragraph as you read each first line

Elaboration with Examples

Step 1: Read the first line of each paragraph; skip words that you do not know

Here's a secret that many won't reveal. An essay is essentially a very long elaboration on a few key points. In reality, the key points can usually be condensed into a few sentences — this is called the "abstract" — the elaboration is usually reserved for those who want to gain a more in-depth understanding of what the text is proposing.

Furthermore, academic writers also have essay structures. Each paragraph serves a purpose. If the essay is well-written, you will be able to gauge its meaning based on the first paragraph alone. In most cases, you will be able to get a good idea of what the paragraph itself is about by zooming in on the first sentence.

Reading the first line of each paragraph does not take up much time, but you would be surprised at how much you can glean from it. We will explore this further using a sample passage:

Through Time and Space: A Perspective on Circulation in Island Southeast Asia

On the fourth of May, 1998, "Macet Total" occurred in Indonesia. The government's announcement that oil subsidies would be drastically reduced caused the lines for fuel, particularly in Jakarta and Surabaya, to be extended through many blocks, causing the traffic to be at a standstill. The underlying tension between circulation and accumulation, particularly accumulation of capital, in President Suharto's New Order had set the stage for Macet Total. The appropriation of capital accumulation has, historically, among the central causes of conflicts, revolts and revolutions throughout the course of history. Hence, that accumulation was one of the tensions that brought about Macet Total should not be too surprising. A more interesting notion in which to examine it is the aspect of circulation.

The concept of circulation can be interpreted as the exchange or interplay of things like goods, relationships, information and so on by means of social or political networking. It is a key idea in attempting to understand island Southeast Asia as a region, as circulation has the potential to induce critical social and political consequences that affect events and outcomes in island Southeast Asia.

Prior to the arrival of colonial powers, Southeast Asia was a region populated by ports run by governments or kingdoms whose main economic activity was international trade. The existence of numerous ports battling it out for trade volume and trade share forced an intense amount of competition and even rivalry. An example of such a rivalry was the rivalry between the Acheh kingdom and the Johor kingdom in the 1500s for control of trade in the Straits of Malacca. What this competition did then was force ports to diversify their goods and to provide more goods that would attract the wealthy merchants from the Arab world, China, India and Europe. It forced ports to look inland in search of new goods. A model of this dynamic is presented by Bennet Bronson in his article, "Exchange at the Upstream and Downstream Ends." Based on this model, the natural enemy of a port, A, is a nearby port, A′, with access to roughly similar inland resources as it. Inland towns are not the natural enemies of A; rather, they are places in which A tries to establish some form of connection. This is where the notion of circulation enters into play. If A is strong or powerful enough, it can simply launch an attack on its inland neighbors.

Yet, Bronson suggests that, in most cases, what A would try to do was to establish some political or colonial tie with its inland neighbors, thereby ensuring a steady stream of trade. Hence, we see that A's focus is simply to establish social relations rather than war. A recognizes the significance of social and political relations to its economic benefits. At places further inland, A might even try to use inter-marriages as a means of establishing trade relations. This form of trade creation through marriage and social networking can also be observed even at the highest levels of hierarchy and at inter-governmental levels. Thus, we see the social and political stakes that arise from circulation. Kingdoms in Southeast Asia would rather establish social and political ties with potential trading partners rather than simply conquer them through force, due to the inherent notion of circulation.

A more contemporary example is the text messaging revolution in the Philippines in the late 1990s and early part of the twenty-first century. This phenomenon can be seen as a form of circulation, whereby due to the low costs of text messaging, a sizable proportion of communication was done through this form. This power was unleashed in 2001, when a large proportion of Philippine society gathered to demand for the resignation of then Philippine President Joseph Estrada, a former movie star. When news of President Estrada's failed impeachment was released, the news spread through text messaging. The constant forwarding of messages generated a creation and recreation of social networks. It all came to a head on those January days in 2001. The idea for the gathering and the dissemination of its whereabouts were spread through forwarded text messages. Had circulation not been an integral part of Philippine culture, it is entirely plausible that this gathering may never have happened. Hence, the concept of circulation, so prevalent in Philippine culture, had a massive impact on the social and political sphere, enabling a multitude of people to band together in opposition of a current political event.

This brings us back to the Macet Total event in Indonesia. This case is particularly fascinating as the streets in Surabaya, for example, were designed to be uni-directional, therefore minimizing the frequency and duration of traffic congestions. Yet, traffic was at a standstill on that May day in 1998. The circulation from this event comes primarily from the then ruling regime under President Suharto. John Sidel suggests that the regime's own tactics in managing or controlling the macet actually facilitated the process and outcome of regime transition. It is in their tactics that circulation is evident. Social networks and business networks that had been established by the Suharto regime enabled businesses that had intimate yet narrowly economic linkages with the regime to accumulate private capital. This is the tension between accumulation and circulation that Sidel believes set the stage for Macet Total. The regime also relied heavily on Chinese entrepreneurs, particularly the ones that they could trust. Remnants of local aristocracies were also incorporated into the business sector of the economy.

By considering circulation, we can observe how and why events unravel as they do and the social and political consequences that are at stake. Given that this has been a consistent theme throughout island Southeast Asia's history, it will, in all likelihood, continue to do so. As such, when we attempt to study or understand the region of island Southeast Asia, we must ensure that the concept of circulation is incorporated. Only then can we begin to gain a more comprehensive and profound insight into its culture, peoples and way of life.

Author: Nicholas Khaw

Let's take a look at how the first line of each paragraph from the sample passage would look like if strung together:

On the fourth of May, 1998, "Macet Total" occurred in Indonesia.

The concept of circulation can be interpreted as the exchange or interplay of things like goods, relationships, information and so on by means of social or political networking.

The Academic Reading Section

> Prior to the arrival of colonial powers, Southeast Asia was a region populated by ports run by governments or kingdoms whose main economic activity was international trade.
>
> Yet, Bronson suggests that, in most cases, what A would try to do was to establish some political or colonial tie with its inland neighbours, thereby ensuring a steady stream of trade.
>
> A more contemporary example is the text messaging revolution in the Philippines in the late 1990s and early part of the twenty-first century.
>
> This brings us back to the Macet Total event in Indonesia.
>
> By considering circulation, we can observe how and why events unravel as they do and the social and political consequences that are at stake.

Skip over the words you don't understand. For example, if you don't understand what Macet Total or Bronson means, then just ignore it for now. Many students make the mistake of pondering over difficult vocabulary or unknown concepts for a long time. It takes up a lot of time and may not help you obtain a better grade, so it is best to make do with what you know. The following steps will help you understand the paragraph better.

Step 2: Circle concepts or key nouns, and underline definitions or elaboration

Performing some form of labeling action often helps the mind to process information better. This also serves the purpose of helping you identify marked-up items more easily when you do "Scanning and Matching" (this will be covered in the next chapter).

For the IELTS, the two items you should focus on are concepts or key nouns, as well as definitions of elaborations. Much of the examination tests your comprehension of concepts (which often come in the form of key nouns). Consider the classification-type questions, and to some extent the "true, false or not given"-type questions as well. More advanced questions, such as subjective questions, may test your ability to understand the overall picture presented within the passage, but even that sort of comprehension begins with understanding the concepts.

Thus, it is imperative that you circle the concepts or key nouns that pop up in the first line. If you see definitions or elaborations on a concept, underline it. Later on, when you need to refer to these concepts, you will be able to do so more easily.

Here's an example. (Note: for illustration purposes, we have put concepts or key nouns in **bold** instead of circling them)

On the fourth of May, 1998, "**Macet Total**" occurred in Indonesia.

The concept of **circulation** can be interpreted as the exchange or interplay of things like goods, relationships, information and so on by means of social or political networking.

Prior to the arrival of colonial powers, **Southeast Asia** was a region populated by ports run by governments or kingdoms whose main economic activity was international trade.

Yet, **Bronson** suggests that, in most cases, what A would try to do was to establish some political or colonial tie with its inland neighbours, thereby ensuring a steady stream of trade.

A more contemporary example is the **text messaging revolution** in the Philippines in the late 1990s and early part of the twenty-first century.

This brings us back to the **Macet Total** event in Indonesia.

By considering **circulation**, we can observe how and why events unravel as they do and the social and political consequences that are at stake.

You can see how this helps. If you come across questions asking about Macet Total, circulation, Southeast Asia, Bronson or the text messaging revolution in the questions, you immediately know where to refer to. More importantly, you know which paragraph is most likely to contain detailed elaboration on that particular concept.

Step 3: Roughly categorize each paragraph as you read each first line

Now what? You've done the first layer of speed reading, which is to categorize and label what you have read in the first line of each paragraph. Now, you need to do a bit more thinking to truly gain a useful understanding of the passage. This can be done by training your mind to categorize each paragraph.

As you will see in the writing section, each paragraph serves a purpose. Understanding the purpose of the paragraph will help you find answers more quickly. For example, if a particular MCQ-type question asks about **what** the concept of circulation is, you know that you should refer to the second paragraph. If the question asks **why** the concept of circulation is important, you can refer to the last paragraph.

How did we arrive at that conclusion so quickly? We did it simply by categorizing as we read. When categorizing, adhere to the following tips:

a) Use question words like **who, what, why, when** and **how** when categorizing paragraphs. This is because the questions are phrased using these key question words. If you use question words to categorize the paragraphs, you will be better able to match them to the questions later on.

b) Use action words such as **describes, explains, compares**. The differences between these action words are as follows:

- Describes — provides a definition
- Explains — gives reasons or factors for why something happened
- Compares — places two items side by side, and presents a comparison

Let's look at an example:

No	First line of the paragraph	Categorization
1	On the fourth of May, 1998, "**Macet Total**" occurred in Indonesia.	Describes what Macet Total is
2	The concept of **circulation** can be interpreted as the exchange or interplay of things like goods, relationships, information and so on by means of social or political networking.	Describes what circulation is
3	Prior to the arrival of colonial powers, **Southeast Asia** was a region populated by ports run by governments or kingdoms whose main economic activity was international trade.	Describes how Southeast was prior to the arrival of colonial powers
4	Yet, **Bronson** suggests that, in most cases, what A would try to do was to establish some political or colonial tie with its inland neighbors, thereby ensuring a steady stream of trade.	Explains what "A" would do

5	A more contemporary example is the **text messaging revolution** in the Philippines in the late 1990s and early part of the twenty-first century.	Describes what the text messaging revolution is
6	This brings us back to the **Macet Total** event in Indonesia.	Describes what Macet Total is
7	By considering **circulation**, we can observe how and why events unravel as they do and the social and political consequences that are at stake.	Explains why circulation is important

In short, by taking a few minutes to complete this exercise, you have a general idea of the overall passage structure:

- The concept of circulation has been defined and its importance has been explained
- Examples used to support the argument include Macet Total and the text messaging revolution
- History of Southeast Asia described
- Ideas from other scholars cited included those from Bronson

That's good enough for a general sense of what the passage is about. Before we move to the next strategy, which is "Scanning and Matching," try applying the speed reading technique in the ***IELTS Trainer*** section.

IELTS Trainer

Passage 1:

Public and Private Management Practices

Management style is an increasingly important area in the study of management. There has been much debate concerning the differences between management styles in the public and the private sectors. Managers, whether public or private, play an important role in the continuation of society as we see it. Private and public sector managers both shape the world and the environment that we live in with the decisions they take on a daily basis — sometimes they make or are blamed for mistakes which may not have been their doing but fall within their oversight. There has been much literature written in modern times about the differences between the approaches to management taken by public and private sector managers. Most of the arguments put forward revolves around which approach is more effective. Recently there have been many calls for public sector management to adopt and implement private sector style management in the public sector in order to deliver better services at a more cost-effective level.

To determine whether public sector and private sector management can be directly compared, consider two articles written on this topic: one by Michael A. Murray published in 1975 in the *Public Administration Review* and another by George A. Boyne published in 2002 in the *Journal of Management Studies*. Murray states that in the past two generations scholars and practitioners have begun to realize that management can be viewed as a generic process whereas historically in America the view was that private sector management and public sector management require two separate approaches. He goes on to further state that many new scholarly articles have been published and more significantly new management schools are being founded based on the assumption that both public and private management have many similarities. He does, however, caution that the shifting in attitudes towards management, from one where private and public sector management are two separate entities to one where there are significant overlaps in the application of management in any institutional setting, has not progressed very quickly due to mutual distrust between both public sector and private sector management practitioners and entrenched interest from those who are threatened by the shift in attitudes such as free standing schools of business and schools of public administration.

On the other hand, Boyne argues that whereas others have reasoned that there are significant differences between public sector management and private sector management in important areas, these allegations have not been backed up by empirical evidence. Therefore, the notion that public management can implement certain practices from private management should be given some thought until it can be proven empirically whether or not public and private management are significantly different.

When looking at these arguments, it can be seen that while both authors are looking at the differences between public sector management and private sector management the purposes of their articles differ. Murray hopes to prove that there are more similarities between public sector management and private sector management than there are differences, while Boyne is seeking to test whether or not the similarities between public sector management and private sector management are limited to the unimportant aspects or whether they also incorporate the important aspects and thus make the case for the implementation of private sector management policies in the public sector.

Looking at how the arguments are dissimilar, it could be possible to hypothesize that the articles differ in their arguments perhaps due to the time period in which the articles were written. Murray was writing his article in 1975 when, presumably, the idea that both public and private sector management had a lot in common was just gaining traction. Whereas Boyne wrote his article in 2002 when the subject of the similarities between public sector and private sector management has been more thoroughly explored via other methods. Thus, Boyne seeks to prove or disprove the notion of similarities between the public sector and the private and the feasibility of the adoption of private sector management practices in public sector management through the use of empirical evidence.

Given the differences in when the two articles were written and published, another factor to consider is the shape of the public and private management landscape at the time the authors were writing. The early decades of the twentieth century saw the "reform movement" in the United States where municipal governments in that country emphasized the benefits of business-like behavior — a similar "corporate revolution" where local governments in the United Kingdom became more interested in private sector management practices which were popular with large companies only in the 1970s.

From these examples we can see that insofar as the adoption of private management practices into public management goes, the process and ideas developed earlier in the United States than in the United Kingdom, which could have influenced the arguments that are raised by the articles. Murray states that the idea that both public and private management have more in common than they have differences has been around for two generations while Boyne states that the central element of the New Public Management Program is the adoption of managerial processes and behaviors from the private sectors into the public sector. The latter also states that "the adoption of private sector

The Academic Reading Section

models had been viewed with much scepticism in the literatures on public administration and public management." Boyne's view can be linked with Murray's statement on resistance from both established public and private management sector policies on integrating due to mutual distrust. Furthermore the decision to adopt private sector management practices into public sector management by the New Public Management Program could be influenced by the results shown by the "reform movement," which was implemented in the United States during the early decades of the twentieth century.

Author: Ariff Hassan

Step 1:

Step 2:

Step 3:

No	First line of the paragraph	Categorization
1		
2		
3		
4		
5		
6		
7		

Passage 2:

Indiana Jones and the Grain of Salt: Public Portrayals of Archaeology

In 1981, a film entitled *The Raiders of the Lost Ark* was released, becoming an instant hit, grossing over $384 million worldwide from its initial theatrical release. This movie, starring the popular Harrison Ford, thrust the field of archaeology into mainstream popular culture. Since then, among all academic fields, the field of archaeology has become the most featured and the most popular in mainstream culture, rivaled, perhaps, only by paleontology. Yet, it is unsurprising that most casual moviegoers would not be interested in what the actual field of archaeology actually entails, being fascinated only by the sensational and the romantic aspects of the field. This therefore begs the question; how much of actual archaeological methods and practices is accurately showcased? Are the archaeological sites and discoveries accurately displayed or are these issues given a more sensationalist interpretation so as to cater to popular mainstream culture? To answer these questions, let us explore the case study of the popular Indiana Jones film, *Indiana Jones and the Last Crusade*, focusing on the movie's portrayal of the archaeological site of Petra.

The actual exact age of the Petra monument is impossible to determine. As noted in Joukowsky (2002), the stratigraphy of the site is difficult to chart as many changes, both geological and manmade, have caused several periods of "reconstruction and reuse" to the buildings. Kenyon, Musil and Hall (1924) attempt to give a rough estimate as to when the Petra buildings were built, placing the estimate at several centuries B.C. They conjecture that there may even have been cave dwellers or buriers even before the city was created. The geographic location of Petra is well-described in the literature. The culture of Petra is also clearly described by Joukowsky and Basile (2004). They state that the Great Temple, the primary feature of Petra in *Indiana Jones and the Last Crusade*, was a center of Nabataean life, complemented by extremely intricate art and architecture within the Nabatean culture. Indeed, this view is supported by Zeitler (1993), who states that Nabataean types of pottery were present as late as the fourth century A.D. Later on, the site was also influenced by Egyptian and Graeco-Roman designs as documented by Kennedy (1926).

Perhaps the most obvious discrepancy between the film's portrayal of Petra and Petra itself is the location of Petra. Petra is located in modern-day

Jordan whereas in the movie, the monument was said to be located in the Republic of Hatay, a province of Turkey. In the movie, the Nazi forces were shown to request permission from the Ruler of Hatay to explore the site and to extract artifacts from the site. As a corollary to this point, the site was said to be located near the city of Alexandretta or modern-day Iskenderiun, which is again located in Turkey. Another aspect of the Petra site in which the movie differs is the notion of the site being a Christian monument above all else. In the movie, the site is said to be the storage place for the Holy Grail and was thus designed by the Crusades. The Lion's heads statues depicted in the movie are also inconsistent with the actual site. As noted in Joukowsky and Basile (2004), the strongest influence on the site comes from the Nabatean culture. Thus, the movie's portrayal of the site as purely Christian is flawed. As an extrapolation of the Christianity aspect of the site, as per the film, this would mean that the site was constructed during the Crusades wars. Yet, there is strong evidence to support the notion that the origin of the site begun a few centuries B.C.

It is important to keep in mind that the film is a work of fiction and not everything portrayed in the film is necessarily accurate or exact. Yet, this might cause some flawed perceptions in the public eye regarding the field of archaeology. In the film, archaeology is deliberately sensationalized and romanticized, understandably so. It depicts, inaccurately, archaeologists as being treasure hunters rather than scientists. The methodology of archaeology in the film is to dig graves and recover legendary artifacts rather than applying a systematic method of excavation in order to retrieve artifacts. While Indiana Jones insists on artifacts being restored for the purpose of museum display, representative of professional archaeologists in general, his methods do not fall in line with the conventional methods of professional archaeology. In the movies, there is no real sense of ownership with regards to the artifacts; the basis of ownership simply goes by whoever steals the artifact, keeps the artifact. Of course, this is a far stretch from what the discipline of archaeology actually entails.

What these discrepancies do is alter the public perception of archaeology and archaeologists. Instead of being displayed as a science of strict discipline and methodology, archaeology is portrayed as a field of sensational treasure hunts and romantic adventures. Thus, the public gets the flawed idea that archaeology is purely adventure and excitement, disregarding the time spent in libraries and laboratories doing research. Granted, the purpose of films is to make as much profit as possible and, thus, providing an accurate view of the subjects might not necessarily be on top of their list of priorities. As such, mainstream portrayals of archaeology must be taken with a grain of salt. If we can do that, then we can continue enjoying films such as the Indiana Jones series while understanding that there exist significant discrepancies between real archaeology and mainstream culture "archaeology."

Author: Nicholas Khaw

Step 1:

Step 2:

Step 3:

No	First line of the paragraph	Categorization
1		
2		
3		
4		
5		

Passage 3:

Body and Paradigm: Internalizing Cultures Externally

We embody our habits. "Body language" is what we unconsciously communicate to people when we speak to them. All the nuances of motion, from the arch of our eyebrows to the curve of our smiles, are the result of an idea, a state of mind which we are in. These ideas may be fleeting emotions, such as the depressed hunch of a student who realizes that he has an untouched writing seminar essay revision due in three hours, or they may also be more permanent embodiments of our surroundings, such as the gait of a person who is adept at capoeira, a Brazilian martial art and dance.

It is crucial to acknowledge that it is an idea that causes a motion. The actor moves with a purpose — his moves are largely subconscious, his actions are to achieve a goal. As an observer, the audience tries to interpret the performer's actions to understand the idea that he is trying to convey. However, the audience does not have direct access to the actor's mind — the actor's idea has to pass through the medium of physical conveyance to the audience. This means that the actor cannot be assured that his idea will be reproduced faithfully in his audience's minds, for it is the action that they are witnessing, not the idea. The significance of an action to the actor might be different to an observer, especially if one compares different cultures. A "thumbs-up" sign, which most people in America would interpret as "good job," is actually the American equivalent of sticking up one's third finger in places such as Greece, Russia and South Italy. Therefore, there is a certain degree of *interpretation* that is taking place when the audience watches the actor. The actor moves his body to express his intended idea, but the audience interprets meaning from the actor's actions *according to their own paradigms*. Hence, there is a disparity between the actor's translation of the (cultural) ideas into his actions and the interpretation of his actions into ideas by his audience. For daily interactions of people within the same cultures, this usually does not pose much of a problem, because both the actor and the audience come from similar cultural backgrounds. But when we deal with different cultures and paradigms, then the risk of misinterpretation becomes higher.

This is where the ethnographer comes in. He acknowledges this disparity, and tries to resolve it by trying to mimic the actions of the performer in order to better comprehend the original idea behind the actions. Essentially, the ethnographer, as the audience, tries to be the actor to overcome the barrier that physical communication poses to the conveyance of ideas.

However, does ethnographic analysis really give a clearer view of the idea behind the actions of a performer? Although ethnographers might claim to be able to truly access the underlying ideas of a culture by mimicking the actions of the people in that culture, the experience of that culture cannot give the ethnographer a "true" sense of the culture's essence. This is because the ethnographer himself is affected by his own paradigms and consequently interprets the experience of his actions according to his own viewpoint. However, this does not mean that ethnography is useless. Whereas the normal observer is only able to see the actor's actions, the ethnographer is privy to additional tactile information, which contributes to his interpretation of the culture. He combines a personal viewpoint with the experience gleaned from corporeal knowledge to create a modified and individualistic paradigm of a culture. Therefore, by looking at how ethnographers experience a culture internally, we can see how the view of culture that is presented to us is not actually an actual re-presentation of culture, but rather a richer re-interpretation of that culture. This is crucial because it is necessary to realize the existence, benefits and flaws of such re-interpretations.

Author: Jee Ian Tam

Step 1:

Step 2:

Step 3:

The Academic Reading Section

No	First line of the paragraph	Categorization
1		
2		
3		
4		

Passage 4:

Can Anthropologists Speak on Behalf of the People They Study?

Anthropology is known as the discipline that specializes in the study of people and culture, and this has been proven true on most levels. However, in social anthropology the question if anthropologists are able to speak on behalf of those communities they have worked with is a situational one. In some situations where the people studied face a difficult situation where they are unable to have a voice in a rigid social system, experience significant social and cultural change or otherwise are subject to strongly polarized opinions and influences, the work and findings of anthropologists can be appropriate to help bring about more equalized social change, hopefully to benefit the community that has been studied. On the other hand, ethnography can also be dangerous as the anthropologist may not present an accurate description or analysis of the people studied.

Whilst anthropological fieldwork often involves the anthropologist becoming integrated with the community being studied, this is often temporary and incomplete. Moreover, anthropologists always carry their own cultural values with them and if these values are imposed on their observations of the people they study in fieldwork, this paves the way to ethnocentrism and potentially biased reports. Our dualistic culture makes us think of nature and culture as separate, if not opposing, components that make society what it is. This is an important thing to remember, as anthropologists are fundamentally members of one cultural group who attempt to study people from another cultural group.

There is also a danger of assuming too much when it comes to unravelling the significance of culture-specific concepts in anthropology and this runs in both directions. Universalists like Levi-Strauss (1969) assume that common features across human cultures can be attributed to some social functioning based on biology or nature. Relativists in their efforts to describe and interpret their findings in ethnographic fieldwork may end up missing the bigger picture or the deeper meaning behind what they observe. Geertz (1993) in his highly interpretative essay on Balinese cockfights seems to have skimmed over the larger social background in favor of focusing on contextualizing the cockfight in Balinese society.

In fact, to be better equipped to study and perhaps speak for other cultures, anthropologists will have to reconsider this whole nature–culture debate that divides them into opposing camps. Either side may be good at finding common ground between cultures or highlighting uniqueness and emphasizing cultural contexts, but neither approach is a good way to gain a better understanding of how human societies work.

As a good example of how our dualistic mindset can impede anthropologists from understanding a particular culture's cosmology in the same way a local person would, Strathern (1980) writes about the Hagen having little to no distinction between nature and culture in their cosmology, yet she attempts to draw parallels to a dualistic model, particularly in agriculture and gender roles where the *mbo–rømi* difference is shown as parallel to male–female duality depending on the situation. This is a common feature of many ethnographies focusing on cosmology. Another example that comes to mind is Howell's (1996) paper on the Chewong of Malaysia, where she indicates Chewong animism as having no nature–culture boundary but a boundary between forest and non-forest cultures and environments. Anthropologists may be able to understand cosmologies in a way that makes sense to them, but such understanding is drawn from forming links to perceived similarities or differences to our own cultural background.

As far as social anthropology is concerned, whether anthropologists can speak on behalf of those they study is likely to remain a debatable topic at best. The legacy of dualism and the extremeness of both the universalist and relativist approaches to anthropology make this conundrum somewhat harder to work out as well. That being said, although anthropologists may never become fully integrated into the societies they study, this brings valuable insights and perspectives on many aspects of that community's social life ignored by

The Academic Reading Section

locals. Such an outsider's perspective is useful for analysis, for asking all sorts of questions that contribute not only to detailed ethnographical works, but also to the formation of future anthropological theory. If such future theories manage to bypass the nature–culture duality that can limit anthropologists, this can bring forth greater possibilities for anthropology as a broad discipline in a post-modern situation where boundaries and dichotomies are getting increasingly blurred. Future anthropologists may find themselves having to speak for peoples and communities more often, when it comes to important matters and interdisciplinary efforts, and hopefully this discipline will prove valuable to human development in the long run.

Author: Shuen-Yi Long

Step 1:

Step 2:

Step 3:

No	First line of the paragraph	Categorization
1		
2		
3		
4		
5		
6		

Passage 5:

Piecemeal Integration in the European Union:
The Cases of Norway and Switzerland

In the eyes of many observers, the Eurozone crisis has severely weakened the European Union. However, despite widespread pessimism and skepticism about the European Union, it has certainly not brought the process of European integration to a halt. The ongoing political crisis in Ukraine that was sparked by President Yanukovych's apparent refusal to sign an association agreement with Brussels is perhaps the clearest reminder of the attractive power that the European Union still exerts on many peoples and governments outside of the 28-member union.

The road to membership is far from straightforward. As a basic precondition, states must meet the so-called "Copenhagen criteria" to be considered viable candidates. They must not only have "stable institutions guaranteeing democracy, the rule of law, [and] human rights," but they must also have "a functioning market economy." Candidates should also demonstrate "the ability to take on ... the obligations of membership." The negotiation process often takes years, and prospective candidates are required to make significant adjustments to domestic laws and institutions to ensure that they are brought in line with existing EU legislation, also known as the *acquis*. The recent experience of Croatia suffices to show just how rigorous and intrusive this process can be. As part of the negotiation process, Zagreb was asked to reform everything from their judicial system to regulations on the size of chicken cages. No state would willingly enter and undergo this process without an exceptionally strong and unwavering commitment to join the EU. The historic "Eastern Enlargement" in 2004, followed by the accession of Romania and Bulgaria in 2007 and most recently Croatia in 2013, is surely a sign that the project of European integration is not about to come shuddering to a halt. Iceland, Montenegro and Turkey have also begun negotiations with the European Commission in the hopes that they too may join the EU.

In light of the above, the decision of two Western European countries — Norway and Switzerland — to stay outside of the EU is especially puzzling. Many often assume that Norway and Switzerland are EU member states until they discover otherwise, given that both have highly developed market economies and strong, stable democratic institutions. Both are among the richest countries in the world. If Norway and Switzerland were to make the decision to become a member state, they would not have to experience the political and economic overhaul that Eastern European states had to undergo in dismantling the legacies of communist authoritarianism. The accession process would surely be nowhere near as difficult as it was for many of the post-communist countries.

It is not for lack of trying that Norway and Switzerland remain non-member states. A key prerequisite for EU membership is that states "[have] the consent of their citizens" in joining the political and economic union. It is precisely this condition that both Oslo and Bern have previously tried and failed to meet. Norway has a history of rejecting deep involvement in the project of European integration. In 1972, "53.5% percent [of the population] voted no to membership in the European Community" in a national referendum. A little over twenty years later, "52.2% of ... voters rejected membership in the European Union." As noted by Pettersen, Jenssen and Listhaug, "Norway remains the only country which has declined membership in the [EU] by a popular vote ... for a second time."

Nevertheless, the Norwegian and Swiss population's decision to refrain from formal EU membership demands an explanation. The preservation of national sovereignty, a tendency deeply rooted in Norwegian history, figured prominently in public debates leading up to the 1994 referendum on EU membership. Concern for sovereignty and democracy was cited by 26.1% of respondents as a reason for opposing EU membership, a proportion over twice as high as the next most frequently cited reason.

Similarly, the Swiss population's rejection of the EEA in December 1992 was also largely due to concerns about national sovereignty and democracy. A May 1992 survey indicated that "a majority of citizens was ready to endorse the EEA agreement." However, the Swiss government proved unable to project a strong message of support for EEA membership. For instance, "two out of seven ministers repeatedly [expressed] their doubts about the EEA" in the period leading up to the referendum. Those opposed to the treaty were able to dominate the public discourse by "[dramatizing] the debate with emotional arguments about the loss of sovereignty and neutrality, the decline of direct democracy, [and] the threat of massive immigration." As in Norway, this argument proved to be persuasive. "The loss of sovereignty" was found to be one of the "main concerns of the voters" in the 1992 referendum.

Although the Norwegian and Swiss electorate both rejected deeper involvement in European integration largely due to concerns about the loss of sovereignty, this has not prevented them from building closer ties to Europe. It was estimated in 2012 that Norway had adopted "about three quarters of [EU] legislation ... into national law as of 2011." Although Norway cannot vote on EU legislation, it has the right to actively "participate ... in the preparatory stage and implementation of new regulations and directives."

Switzerland has also taken steps to better align itself with the European Union. In addition to actively adopting EU law into national law, Switzerland has signed a large number of bilateral treaties with the EU. These treaties cover a wide range of issue areas. For example, the 2010 treaty relates to "education, vocational training and youth," whereas a package of treaties signed in 1999 address areas such as "agriculture, overland transport, civil aviation, [and] research."

Norway and Switzerland have both sought to draw closer to Europe in ways that do not run counter to their publics' desire to retain national sovereignty. However, it is questionable, in light of ongoing trends, whether integration with Europe on their own terms is a sustainable approach. As the EU seeks to centralize the regulation of more cross-national issues, domestic actors in non-member states will face considerable difficulties, creating political pressure to more clearly define the country's relationship to European institutions. Norway, which acts on the legal basis of the EEA agreement, may be able to better absorb and influence, albeit to a limited degree, the evolution of EU laws. However, if the regulatory boundary of the EU sharpens further, both Norway and Switzerland are likely to face difficulties in trying to reap the benefits of ties with the EU market while avoiding formal membership.

Author: Raymond Ha

The Academic Reading Section

Step 1:

Step 2:

Step 3:

No	First line of the paragraph	Categorization
1		
2		
3		
4		
5		
6		
7		
8		
9		

Answers:

1.
Step 1:
Management style is an increasingly important area in the study of management.

To determine whether public sector and private sector management can be directly compared, consider two articles written on this topic: one by Michael A. Murray published in 1975 in the *Public Administration Review* and another by George A. Boyne published in 2002 in the *Journal of Management Studies*.

On the other hand, Boyne argues that whereas others have reasoned that there are significant differences between public sector management and private sector management in important areas, these allegations have not been backed up by empirical evidence.

When looking at these arguments it can be seen that while both authors are looking at the differences between public sector management and private sector management the purposes of their articles differ.

Looking at how the arguments are dissimilar, it could be possible to hypothesize that the articles differ in their arguments perhaps due to the time period in which the articles were written.

Given the difference in when the two articles were written and published another factor to consider is the shape of the public and private management landscape at the time the authors were writing.

From these examples we can see that insofar as the adoption of private management practices into public management goes, the process and ideas developed earlier in the United States than in the United Kingdom, which could have influenced the arguments that are raised by the different articles.

Step 2:
Management style is an <u>increasingly important area in the study of management</u>.

To <u>determine whether public sector and private sector management can be directly compared</u>, consider two articles written on this topic: one by **Michael A. Murray published in 1975 in the** *Public Administration Review* and another by **George A. Boyne published in 2002 in the** *Journal of Management Studies*.

On the other hand, **Boyne** argues that whereas <u>others have reasoned that there are significant differences between public sector management and private sector management</u> in important areas, <u>these allegations have not been backed up by empirical evidence</u>.

When looking at these arguments it can be seen that while **both authors** are <u>looking at the differences between public sector management and private sector management the purpose of their articles differ</u>.

Looking at how the **arguments** are dissimilar, it could be possible to hypothesize that the articles <u>differ in their arguments perhaps due to the time period in which the articles were written.</u>

Given the difference in when the two articles were written and published **another factor to consider** is <u>the shape of the public and private management landscape at the time the authors were writing.</u>

From these examples we can see that insofar as **the adoption of private management practices into public management** goes, the <u>process and ideas</u>

The Academic Reading Section

developed earlier in the United States than in the United Kingdom, which could have influenced the arguments that are raised by the different articles.

Step 3:

No	First line of the paragraph	Categorization
1	**Management style** is an <u>increasingly important area in the study of management.</u>	Explains that management style is becoming an important topic
2	To <u>determine whether public sector and private sector management can be directly compared,</u> consider two articles written on this topic: one by **Michael A. Murray published in 1975 in the *Public Administration Review*** and another by **George A. Boyne published in 2002 in the *Journal of Management Studies*.**	Compares public and private sector management based on two articles
3	On the other hand, **Boyne** argues that whereas <u>others have reasoned that there are significant differences between public sector management and private sector management</u> in important areas, <u>these allegations have not been backed up by empirical evidence.</u>	Explains why there is a weakness that Boyne has observed in the argument that there are significant differences between public and private sector management
4	When looking at these arguments it can be seen that while **both authors** are <u>looking at the differences between public sector management and private sector management the purpose of their articles differ.</u>	Explains that the two authors have different purposes
5	Looking at how the **arguments** are dissimilar, it could be possible to hypothesize that the articles <u>differ in their arguments perhaps due to the time period in which the articles were written.</u>	Explains why the authors have different arguments
6	Given the difference in when the two articles were written and published **another factor to consider** is <u>the shape of the public and private management landscape at the time the authors were writing.</u>	Explains a second reason as to why the authors have different arguments

| 7 | From these examples we can see that insofar as **the adoption of private management practices into public management** goes, the <u>process and ideas developed earlier in the United States than in the United Kingdom, which could have influenced the arguments that are raised by the different articles.</u> | Explains a third reason as to why the authors' arguments are different |

2.
Step 1:
In 1981, a film entitled *The Raiders of the Lost Ark* was released, becoming an instant hit, grossing over $384 million worldwide from its initial theatrical release.

The actual exact age of the Petra monument is impossible to determine.

Perhaps the most obvious discrepancy between the film's portrayal of Petra and Petra itself is the location of Petra.

It is important to keep in mind that the film is a work of fiction and not everything portrayed in the film is necessarily accurate or exact.

What these discrepancies do is alter the public perception of archaeology and archaeologists.

Step 2:
In <u>1981</u>, a <u>film</u> entitled ***The Raiders of the Lost Ark*** <u>was released</u>, <u>becoming an instant hit</u>, <u>grossing over $384 million worldwide from its initial theatrical release.</u>

The <u>actual exact age</u> of the **Petra monument** is <u>impossible to determine.</u>

Perhaps <u>the most obvious discrepancy between the</u> <u>film's</u> **portrayal of Petra and Petra** itself is the <u>location of Petra.</u>

It is important to <u>keep in mind</u> that the **film** is <u>a work of fiction</u> and <u>not everything portrayed in the film is necessarily accurate or exact.</u>

What these **discrepancies** do is <u>alter the public perception of archaeology and archaeologists.</u>

The Academic Reading Section

Step 3:

No	First line of the paragraph	Categorization
1	In <u>1981</u>, a <u>film</u> entitled **The Raiders of the Lost Ark** <u>was released, becoming an instant hit, grossing over $384 million worldwide from its initial theatrical release.</u>	Describes what *The Raiders of the Lost Ark* is
2	The <u>actual exact age</u> of the **Petra monument** is <u>impossible to determine.</u>	Explains that we do not know the age of the Petra monument
3	Perhaps <u>the most obvious discrepancy between the</u> film's **portrayal of Petra and Petra** itself is the <u>location of Petra.</u>	Explains the biggest difference between the film's portrayal of Petra and Petra itself
4	It is important to <u>keep in mind</u> that the **film** is <u>a work of fiction</u> and <u>not everything portrayed in the film is necessarily accurate or exact.</u>	Reminds the reader that the film is not factual
5	What these **discrepancies** do is <u>alter the public perception of archaeology and archaeologists.</u>	Explains the consequences of these discrepancies

3.
Step 1:
We embody our habits.
    It is crucial to acknowledge that it is an idea that causes a motion.
    This is where the ethnographer comes in.
    However, does ethnographic analysis really give a clearer view of the idea behind the actions of a performer?

Step 2:
We <u>embody</u> our **habits.**
    It is <u>crucial to acknowledge</u> that it is an **idea** that <u>causes a motion.</u>
    This is <u>where</u> the **ethnographer** <u>comes in.</u>
    However, does **ethnographic analysis** really <u>give a clearer view of the idea behind the actions of a performer?</u>

Step 3:

No	First line of the paragraph	Categorization
1	We <u>embody</u> our **habits**.	Describes the relationship between us and our habits
2	It is <u>crucial to acknowledge</u> that it is an **idea** that <u>causes a motion.</u>	Describes the link between ideas and motion
3	This is <u>where</u> the **ethnographer** <u>comes in.</u>	Explains why the ethnographer is important
4	However, does **ethnographic analysis** really <u>give a clearer view of the idea behind the actions of a performer?</u>	Questions whether ethnographic analysis can help us understand the actions of a performer

4.

Step 1:

Anthropology is known as the discipline that specializes in the study of people and culture, and this has been proven true on most levels.

Whilst anthropological fieldwork often involves the anthropologist becoming integrated with the community being studied, this is often temporary and incomplete.

There is also a danger of assuming too much when it comes to unravelling the significance of culture-specific concepts in anthropology and this runs in both directions.

In fact, to be better equipped to study and perhaps speak for other cultures, anthropologists will have to reconsider this whole nature–culture debate that divides them into opposing camps.

As a good example of how our dualistic mindset can impede anthropologists from understanding a particular culture's cosmology in the same way a local person would, Strathern (1980) writes about the Hagen having little to no distinction between nature and culture in their cosmology, yet she attempts to draw parallels to a dualistic model, particularly in agriculture and gender roles where the *mbo–rømi* difference is shown as parallel to male–female duality depending on the situation.

As far as social anthropology is concerned, whether anthropologists can speak on behalf of those they study is likely to remain a debatable topic at best.

The Academic Reading Section

Step 2:

Anthropology is known as <u>the discipline that specializes in the study of people and culture,</u> and this has <u>been proven true on most levels.</u>

Whilst **anthropological fieldwork** often <u>involves the anthropologist becoming integrated with the community being studied,</u> this is often <u>temporary and incomplete.</u>

There is also <u>a danger of assuming too much</u> when it comes to <u>unravelling the significance of</u> **culture-specific concepts** in **anthropology** and this <u>runs in both directions.</u>

In fact, to be <u>better equipped to study and perhaps speak for other cultures,</u> **anthropologists** will have to <u>reconsider this whole</u> **nature-culture debate** <u>that divides them into opposing camps.</u>

As <u>a good example of how our</u> **dualistic mindset** <u>can impede anthropologists from understanding a particular culture's</u> **cosmology** <u>in the same way a local person would,</u> **Strathern** (1980) writes about **the Hagen** <u>having little to no distinction between nature and culture</u> in their **cosmology**, yet she <u>attempts to draw parallels to a</u> **dualistic model**, particularly <u>in agriculture and gender roles</u> where the <u>*mbo–rømi*</u> difference is shown as parallel to male–female duality depending on the situation.

As far as <u>social anthropology is concerned,</u> whether **anthropologists** can speak on behalf of those they study is likely to <u>remain a debatable topic at best.</u>

Step 3:

No	First line of the paragraph	Categorization
1	**Anthropology** is known as <u>the discipline that specializes in the study of people and culture,</u> and this has <u>been proven true on most levels.</u>	Describes what anthropology is
2	Whilst **anthropological fieldwork** often <u>involves the anthropologist becoming integrated with the community being studied,</u> this is often <u>temporary and incomplete.</u>	Describes a potential weakness of the anthropological fieldwork
3	There is also <u>a danger of assuming too much</u> when it comes to <u>unravelling the significance of</u> **culture specific concepts** in **anthropology** and this <u>runs in both directions.</u>	Explains the danger of assuming too much when unravelling the significance of culture-specific concepts in anthropology

4	In fact, to be <u>better equipped to study and perhaps speak for other cultures,</u> **anthropologists** will have to <u>reconsider this whole</u> **nature–culture debate** <u>that divides them into opposing camps.</u>	Explains the nature–culture debate that divides anthropologists
5	As <u>a good example of how our</u> **dualistic mindset** <u>can impede anthropologists from understanding a particular culture's cosmology in the same way a local person would,</u> **Strathern** (1980) writes about **the Hagen** <u>having little to no distinction between nature and culture</u> in their **cosmology**, yet she <u>attempts to draw parallels to a</u> **dualistic model**, particularly <u>in agriculture and gender roles</u> where the *mbo–rømi* <u>difference is shown as parallel to male–female duality depending on the situation.</u>	Explains how dualistic mindset works
6	As far as <u>social anthropology is concerned,</u> whether **anthropologists** can <u>speak on behalf of those they study</u> is likely to remain <u>a debatable topic at best.</u>	Explains whether or not anthropologists can speak on behalf of those they study is a debatable topic

5.
Step 1:
In the eyes of many observers, the Eurozone crisis has severely weakened the European Union.

The road to membership is far from straightforward. As a basic precondition, states must meet the so-called "Copenhagen criteria" to be considered viable candidates.

In light of the above, the decision of two Western European countries — Norway and Switzerland — to stay outside of the EU is especially puzzling.

It is not for lack of trying that Norway and Switzerland remain non-member states.

Nevertheless, the Norwegian and Swiss population's decision to refrain from formal EU membership demands an explanation.

The Academic Reading Section

Similarly, the Swiss population's rejection of the EEA in December 1992 was also largely due to concerns about national sovereignty and democracy.

Although the Norwegian and Swiss electorate both rejected deeper involvement in European integration largely due to concerns about the loss of sovereignty, this has not prevented them from building closer ties to Europe.

Switzerland has also taken steps to better align itself with the European Union.

Norway and Switzerland have both sought to draw closer to Europe in ways that do not run counter to their publics' desire to retain national sovereignty.

Step 2:

In the eyes of many observers, the **Eurozone crisis** has severely weakened the European Union.

The road to membership is far from straightforward.

In light of the above, **the decision of two Western European countries — Norway and Switzerland** — to stay outside of the EU is especially puzzling.

It is not for lack of trying that **Norway and Switzerland** remain non-member states.

Nevertheless, **the Norwegian and Swiss population's decision** to refrain from formal EU membership demands an explanation.

Similarly, **the Swiss population's rejection of the EEA** in December 1992 was also largely due to concerns about national sovereignty and democracy.

Although **the Norwegian and Swiss electorate** both rejected deeper involvement in European integration largely due to concerns about the loss of sovereignty, this has not prevented them from building closer ties to Europe.

Switzerland has also taken steps to better align itself with the European Union.

Norway and Switzerland have both sought to draw closer to Europe in ways that do not run counter to their publics' desire to retain national sovereignty.

Step 3:

No	First line of the paragraph	Categorization
1	In the eyes of many observers, the **Eurozone crisis** has severely weakened the European Union.	Describes the impact of the Eurozone crisis on the European Union

2	**The road to membership** is <u>far from straightforward</u>.	Explains that obtaining membership is not an easy process
3	<u>In light of the above,</u> **the decision of two Western European countries — Norway and Switzerland** — to <u>stay outside of the EU is especially puzzling.</u>	Highlights that Norway and Switzerland's decision to stay outside of the EU is puzzling
4	It is <u>not for lack of trying</u> that **Norway and Switzerland** <u>remain non-member states.</u>	Explains that Norway and Switzerland remain non-member states not because they did not try
5	Nevertheless, **the Norwegian and Swiss population's decision** to <u>refrain from formal EU membership demands an explanation.</u>	Explains that we need to understand why the Norwegian and Swiss populations refrain from formal EU membership
6	Similarly, **the Swiss population's rejection of the EEA** <u>in December 1992</u> was also <u>largely due to concerns about national sovereignty and democracy.</u>	Explains why the Swiss population rejected the EEA in December 1992
7	Although **the Norwegian and Swiss electorate** both <u>rejected deeper involvement in European integration</u> largely due to <u>concerns about the loss of sovereignty,</u> this has <u>not prevented them from building closer ties to Europe.</u>	Explains that Norway and Switzerland manage to build closer ties to Europe despite not being integrated into the EU
8	**Switzerland** has also <u>taken steps to better align itself with the European Union.</u>	Explains what Switzerland has done
9	**Norway and Switzerland** have both <u>sought to draw closer to Europe</u> in ways that <u>do not run counter to their publics' desire</u> to <u>retain national sovereignty.</u>	Explains what Norway and Switzerland have done to draw closer to Europe

2 Scanning and Matching

Speed reading isn't enough. You need to know how to transform your comprehension of the passage into concrete results. To do that, you must learn how to scan and match.

You may be wondering about the difference between speed reading and scanning. On one hand, with speed reading, your goal is solely to comprehend the passage in rough terms. You don't need to know every single small detail, but rather gain a broad understanding. On the other hand, with scanning, you must be *looking* for something within the passage. Usually, you do this by identifying a keyword in the questions or answer options given. Subsequently, you scan through the passage trying to look for that specific keyword. This is what we call "matching." Chances are, if you can find that keyword within the passage, the answer should be right where you found the keyword, or somewhere nearby.

In this chapter, we will cover the specific techniques required for effective scanning and matching.

Simple Steps

1. Underline keywords in the question and/or answer options
2. Scan the passage for those specific keywords
3. Search for the answer within the vicinity of the keywords in the passage

Elaboration with Examples

We will refer to the same passage on circulation in Southeast Asia, and demonstrate how the "Scanning and Matching" strategy can be applied by answering some sample questions.

Sample passage:

Through Time and Space: A Perspective on Circulation in Island Southeast Asia

On the fourth of May, 1998, "Macet Total" occurred in Indonesia. The government's announcement that oil subsidies would be drastically reduced caused the lines for fuel, particularly in Jakarta and Surabaya, to be extended through many blocks, causing the traffic to be at a standstill. The underlying tension between circulation and accumulation, particularly accumulation of capital, in President Suharto's New Order had set the stage for Macet Total. The appropriation of capital accumulation has, historically, among the central causes of conflicts, revolts and revolutions throughout the course of history. Hence, that accumulation was one of the tensions that brought about Macet Total should not be too surprising. A more interesting notion in which to examine it is the aspect of circulation.

The concept of circulation can be interpreted as the exchange or interplay of things like goods, relationships, information and so on by means of social or political networking. It is a key idea in attempting to understand island Southeast Asia as a region, as circulation has the potential to induce critical social and political consequences that affect events and outcomes in island Southeast Asia.

Prior to the arrival of colonial powers, Southeast Asia was a region populated by ports run by governments or kingdoms whose main economic activity was international trade. The existence of numerous ports battling it out for trade volume and trade share forced an intense amount of competition and even rivalry. An example of such a rivalry was the rivalry between the Acheh kingdom and the Johor kingdom in the 1500s for control of trade in the Straits of Malacca. What this competition did then was force ports to diversify their goods and to provide more goods that would attract the wealthy merchants from the Arab world, China, India and Europe. It forced ports to look inland in search of new goods. A model of this dynamic is presented by Bennet Bronson in his article, "Exchange at the Upstream and Downstream Ends." Based on this model, the natural enemy of a port, A, is a nearby port, A', with access to roughly similar inland resources as it. Inland towns are not the natural enemies of A; rather, they are places in which A tries to establish some form of connection. This is where the notion of circulation enters into play. If A is strong or powerful enough, it can simply launch an attack on its inland neighbors.

Yet, Bronson suggests that, in most cases, what A would try to do was to establish some political or colonial tie with its inland neighbors, thereby ensuring a steady stream of trade. Hence, we see that A's focus is simply to establish social relations rather than war. A recognizes the significance of social and political relations to its economic benefits. At places further inland, A might even try to use inter-marriages as a means of establishing trade relations. This form of trade creation through marriage and social networking can also be observed even at the highest levels of hierarchy and at inter-governmental levels. Thus, we see the social and political stakes that arise from circulation. Kingdoms in Southeast Asia would rather establish social and political ties with potential trading partners rather than simply conquer them through force, due to the inherent notion of circulation.

A more contemporary example is the text messaging revolution in the Philippines in the late 1990s and early part of the twenty-first century. This phenomenon can be seen as a form of circulation, whereby due to the low costs of text messaging, a sizable proportion of communication was done through this form. This power was unleashed in 2001, when a large proportion of Philippine society gathered to demand for the resignation of then Philippine President Joseph Estrada, a former movie star. When news of President Estrada's failed impeachment was released, the news spread through text messaging. The constant forwarding of messages generated a creation and recreation of social networks. It all came to a head on those January days in 2001. The idea for the gathering and the dissemination of its whereabouts were spread through forwarded text messages. Had circulation not been an integral part of Philippine culture, it is entirely plausible that this gathering may never have happened. Hence, the concept of circulation, so prevalent in Philippine culture, had a massive impact on the social and political sphere, enabling a multitude of people to band together in opposition of a current political event.

This brings us back to the Macet Total event in Indonesia. This case is particularly fascinating as the streets in Surabaya, for example, were designed to be uni-directional, therefore minimizing the frequency and duration of traffic congestions. Yet, traffic was at a standstill on that May day in 1998. The circulation from this event comes primarily from the then ruling regime under President Suharto. John Sidel suggests that the regime's own tactics in managing or controlling the macet actually facilitated the process and outcome of regime transition. It is in their tactics that circulation is evident. Social networks and business networks that had been established by the Suharto regime enabled businesses that had intimate yet narrowly economic linkages with the regime to accumulate private capital. This is the tension between accumulation and circulation that Sidel believes set the stage for Macet Total. The regime also relied heavily on Chinese entrepreneurs, particularly the ones that they could trust. Remnants of local aristocracies were also incorporated into the business sector of the economy.

By considering circulation, we can observe how and why events unravel as they do and the social and political consequences that are at stake. Given that this has been a consistent theme throughout island Southeast Asia's history, it will, in all likelihood, continue to do so. As such, when we attempt to study or understand the region of island Southeast Asia, we must ensure that the concept of circulation is incorporated. Only then can we begin to gain a more comprehensive and profound insight into its culture, peoples and way of life.

Author: Nicholas Khaw

Step 1: Underline keywords in the question and/or answer options

The first thing you need to do is to underline the keywords. This can be found in the question or the answer options. Recall that some questions do not come with answer options at all. Under such circumstances, you will have to make do with whatever you can find within the question itself.

Most students have heard of underlining keywords but many do not know what a keyword is. It is absolutely crucial for you to know this well, because if you select the wrong or misleading keyword, the "Scanning and Matching" technique will not work well. As a general rule, keywords that can help you include:

a) Names
- Alexander the Great
- Genghis Khan
- Asian Financial Crisis
- Internet revolution
- Nike

b) Concepts
- Feminism
- Liberty
- Capitalism
- Apostasy

c) Dates
     - 26th of April
     - 1929
     - December 1998
  d) Numbers
     - 1.7 million
     - 9,210
     - 11
     - Four
  e) Unusual words
     - Aerate
     - Slimy
     - Congratulate
     - Mentality

Step 2: Scan the passage for those specific keywords

Here is where you test the strength of your ability in identifying keywords. If the keyword you've selected is repeated far too many times within the passage, go back to the drawing board and reconsider your selection.

One tip to help you scan the passage more quickly is by matching the order in which the question appears within the passage itself. For example, if you are working on the first question, it is more likely that the answer is within the first few paragraphs of the passage. Therefore, you can begin by scanning the first few paragraphs. Conversely, if you have reached the last question for the section, save some time by first scanning the last few paragraphs in the passage.

Step 3: Search for the answer within the vicinity of the keywords in the passage

A mistake that students often make is that they become overly excited once they find a match within the passage. They may immediately try to extract the answer from that sentence itself.

The correct strategy to employ is to look *around* the keyword match, as well as within the sentence where you found the match. The passage is not likely to be completely straightforward all the time, and a more in-depth understanding of the context is required. Try your best to at least read the entire paragraph.

Let's see how these steps play out in actual IELTS questions.

The Academic Reading Section

Sample questions

The sample questions will cut across the four types of questions typically asked in the IELTS. This is in order to show you how the "Scanning and Matching" strategy is universally applicable.

Type 1: True, False or Not Given?

Do the following statements agree with the claims of the writer in the sample passage?

YES   if the statement agrees with the claims of the writer
NO   if the statements contradicts the claims of the writer
NOT GIVEN   if it is impossible to say what the writer thinks about this

Statement: <u>Capital accumulation</u> contributed to <u>Macet Total.</u>

Step 1:
Underline "capital accumulation" and "Macet Total," since these are unusual nouns. Based on the speed reading you have completed in the previous section, you know that paragraphs 1 and 6 relate to Macet Total. For this reason, you can zoom in on those two paragraphs immediately.

Step 2:
The next step is to scan the passage for the keywords you have underlined. Once again, because speed reading has helped you to filter on paragraphs 1 and 6 based on the keywords "Macet Total," you can first scan those paragraphs for the next keywords, "capital accumulation."

Based on paragraph 1 alone, you will notice that "capital accumulation" is mentioned several times:

> On the fourth of May, 1998, "Macet Total" occurred in Indonesia. The government's announcement that oil subsidies would be drastically reduced caused the lines for fuel, particularly in Jakarta and Surabaya, to be extended through many blocks, causing the traffic to be at a standstill. The underlying tension between circulation and <u>accumulation,</u> particularly <u>accumulation of capital,</u> in President Suharto's New Order had set the stage for Macet Total. The appropriation of <u>capital accumulation</u> has, historically, among the central causes of conflicts, revolts and revolutions throughout

the course of history. Hence, that accumulation was one of the tensions that brought about Macet Total should not be too surprising.

Step 3:
Lastly, scan the area where you have located the keywords. Look for information that can help you determine whether or not the statement is given in the passage, and whether or not it is true.

Let's take a closer look:

The underlying tension between circulation and <u>accumulation,</u> particularly <u>accumulation of capital,</u> in President Suharto's New Order had **set the stage** for Macet Total. The appropriation of <u>capital accumulation</u> has, historically, among the **central causes** of conflicts, revolts and revolutions throughout the course of history.

Even if you did not know that "set the stage" is another way of saying that capital accumulation was one of the contributing factors, the phrase "central causes" should make it clear that capital accumulation did contribute to Macet Total. Therefore, the statement is true.

By layering the Scanning and Matching technique on top of speed reading, you reduced the number of paragraphs you had to read in detail from sevan to just one. This allows you to save time and also have a higher level of focus.

Type 2: MCQ

According to <u>Bennet Bronson,</u> why would "A" choose to <u>establish ties</u> with its neighbors instead of <u>launching an attack?</u>

A. A understands the importance of <u>social and political relations</u> to its economic benefits
B. A was forced to look <u>inland</u> in search of goods
C. A aimed to use <u>inter-marriages</u> as a way of establishing trade relations
D. There was <u>rivalry</u> between the <u>Johor and Acheh kingdoms</u>

Step 1:
This strategy can also work for the MCQ. Once again, we underline keywords in the question — and this time, the answer options as well.

If the questions and answer options are very lengthy in the sense that they have many words that appear to be keywords, be more economical on the answer options but don't cut corners with the question. The question is like a compass, and it is crucial in directing you to the correct answer whereas answer options could be matched to sections in the passage, but may not even be remotely accurate. This is especially so if the answer options are very close to each other in meaning and more complex.

Therefore, when in a rush or in doubt, always place more emphasis on the question.

Step 2:
As before, scan and match the keywords to the passage. Begin with the question keywords first.

Question keywords:

A model of this dynamic is presented by <u>Bennet Bronson</u> in his article, "Exchange at the Upstream and Downstream Ends." Based on this model, the natural enemy of a port, A, is a nearby port, A', with access to roughly similar inland resources as it. Inland towns are not the natural enemies of A; rather, they are places in which A tries to establish some form of connection. This is where the notion of circulation enters into play. If A is strong or powerful enough, it can simply <u>launch an attack</u> on its inland neighbors.

Yet, <u>Bronson</u> suggests that, in most cases, what A would try to do was to <u>establish</u> some political or colonial <u>tie</u> with its inland neighbors, thereby ensuring a steady stream of trade. Hence, we see that A's focus is simply to establish social relations rather than war. A recognizes the significance of social and political relations to its economic benefits.

By doing this, you have narrowed down the passage to the above section, which is much more manageable than 1,000 words or so.

Next, when you scan for keywords found in the answer options, attempt to focus on the section above or in its vicinity.

Answer option A keywords: A understands the importance of <u>social and political relations</u> to its <u>economic benefits.</u>

Yet, Bronson suggests that, in most cases, what A would try to do was to establish some political or colonial tie with its inland neighbors, **thereby**

Scanning and Matching

ensuring a steady stream of trade. **Hence,** we see that A's focus is simply to establish social relations rather than war. A recognizes the significance of social and political relations to its economic benefits.

Answer option A looks like a good choice not just because you can match its keywords to the section that you found the question's keywords in, but also because it answers the question. Let's examine this more closely:

Yet, Bronson suggests that, in most cases, what A would try to do was to establish some political or colonial tie with its inland neighbors, thereby ensuring a steady stream of trade. → The author sets up a puzzle by using the transition word "yet," which is a synonym of "instead." In other words, the author indirectly asks: why would A want to establish some political or colonial tie with its inland neighbors? The first clue as to why this is case appears at the end of the sentence, "thereby ensuring a steady stream of trade."

Hence, we see that A's focus is simply to establish social relations rather than war. → Like "thereby," "hence" is a precursor to explaining the reason behind a phenomenon. Answer option A begins to look even more attractive as the passage states that the focus on establishing "social relations" was more important than war.

A recognizes the significance of social and political relations to its economic benefits. → This confirms A as the answer. It is essentially a summary of the reasons that have been stated in the previous two sentences.

Answer option B keywords: A was forced to look inland in search of goods.
Even though answer option A is the correct answer, we can nonetheless perform the same exercise on the remaining answer options to confirm that they are inaccurate.
This exercise is also meant to demonstrate that often, you will be able to scan and match keywords. But, this does not mean that the answer options are necessarily correct.

It forced ports to look inland in search of new goods. A model of this dynamic is presented by Bennet Bronson in his article, "Exchange at the Upstream and Downstream Ends." Based on this model, the natural enemy of a port, A, is a nearby port, A', with access to roughly similar inland resources as it. Inland towns are not the natural enemies of A; rather, they are places in which A tries to establish some form of connection. This is where the notion of circulation enters into play.

If A is strong or powerful enough, it can simply launch an attack on its inland neighbors.

Yet, Bronson suggests that, in most cases, what A would try to do was to establish some political or colonial tie with its inland neighbors, thereby ensuring a steady stream of trade.

On the surface, this appears as if it could be the answer, but let's take a closer look. Was the fact that ports were forced to look inland the reason why A chose to establish closer ties? Or, is answer option A — the fact that A could see the economic benefits brought by social and political relations — a more direct reason?

The answer is that while answer option B comes close, it does not beat answer option A because you need a few layers of processing before you get to the real reason as to why A did not launch an attack.

Answer option C keywords: A aimed to use inter-marriages as a way of establishing trade relations.

A recognizes the significance of social and political relations to its economic benefits. At places further inland, A might even try to use inter-marriages as a means of establish trade relations. This form of trade creation **through marriage** and social networking can also be observed even at the highest levels of hierarchy and at inter-governmental levels.

After identifying the relevant paragraph, once again, study the area around which the keywords were located and determine whether it is the accurate answer. You will realize that this section on inter-marriages is an elaboration on what A has done upon recognizing the significance of social and political relations to its economic benefits. The word "through" further emphasizes that inter-marriage is a method or example of an action taken, rather than the cause itself.

Hence, while answer option C is another close one, answer option A remains the most accurate choice.

Answer option D keywords: There was rivalry between the Johor and Acheh kingdoms.

The existence of numerous ports battling it out for trade volume and trade share forced an intense amount of competition and even rivalry. **An example** of such a rivalry was the rivalry between the Acheh kingdom and the Johor kingdom in the 1500s for control of trade in the Straits of Malacca. What this competition did then was force ports to diversify their goods and to provide more goods that would attract the wealthy merchants from the Arab world, China, India and Europe. It forced ports to look inland in search of new goods.

The phrase "for example" alerts you to the fact that the Johor and Acheh kingdom rivalry is used as an illustration of the earlier point, which is that the existence of numerous ports had led to competition as well as rivalry. Is this linked to why A would establish ties rather than launch an attack?

Like answer option B, only remotely so. Indeed, rivalry did force ports to look further inland and to consider social and political ties as a means of obtaining economic benefits. But as you can see, you need a few layers of reasoning before you can get to that answer. For this reason, answer option A remains the best option amongst the four.

Scanning and Matching is a very useful technique indeed. But, as you can see from this exercise, you do have to read the narrowed-down passage in detail to arrive at the answer, especially if the answer options given are very close to each other.

Type 3: Classification

Next, let's examine how "Scanning and Matching" can be applied to classification questions.

In a way, classification questions are relatively easier because it essentially asks you to define or provide descriptions that match certain concepts or nouns. There is no such thing as a "not given" option, which makes it easier. Furthermore, unlike the MCQs, there is no variation in terms of asking a broad range of questions including "why," "how," "who" and "when."

Step 1:
Like the other questions, however, begin by underlining keywords in the question and statements provided. Owing to the nature of classification

The Academic Reading Section

questions, you would most likely end up underlining all the concepts listed in the question.

Classify the following as descriptive of

A   Macet Total
B   Text messaging revolution in the Philippines

Write the correct letter A or B next to the following statements:

Statement 1: Triggered by the announcement that <u>oil subsidies</u> would be reduced
Statement 2: Involved call for president to <u>resign</u>

Step 2:
Scan and match the keywords to the passage. This time, begin by first narrowing it down to sections of the passage that have both keywords — one from the question, and one from the possible statements. An example is as follows:

On the fourth of May, 1998, "<u>Macet Total</u>" occurred in Indonesia. The government's announcement that <u>oil subsidies</u> would be drastically reduced **caused** the lines for fuel, particularly in Jakarta and Surabaya, to be extended through many blocks, causing the traffic to be at a standstill.

You can see how scanning and matching both keywords at once helps you narrow down the passage much more quickly and effectively. You can immediately determine whether or not the statement matches the concept. In this case, Macet Total is certainly linked to oil subsidies. If you read the paragraph more closely, it clearly states that the government's announcement that oil subsidies would be drastically reduced **caused** the lines for fuel.

This works as well for the second statement regarding the text messaging revolution:

A more contemporary example is the <u>text messaging revolution in the Philippines</u> in the late 1990s and early part of the twenty-first century. This phenomenon can be seen as a form of circulation, whereby due to the low costs of text messaging, a sizable proportion of communication was done through this form. This power was unleashed in 2001, when a large proportion of Philippine society gathered to demand for the <u>resignation</u> of then Philippine President Joseph Estrada, a former movie star.

Once again, by using scanning and matching, you can easily confirm that the text messaging revolution in the Philippines did involve a call for the president to resign. You will also notice that the keyword "resign" appeared in the form a noun ("resignation") rather than the verb itself. Nonetheless, both bear the same meaning and hence the statement matches the concept.

Type 4: Subjective

"Scanning and Matching" is so versatile that it can be used for subjective questions as well. Let's take a look at how it works.

Step 1:
In a subjective question, you don't have any answer options. You may only have an incomplete sentence or an open-ended question. Work with whatever you have and underline the keywords as usual.

However, you should also attempt to highlight the key transition or question words as well. These will help you understand what the question is looking for, especially if it is an incomplete sentence, which students often find challenging because no direct question is posed.

> Complete the sentences below. Write no more than two words from the passage for each answer.
>
> Sentence 1: In the <u>late 1990s, many people used text messaging</u> as a form of communication **because** of its …………………………………..
>
> Sentence 2: <u>Circulation</u> **has been** a ………………………….. throughout island <u>Southeast Asia's history.</u>

By doing this, you know that Sentence 1 requires you to find the **reason as to why** many people used text messaging in the late 1990s. In addition, you also know that Sentence 2 requires you to find out **what role circulation has played** in the history of Southeast Asia, with an emphasis on "has been" — meaning that this has happened in the past, and continues to happen today.

The Academic Reading Section

Step 2:
Now, scan and match the keywords to the passage.

Sentence 1:

> A more contemporary example is the <u>text messaging revolution in the Philippines in the late 1990s</u> and early part of the twenty-first century. This phenomenon can be seen as a form of circulation, whereby **due to** <u>the low costs of text messaging, a sizable proportion of communication</u> was done through this form.

Sentence 2:

> By considering <u>circulation,</u> we can observe how and why events unravel as they do and the social and political consequences that are at stake. Given that this **has been** a consistent theme throughout <u>island Southeast Asia's history,</u> it will, in all likelihood, continue to do so.

Step 3:
Now, study the relevant section. Recall that the statement is asking for the **reason why** many people used text messaging in the late 1990s. With this in mind, the words "due to" should stand out to you — this is precisely where the reasons for the text messaging revolution are revealed.

By doing this, you now know that the reason is the "low costs of text messaging." Make sure that you select only the two most important words for your answer, which are "low costs."

You can do the same for the Sentence 2. The only place where both "circulation" and "Southeast Asia's history" appear is in the final paragraph. Zoom in on this section and you will notice that there is also a reference to the continuous past ("has been"). Focus further on that sentence, and you will arrive at the correct answer, which is "consistent theme."

To conclude, the complete answers are as follows:

Sentence 1: In the <u>late 1990s, many people used text messaging</u> as a form of communication **because** of its low costs.

Sentence 2: <u>Circulation</u> **has been** a consistent theme throughout island <u>Southeast Asia's history.</u>

IELTS Trainer

A compilation of various question types have been included below, based on the passages that you have already come across in the first chapter, "Speed Reading." Using the "Scanning and Matching" technique to arrive at the correct answer. Passage 1:

Public and Private Management Practices

Management style is an increasingly important area in the study of management. There has been much debate concerning the differences between management styles in the public and the private sector. Managers, whether public or private play an important role in the continuation of society as we see it. Private and public sector managers both shape the world and the environment that we live in with the decisions they take on a daily basis — sometimes they make or are blamed for mistakes which may not have been their doing but fall within their oversight. There has been much literature written in modern times about the differences between the approaches to management taken by public and private sector managers. Most of the arguments put forward revolve around which approach is more effective. Recently there have been many calls for public sector management to adopt and implement private sector style management in the public sector in order to deliver better services at a more cost-effective level.

To determine whether public sector and private sector management can be directly compared, consider two articles written on this topic: one by Michael A. Murray published in 1975 in the *Public Administration Review* and another by George A. Boyne published in 2002 in the *Journal of Management Studies*. Murray states that in the past two generations scholars and practitioners have begun to realize that management can be viewed as a generic process whereas historically in America the view was that private sector management and public sector management require two separate approaches. He goes on to further state that many new scholarly articles have been published and more significantly new management schools are being founded based on the assumption that both public and private management have many similarities. He does, however, caution that the shifting in attitudes towards management, from one where private and public sector management are two separate entities to one where there are significant overlaps in the application of management in any institutional setting, has not progressed very quickly due to mutual distrust between both public sector and private sector management practitioners and entrenched interest from those who are threatened by the shift in attitudes such as free standing schools of business and schools of public administration.

On the other hand, Boyne argues that whereas others have reasoned that there are significant differences between public sector management and private sector management in important areas, these allegations have not been backed up by empirical evidence. Therefore, the notion that public management can implement certain practices from private management should be given some thought until it can be proven empirically whether or not public and private management are significantly different.

When looking at these arguments it can be seen that while both authors are looking at the differences between public sector management and private sector management the purposes of their articles differ. Murray hopes to prove that there are more similarities between public sector management and private sector management than there are differences while Boyne is seeking to test whether or not the similarities between public sector management and private sector management are limited to the unimportant aspects or whether they also incorporate the important aspects and thus make the case for the implementation of private sector management policies in the public sector.

Looking at how the arguments are dissimilar, it could be possible to hypothesize that the articles differ in their arguments perhaps due to the time period in which the articles were written. Murray was writing his article in 1975 when, presumably, the idea that both public and private sector management had a lot in common was just gaining traction. Whereas Boyne wrote his article in 2002 when the subject of the similarities between public sector and private sector management has been more thoroughly explored via other methods. Thus, Boyne seeks to prove or disprove the notion of similarities between the public sector and the private and the feasibility of the adoption of private sector management practices in public sector management through the use of empirical evidence.

Given the differences in when the two articles were written and published, another factor to consider is the shape of the public and private management landscape at the time the authors were writing. The early decades of the twentieth century saw the "reform movement" in the United States where municipal governments in that country emphasized the benefits of business-like behavior — a similar "corporate revolution" where local governments in the United Kingdom became more interested in private sector management practices which were popular with large companies only in the 1970s.

From these examples we can see that insofar as the adoption of private management practices into public management goes, the process and ideas developed earlier in the United States than in the United Kingdom, which could have influenced the arguments that are raised by the articles. Murray states that the idea that both public and private management have more in common than they have differences has been around for two generations while Boyne states that the central element of the New Public Management Program is the adoption of managerial processes and behaviors from the private sectors into the public sector. The latter also states that "the adoption of private sector models had been viewed with much scepticism in the literatures on public administration and public management." Boyne's view can be linked with Murray's statement on resistance from both established public and private management sector policies on integrating due to mutual distrust. Furthermore the decision to adopt private sector management practices into public sector management by the New Public Management Program could be influenced by the results shown by the "reform movement," which was implemented in the United States during the early decades of the twentieth century.

Author: Ariff Hassan

Questions 1–8

Match the following arguments or statements to the correct scholar

    A. Michael A. Murray
    B. George A. Boyne
    C. None of the above

Write the correct letter, **A, B or C**, in boxes 1–8 on your answer sheet

1. In America, the general belief is that private sector management and public sector management require different approaches
2. Management styles can differ vastly between Western and Eastern cultures

The Academic Reading Section

3. Public management should implement certain practices from private management
4. The adaptation of private sector models were viewed with skepticism in academic literature
5. The article was written in 2002
6. There is mutual distrust between both public sector and private sector management practitioners
7. American management systems have progressed at a much faster rate due to its immigration policies
8. Management schools are being established based on the assumption that both public and private management have many similarities

Answers for Questions 1–8
1. A
2. C
3. C
4. B
5. B
6. A
7. C
8. A

Passage 2:

Indiana Jones and the Grain of Salt: Public Portrayals of Archaeology

In 1981, a film entitled *The Raiders of the Lost Ark* was released, becoming an instant hit, grossing over $384 million worldwide from its initial theatrical release. This movie, starring the popular Harrison Ford, thrust the field of archaeology into mainstream popular culture. Since then, among all academic fields, the field of archaeology has become the most featured and the most popular in mainstream culture, rivaled, perhaps, only by paleontology. Yet, it is unsurprising that most casual moviegoers would not be interested in what the actual field of archaeology actually entails, being fascinated only by the sensational and the romantic aspects of the field. This therefore begs the question; how much of actual archaeological methods and practices is accurately showcased? Are the archaeological sites and discoveries accurately displayed or are these issues given a more sensationalist interpretation so as to cater to popular mainstream culture? To answer these questions, let us explore the case study of the popular Indiana Jones film, *Indiana Jones and the Last Crusade*, focusing on the movie's portrayal of the archaeological site of Petra.

The actual exact age of the Petra monument is impossible to determine. As noted in Joukowsky (2002), the stratigraphy of the site is difficult to chart as many changes, both geological and man-made, have caused several periods of "reconstruction and reuse" to the buildings. Kenyon, Musil and Hall (1924) attempt to give a rough estimate as to when the Petra buildings were built, placing the estimate at several centuries B.C. They conjecture that there may even have been cave dwellers or buriers even before the city was created. The geographic location of Petra is well-described in the literature. The culture of Petra is also clearly described by Joukowsky and Basile (2004). They state that the Great Temple, the primary feature of Petra in *Indiana Jones and the Last Crusade* was a center of Nabataean life, complemented by extremely intricate art and architecture within the Nabatean culture. Indeed, this view is supported by Zeitler (1993) who states that Nabataean types of pottery were present as late as the 4th century A.D. Later on, the site was also influenced by Egyptian and Graeco-Roman designs as documented by Kennedy (1926).

Perhaps the most obvious discrepancy between the film's portrayal of Petra and Petra itself is the location of Petra. Petra is located in modern-day Jordan whereas in the movie, the monument was said to be located in the Republic of Hatay, a province of Turkey. In the movie, the Nazi forces were shown to request permission from the Ruler of Hatay to explore the site and to extract artifacts from the site. As a corollary to this point, the site was said to be located near the city of Alexandretta or modern-day Iskenderiun, which is again located in Turkey. Another aspect of the Petra site in which the movie differs is the notion of the site being a Christian monument above all else. In the movie, the site is said to be the storage place for the Holy Grail and was thus designed by the Crusades. The Lion's heads statues depicted in the movie are also inconsistent with the actual site. As noted in Joukowsky and Basile (2004), the strongest influence on the site comes from the Nabatean culture. Thus, the movie's portrayal of the site as purely Christian is flawed. As an extrapolation of the Christianity aspect of the site, as per the film, this would mean that the site was constructed during the Crusades wars. Yet, there is strong evidence to support the notion that the origin of the site begun a few centuries B.C.

It is important to keep in mind that the film is a work of fiction and not everything portrayed in the film is necessarily accurate or exact. Yet, this might cause some flawed perceptions in the public eye regarding the field of archaeology. In the film, archaeology is deliberately sensationalized and romanticized, understandably so. It depicts, inaccurately, archaeologists as being treasure hunters rather than scientists. The methodology of archaeology in the film is to dig graves and recover legendary artifacts rather than applying a systematic method of excavation in order to retrieve artifacts. While Indiana Jones insists on artifacts being restored for the purpose of museum display, representative of professional archaeologists in general, his methods do not fall in line with the conventional methods of professional archaeology. In the movies, there is no real sense of ownership with regards to the artifacts; the basis of ownership simply goes by whoever steals the artifact, keeps the artifact. Of course, this is a far stretch from what the discipline of archaeology actually entails.

What these discrepancies do is alter the public perception of archaeology and archaeologists. Instead of being displayed as a science of strict discipline and methodology, archaeology is portrayed as a field of sensational treasure hunts and romantic adventures. Thus, the public gets the flawed idea that archaeology is purely adventure and excitement, disregarding the time spent in libraries and laboratories doing research. Granted, the purpose of films is to make as much profit as possible and thus, providing an accurate view of the subjects might not necessarily be on top of their list of priorities. As such, mainstream portrayals of archaeology must be taken with a grain of salt. If we can do that, then we can continue enjoying films such as the Indiana Jones series while understanding that there exist significant discrepancies between real archaeology and mainstream culture "archaeology."

Author: Nicholas Khaw

Questions 9–16

Choose the correct letter, **A, B, C or D.**

Write the correct letter in boxes 9–16 on your answer sheet.

9. How did archaeology enter mainstream popular culture?
   A. Harrison Ford began dabbling in archaeology
   B. *The Raiders of the Lost Ark* became an instant hit worldwide
   C. Indiana Jones produced some effective commercials
   D. Monuments such as Petra captured the public's eye

10. Which of the following statements is **not** true?
    A. Harrison Ford is a famous actor
    B. *The Raiders of the Lost Ark* took some time to gain fame and recognition worldwide
    C. No one knows the exact age of the Petra monument
    D. In the movie, the location of Petra is different from its location in real life

11. What is the writer's motivation for writing this article?
    A. To explore how much of actual archaeological methods and practices is accurately showcased
    B. To raise public awareness about *The Raiders of the Lost Ark*
    C. To make the field of archaeology more popular in mainstream culture
    D. To educate the public regarding the archaeology of Petra

12. What role did the Great Temple play in the film?
    A. To give a rough estimate as to when the Petra buildings were built
    B. As the storage place for the Holy Grail
    C. As the center of Nabataean life and culture
    D. All of the above

13. The following are discrepancies between the film and reality, except
    A. The location of Petra
    B. The role of archaeologists
    C. The age of the Petra monument
    D. The Lion's head statues

The Academic Reading Section

14. Why does the writer argue that it is not wholly possible for the Petra monument to be a fully Christian site?
    A. Christianity did not exist during the movie's time period
    B. There were Egyptian and Graeco-Roman designs
    C. The actual monument was located in Turkey
    D. The origin of the site begun a few centuries B.C.

15. According to the writer, what would a true archaeologist do?
    A. Dig graves and recover legendary artifacts
    B. Give a rough estimate as to when the Petra buildings were built
    C. Sensationalize and romanticize the profession
    D. Apply a systematic method of excavation in order to retrieve artifacts

16. According to the writer, what is the purpose of the film, *The Raiders of the Lost Ark*?
    A. To thrust the field of archaeology into mainstream popular culture
    B. To popularize Harrison Ford
    C. To make as much profit as possible
    D. To sensationalize and romantics archaeology

Answers for Questions 9–16
9. B
10. B
11. A
12. C
13. C
14. D
15. D
16. C

Passage 3:

Body and Paradigm: Internalizing Cultures Externally

We embody our habits. "Body language" is what we unconsciously communicate to people when we speak to them. All the nuances of motion, from the arch of our eyebrows to the curve of our smiles, are the result of an idea, a state of mind which we are in. These ideas may be fleeting emotions, such as the depressed hunch of a student who realizes that he has an untouched writing seminar essay revision due in three hours, or they may also be more permanent embodiments of our surroundings, such as the gait of a person who is an adept at capoeira, a Brazilian martial art and dance.

It is crucial to acknowledge that it is an idea that causes a motion. The actor moves with a purpose — his moves are largely subconscious, his actions are to achieve a goal. As an observer, the audience tries to interpret the performer's actions to understand the idea that he is trying to convey. However, the audience does not have direct access to the actor's mind — the actor's idea has to pass through the medium of physical conveyance to the audience. This means that the actor cannot be assured that his idea will be reproduced faithfully in his audience's minds, for it is the action that they are witnessing, not the idea.

The significance of an action to the actor might be different to an observer, especially if one compares different cultures. A "thumbs-up" sign, which most people in America would interpret as "good job," is actually the American equivalent of sticking up one's third finger in places such as Greece, Russia and South Italy. Therefore, there is a certain degree of *interpretation* that is taking place when the audience watches the actor. The actor moves his body to express his intended idea, but the audience interprets meaning from the actor's actions *according to their own paradigms*. Hence, there is a disparity between the actor's translation of the (cultural) ideas into his actions and the interpretation of his actions into ideas by his audience. For daily interactions of people within the same cultures, this usually does not pose much of a problem, because both the actor and the audience come from similar cultural backgrounds. But when we deal with different cultures and paradigms, then the risk of misinterpretation becomes higher.

This is where the ethnographer comes in. He acknowledges this disparity, and tries to resolve it by trying to mimic the actions of the performer in order to better comprehend the original idea behind the actions. Essentially, the ethnographer, as the audience, tries to be the actor to overcome the barrier that physical communication poses to the conveyance of ideas.

However, does ethnographic analysis really give a clearer view of the idea behind the actions of a performer? Although ethnographers might claim to be able to truly access the underlying ideas of a culture by mimicking the actions of the people in that culture, the experience of that culture cannot give the ethnographer a "true" sense of the culture's essence. This is because the ethnographer himself is affected by his own paradigms and consequently interprets the experience of his actions according to his own viewpoint. However, this does not mean that ethnography is useless. Whereas the normal observer is only able to see the actor's actions, the ethnographer is privy to additional tactile information, which contributes to his interpretation of the culture. He combines a personal viewpoint with the experience gleaned from corporeal knowledge to create a modified and individualistic paradigm of a culture. Therefore, by looking at how ethnographers experience a culture internally, we can see how the view of culture that is presented to us is not actually an actual re-presentation of culture, but rather a richer re-interpretation of that culture. This is crucial because it is necessary to realize the existence, benefits and flaws of such re-interpretations.

Author: Jee Ian Tam

Questions 17–22

Complete the sentences below.

Write **NO MORE THAN TWO WORDS** from the passage for each answer.

Write your answers in boxes 17–22 on your answer sheet.

17. When we speak to others, we unconsciously use .... to communicate as well.
18. In America, people interpret a .... sign as a way to say "good job."
19. When the audience watches an actor, ... takes place.
20. Where different cultures are involved, there is a risk of ....
21. The .... attempts to overcome the barrier that physical communication poses to the conveyance of ideas.
22. The ethnographer combines a .... with the experience extracted from corporeal knowledge to create a modified and individualistic paradigm of a culture.

Answers for Questions 17–22

17. Body language
18. Thumbs-up
19. Interpretation
20. Misinterpretation
21. Ethnographer
22. Personal viewpoint

Passage 4:

Can Anthropologists Speak on Behalf of the People They Study?

Anthropology is known as the discipline that specializes in the study of people and culture, and this has been proven true on most levels. However, in social anthropology the question if anthropologists are able to speak on behalf of those communities they have worked with is a situational one. In some situations where the people studied face a difficult situation where they are unable to have a voice in a rigid social system, experience significant social and cultural change or otherwise are subject to strongly polarized opinions and influences, the work and findings of anthropologists can be appropriate to help bring about more equalized social change, hopefully to benefit the community that has been studied. On the other hand, ethnography can also be dangerous as the anthropologist may not present an accurate description or analysis of the people studied.

Whilst anthropological fieldwork often involves the anthropologist becoming integrated with the community being studied, this is often temporary and incomplete. Moreover, anthropologists always carry their own cultural values with them and if these values are imposed on their observations of the people they study in fieldwork, this paves the way to ethnocentrism and potentially biased reports. Our dualistic culture makes us think of nature and culture as separate, if not opposing, components that make society what it is. This is an important thing to remember, as anthropologists are fundamentally members of one cultural group who attempt to study people from another cultural group.

There is also a danger of assuming too much when it comes to unravelling the significance of culture-specific concepts in anthropology and this runs in both directions. Universalists like Levi-Strauss (1969) assume that common features across human cultures can be attributed to some social functioning based on biology or nature. Relativists in their efforts to describe and interpret their findings in ethnographic fieldwork may end up missing the bigger picture or the deeper meaning behind what they observe. Geertz (1993) in his highly interpretative essay on Balinese cockfights seems to have skimmed over the larger social background in favor of focusing on contextualizing the cockfight in Balinese society.

In fact, to be better equipped to study and perhaps speak for other cultures, anthropologists will have to reconsider this whole nature–culture debate that divides them into opposing camps. Either side may be good at finding common ground between cultures or highlighting uniqueness and emphasizing cultural contexts, but neither approach is a good way to gain a better understanding of how human societies work.

As a good example of how our dualistic mindset can impede anthropologists from understanding a particular culture's cosmology in the same way a local person would, Strathern (1980) writes about the Hagen having little to no distinction between nature and culture in their cosmology, yet she attempts to draw parallels to a dualistic model, particularly in agriculture and gender roles where the *mbo–rømi* difference is shown as parallel to male–female duality depending on the situation. This is a common feature of many ethnographies focusing on cosmology. Another example that comes to mind is Howell's (1996) paper on the Chewong of Malaysia, where she indicates Chewong animism as having no nature–culture boundary but a boundary between forest and non-forest cultures and environments. Anthropologists may be able to understand cosmologies in a way that makes sense to them, but such understanding is drawn from forming links to perceived similarities or differences to our own cultural background.

As far as social anthropology is concerned, whether anthropologists can speak on behalf of those they study is likely to remain a debatable topic at best. The legacy of dualism and the extremeness of both the universalist and relativist approaches to anthropology make this conundrum somewhat harder to work out as well. That being said, although anthropologists may never become fully integrated into the societies they study, this brings valuable insights and perspectives on many aspects of that community's social life ignored by locals. Such an outsider's perspective is useful for analysis, for asking all sorts of questions that contribute not only to detailed ethnographical works, but also to the formation of future anthropological theory. If such future theories manage to bypass the nature–culture duality that can limit anthropologists, this can bring forth greater possibilities for anthropology as a broad discipline in a post-modern situation where boundaries and dichotomies are getting increasingly blurred. Future anthropologists may find themselves having to speak for peoples and communities more often, when it comes to important matters and interdisciplinary efforts, and hopefully this discipline will prove valuable to human development in the long run.

Author: Shuen-Yi Long

Questions 23–29

Do the following statements agree with the claims of the writer in Passage 4?

YES	if the statement agrees with the claims of the writer
NO	if the statements contradicts the claims of the writer
NOT GIVEN	if it is impossible to say what the writer thinks about this

23. An anthropologist normally integrates into the community that is being studied.
24. An anthropologist may be able to bring about more equalized social change through their work.
25. Anthropologists separate themselves from their own personal cultural values.
26. Dualistic culture refers to anthropologists who study two cultures simultaneously.
27. Universalists believe that all humans have similar cultural values.
28. The Hagen example shows how a dualistic mindset can be a disadvantage for the anthropologist.
29. Howell, who wrote the paper on the Chewong of Malaysia, is a universalist.

The Academic Reading Section

Answers for Questions 23–29

23. YES
24. YES
25. NO
26. NO
27. NO
28. YES
29. NOT GIVEN

Passage 5:

Piecemeal Integration in the European Union: The Cases of Norway and Switzerland

In the eyes of many observers, the Eurozone crisis has severely weakened the European Union. However, despite widespread pessimism and skepticism about the European Union, it has certainly not brought the process of European integration to a halt. The ongoing political crisis in Ukraine that was sparked by President Yanukovych's apparent refusal to sign an association agreement with Brussels is perhaps the clearest reminder of the attractive power that the European Union still exerts on many peoples and governments outside of the 28-member union.

The road to membership is far from straightforward. As a basic precondition, states must meet the so-called "Copenhagen criteria" to be considered viable candidates. They must not only have "stable institutions guaranteeing democracy, the rule of law, [and] human rights," but they must also have "a functioning market economy." Candidates should also demonstrate "the ability to take on ... the obligations of membership." The negotiation process often takes years, and prospective candidates are required to make significant adjustments to domestic laws and institutions to ensure that they are brought in line with existing EU legislation, also known as the *acquis*. The recent experience of Croatia suffices to show just how rigorous and intrusive this process can be. As part of the negotiation process, Zagreb was asked to reform everything from their judicial system to regulations on the size of chicken cages. No state would willingly enter and undergo this process without an exceptionally strong and unwavering commitment to join the

EU. The historic "Eastern Enlargement" in 2004, followed by the accession of Romania and Bulgaria in 2007 and most recently Croatia in 2013, is surely a sign that the project of European integration is not about to come shuddering to a halt. Iceland, Montenegro, and Turkey have also begun negotiations with the European Commission in the hopes that they too may join the EU.

In light of the above, the decision of two Western European countries — Norway and Switzerland — to stay outside of the EU is especially puzzling. Many often assume that Norway and Switzerland are EU member states until they discover otherwise, given that both have highly developed market economies and strong, stable democratic institutions. Both are among the richest countries in the world. If Norway and Switzerland were to make the decision to become a member state, they would not have to experience the political and economic overhaul that Eastern European states had to undergo in dismantling the legacies of communist authoritarianism. The accession process would surely be nowhere near as difficult as it was for many of the post-communist countries.

It is not for lack of trying that Norway and Switzerland remain non-member states. A key prerequisite for EU membership is that states "[have] the consent of their citizens" in joining the political and economic union. It is precisely this condition that both Oslo and Bern have previously tried and failed to meet. Norway has a history of rejecting deep involvement in the project of European integration. In 1972, "53.5% percent [of the population] voted no to membership in the European Community" in a national referendum. A little over twenty years later, "52.2% of ... voters rejected membership in the European Union." As noted by Pettersen, Jenssen and Listhaug, "Norway remains the only country which has declined membership in the [EU] by a popular vote…for a second time."

Nevertheless, the Norwegian and Swiss population's decision to refrain from formal EU membership demands an explanation. The preservation of national sovereignty, a tendency deeply rooted in Norwegian history, figured prominently in public debates leading up to the 1994 referendum on EU membership. Concern for sovereignty and democracy was cited by 26.1% of respondents as a reason for opposing EU membership, a proportion over twice as high as the next most frequently cited reason.

Similarly, the Swiss population's rejection of the EEA in December 1992 was also largely due to concerns about national sovereignty and democracy. A May 1992 survey indicated that "a majority of citizens was ready to endorse the EEA agreement." However, the Swiss government proved unable to project a strong message of support for EEA membership. For instance, "two out of seven ministers repeatedly [expressed] their doubts about the EEA" in the period leading up to the referendum. Those opposed to the treaty were able to dominate the public discourse by "[dramatizing] the debate with emotional arguments about the loss of sovereignty and neutrality, the decline of direct democracy, [and] the threat of massive immigration." As in Norway, this argument proved to be persuasive. "The loss of sovereignty" was found to be one of the "main concerns of the voters" in the 1992 referendum.

Although the Norwegian and Swiss electorate both rejected deeper involvement in European integration largely due to concerns about the loss of sovereignty, this has not prevented them from building closer ties to Europe. It was estimated in 2012 that Norway had adopted "about three quarters of [EU] legislation … into national law as of 2011." Although Norway cannot vote on EU legislation, it has the right to actively "participate … in the preparatory stage and implementation of new regulations and directives."

Switzerland has also taken steps to better align itself with the European Union. In addition to actively adopting EU law into national law, Switzerland has signed a large number of bilateral treaties with the EU. These treaties cover a wide range of issue areas. For example, the 2010 treaty relates to "education, vocational training and youth," whereas a package of treaties signed in 1999 address areas such as "agriculture, overland transport, civil aviation, [and] research."

Norway and Switzerland have both sought to draw closer to Europe in ways that do not run counter to their publics' desire to retain national sovereignty. However, it is questionable, in light of ongoing trends, whether integration with Europe on their own terms is a sustainable approach. As the EU seeks to centralize the regulation of more cross-national issues, domestic actors in non-member states will face considerable difficulties, creating political pressure to more clearly define the country's relationship to European institutions. Norway, which acts on the legal basis of the EEA agreement, may be able to better absorb and influence, albeit to a limited degree, the evolution of EU laws. However, if the regulatory boundary of the EU sharpens further, both Norway and Switzerland are likely to face difficulties in trying to reap the benefits of ties with the EU market while avoiding formal membership.

Author: Raymond Ha

Questions 29–35

Complete the sentences below.

Write **NO MORE THAN TWO WORDS** from the passage for each answer.

Write your answers in boxes 29–35 on your answer sheet.

29. Based on public perspective, the European Union has been weakened by the ………………………..
30. In order to be considered a viable candidate for the European Union, candidates must fulfill the basic precondition also known as the ………………………..
31. The ……………………….. refers to being domestic laws and institution in line with European Union legislation.
32. In order to join the European Union, Eastern European states had to first dismantle ………………………..
33. Historically, Norwegians have tended to feel very strongly about the preservation of ………………………..
34. In 1992, Norwegian voters expressed their views on European Union membership via a ………………………..
35. Despite not having formal membership, Switzerland has signed a number of ……………………….. with the European Union.

Answers for Questions 29–35

29. Eurozone crisis
30. Copenhagen criteria
31. Acquis
32. Communist authoritarianism
33. National sovereignty
34. Referendum/national referendum
35. Bilateral treaties

3 Two-Layer Processing

The IELTS isn't so simple. Not every answer is dished out to you in a very direct manner. At times, you may be expected to infer or even provide an opinion on certain items. Let's take a look at a brief example below to see what this could look like:

Sample passage:

> Hybrid vehicles have been slowly increasing in popularity, with a number of major car manufacturers producing models that fit into this category. Many governments around the world have introduced favorable tax policies to encourage the general public to give hybrid vehicles a chance. Some have even gone so far as to give a complete tax relief for hybrid vehicles, which has resulted in an increase in the number of hybrid vehicles on the road. Indeed, this is a much welcome initiative to help tackle rising air pollution levels and to ensure a much healthier future for the next generation.

What is the writer's general view on hybrid vehicles?

A. Hybrid vehicles should be supported as a means to help reduce pollution
B. Hybrid vehicles are a burden, as they take up a significant amount of government funding
C. Hybrid vehicles are attractive to the general public
D. Air pollution levels are rising and this problem needs to be solved

As you can see from the example above, nowhere does it state outright that "here is the general view of the passage." That is why using the "Scanning and Matching" technique alone will not help you answer the question correctly.

Instead, you will have to apply a more sophisticated approach as outlined below. We will guide you through the steps needed to answer a sample question like the above in a timely and accurate manner.

Simple Steps

1. Assess the answer options, if any
2. Rephrase the question; break it up into sub-questions if necessary
3. Use the "Scanning and Matching" technique to find answers to Step 1

Elaboration with Examples

Step 1: Assess the answer options, if any

The key to answering analytical questions is to break them down into smaller pieces. Because these questions require more than one layer of processing, breaking these questions down will help you understand the answers you need to find in a more direct manner. This is necessary because subjective and open-ended questions can be vague. For example, what do you think the question means by a "general view"? A general view can include whether the writer thinks hybrid vehicles are beneficial or not. It can also include the writer's view on whether or not hybrid vehicles are cost-efficient. Or, it could be regarding the writer's view on whether or not hybrid vehicles are designed well and look attractive. As you can see, a "general view" can be about *anything*.

Therefore, before rephrasing the question, try to first digest as many clues as you can. If the question at hand is an MCQ like the one above, you can use the answer options to help you narrow down the information that you should be looking for. It is similar to working backwards to figure out what the question is asking.

Refer to the answer options given above:

A. Hybrid vehicles should be supported as a means to help reduce pollution
   Comment: Should hybrid vehicles be supported, and if so, why?
B. Hybrid vehicles are a burden, as they take up a significant amount of government funding
   Comment: Are hybrid vehicles a burden, and if so, why?
C. Hybrid vehicles are attractive to the general public
   Comment: Does the general public find hybrid vehicles attractive?
D. Air pollution levels are rising and this problem needs to be solved
   Comment: What is the current situation regarding air pollution?

Based on the answer options, you can already see some trends. It is likely that there is more than one answer option that is true. When this happens, many students get caught because they hurriedly choose the first true option they see, which may not be correct. To clarify, a "true" option is one that is factually true according to the passage. The "correct" option is one that is true, and answers the question correctly.

For instance, answer option C is true. The passage does state that the number of hybrid vehicles on the road has increased, which implies that they are attractive to the public. But, it is not exactly the passage's view because it only refers to one small aspect of hybrid vehicles. In fact, it is more of the *general public*'s view. For this reason, we can eliminate this option.

Let's take a look at another example. Answer option D is true — air pollution levels are indeed rising and the passage does imply that it needs to be solved. But, recall that the question is about the writer's general view on **hybrid vehicles**. Because answer option D is about air pollution levels, you can rule it out.

The remaining answer options seem fairly relevant. For now, let's take them all into account as we move into Step 2.

Step 2: Rephrase the question; break it up into sub-questions if necessary

Based on the remaining answer options A and B, try to rephrase the question from the sample passage above. Break it up into smaller pieces if you have to.

Original: **What is the passage's general view on hybrid vehicles?**

Rephrased:

   a. Is the passage positive or negative on hybrid vehicles?
   b. Why so?

Applying the scanning and matching technique here would result in the following:

> Answer option A: Hybrid vehicles should be supported as a means to help reduce <u>pollution</u>
>
> Indeed, this is a **much welcome** initiative to help tackle rising air <u>pollution</u> levels and to ensure a **much healthier future** for the next generation.

The keyword "pollution" matches to the last sentence of the paragraph. Begin by hunting for clues within this sentence, and you will notice positive phrases such as "much welcome" and "much healthier future." This sentence alone will help you answer the rephrased questions:

a. Is the passage positive or negative on hybrid vehicles?
Answer: It is positive.
b. Why so?
Answer: Hybrid vehicles can help reduce pollution, which can result in a much healthier future for the next generation

Answer option A looks like a very good candidate. But, let's assess answer option B as well, just in case.

Answer option B: Hybrid vehicles are a burden, as they take up a significant amount of government funding

Many governments around the world have introduced **favorable** tax policies to encourage the general public to give hybrid vehicles a chance.

If you were to "Scan and Match," you could match "government" to the second sentence of the paragraph. However, you would be hard-pressed to find any words or phrases hinting that the passage views hybrid vehicles as a burden. On the contrary, the terms used seem to be positive, such as "favorable." This is in addition to "welcome initiative," which was found in the sentence you scanned for answer option A.

Therefore, the answer option that is both true and correct is answer option A.

You can also use "Two-Layer Processing" as a strategy for subjective questions that involve sentence completion. Refer to the following sample passage and question:

Sample passage:

Many people around the world drink coffee, which has become a staple in numerous households. In fact, some of the most well-known brands today are related to coffee companies. This includes Starbucks, Costa Coffee and Coffee Bean. But, have you ever paused to wonder why we like coffee so much? It cannot be solely because of its taste. If you think about it, coffee leaves a bitter and acidic aftertaste. It also requires a great deal of effort to make. First, you have to harvest the beans. Next, you have to roast the beans before grinding them carefully. Lastly, you have to brew them at the perfect temperature and sometimes even add milk before it is ready for consumption. It is possible that there are some who like coffee because of the role it plays as a stimulant. Indeed, drinking coffee can help us feel more alert and awake. But, why do we choose coffee when there are so many other alternatives such as tea and energy drinks?

Sample questions:

Fill in the blanks. Choose no more than two words from the passage.

1. In many households, coffee is a ....
2. After brewing coffee, some people may choose to add .... before drinking it.

Even though this is a subjective question without any answer options, we can still apply the strategy. Without Step 1 (assessing the answer options), our task will be made slightly more challenging but not impossible at all.

Step 2: Rephrase the question; break it up into sub-questions if necessary

The best way to approach a sentence completion question is to turn it into a question. Some students may find sentence completion questions challenging precisely because it is not a direct question. Often, time is wasted trying to figure out *what* the question is asking.

To turn a sentence completion question into a direct question, place yourself in the shoes of the examiner and think about how you would test the student for comprehension of the same information, but in the form of, say, an MCQ-type question.

In this case, we can rephrase the sentence completion questions as follows:

1. What role does coffee play in many households?
2. After brewing, what do some people add to coffee before drinking it?

By doing this, you can clearly understand what the question is looking for. The process of transforming a sentence completion question into an actual question also implicitly forces you to narrow down what you are supposed to look for. You may not realize it, but you have to use "question words" in the process of forming questions — who, what, when, how and so on and so forth. At the very least, you roughly know now what you should look for, whether it is a person's name, a date or time, or an object.

Step 3: Use the Scanning and Matching technique to find answers to Step 1

Apply the "Scanning and Matching" strategy to the newly formed questions in Step 2.

1. What role does coffee play in many <u>households?</u>

    Many people around the world drink coffee, which has become a staple in numerous <u>households</u>.

After having zoomed in on a specific sentence by using "Scanning and Matching," you will notice that coffee is described as a **staple**. This is in fact the answer to the sentence completion question.

Let's take a look at the second example.

2. <u>After brewing,</u> what do some people <u>add to coffee</u> before drinking it?

    Lastly, you have to <u>brew</u> them at the perfect temperature and sometimes even add milk before it is ready for consumption.

This question is even more straightforward because the keyword "add" matches the passage. It becomes clear that the missing word is "milk."

IELTS Trainer

Apply the "Two-Layer Processing" technique to answer the questions which are based on the following reading passage.

Elevated Temperature as a Trigger of Coral Bleaching

Coral reefs are well known for their natural beauty. However, not many are aware that the survival of our coral reefs is under threat. In 2003, a mass coral bleaching event occurred in Bermuda. According to documentation, the first recorded event was in 1988, followed by 1991, 1992, 1995 and 1998. Mass coral bleaching also occurred in the Great Barrier Reef of Australia in 1998, 2002, 2004 and 2006.

Bleaching is the loss of color due to the partial to total elimination of the zooxanthellae ("zoox"), the algal pigments in yellow pencil coral. The zoox provides up to 90 percent of the energy needed by the coral. It is a relationship of mutual benefit because in return, the zoox receives shelter from the coral. Unless the stress trigger is removed or the coral recovers sufficiently from the shock, the coral will die because it relies heavily on the symbiosis with the zoox. There are three potential effects of elevated temperatures which are symptoms of coral bleaching: (1) Decrease in skeletal growth; (2) Reduction in zoox density; and (3) Chlorophyll A concentration.

The frequency of these coral bleaching events in more than one location around the world shows that it is not just a coincidence that these bleaching events have been occurring. There has to be one or more triggers causing these events to happen. In light of the recent concern in the rise in sea surface temperatures worldwide, temperature has been strongly correlated with coral bleaching, although the correlation is yet to be fully understood. There could be other factors in play, such as disease, changes in salinity and sedimentation from underwater activities like dredging. However, extremes of temperatures, both heat shocks and cold shocks, have been identified as a trigger of coral bleaching.

It is possible that bleached coral could recover if environmental conditions revert to normal, but it is unlikely that the coral would return to its optimal state. Since coral reefs not only have a crucial role in shaping the existent ecosystems today but also represent important sources of income and resources, it is crucial that the nature of the correlation between temperature and coral bleaching is understood. Furthermore, despite only making up less than 1 percent of the underwater ecosystem, coral reefs are home to 25 percent of marine animals and protect our shorelines.

Studies have shown global warming is on the rise, and that uncurbed pollution could adversely affect our planet's climate. In recent years, there has been no shortage of apocalyptic movies in popular culture that demonstrate the vivid consequences of what could happen if humankind were to let pollution get out of control. One such movie is *Interstellar*, which depicts a world that has become immensely polluted that the earth can no longer produce food. If warning signals like mass coral bleaching are ignored, such movies may no longer remain fiction.

Questions

1. How do we know that mass coral bleaching is not a one-off isolated event?
   A. It has happened multiple times in different places
   B. It correlates with increases in temperature
   C. There could be other factors at play
   D. Bleached coral cannot recover very easily

Step 1: Assess the answer options

Step 2: Rephrase the question

Step 3: Scan and Match

2. What is the passage's main view on coral reefs?
   A. It is being destroyed by global warming
   B. It is an important resource and needs to be protected
   C. Coral reefs have undergone many episodes of bleaching
   D. More research is needed to save the coral reefs

Step 1: Assess the answer options

Step 2: Rephrase the question

Step 3: Scan and Match

3. Which of the following statements proves that zooxanthellae is important to coral?
   A. Once the zoox is expelled, the coral will have a hard time recovering
   B. Zoox provides up to 90 percent of the energy needed by coral
   C. Zoox is immune to fluctuations in temperature
   D. Coral reefs house 25 percent of marine organisms

Step 1: Assess the answer options

Step 2: Rephrase the question

Step 3: Scan and Match

4. Which of the following is dependent on coral reefs?
   A. The underwater ecosystem
   B. Divers
   C. Climate scientists
   D. Marine animals

Step 1: Assess the answer options

The Academic Reading Section

Step 2: Rephrase the question

Step 3: Scan and Match

5. It is possible that coral bleaching has occurred if you observe a fall in zoox density or ....

~~*Step 1: Assess the answer options*~~ *(not applicable as the question does not have answer options)*

Step 2: Rephrase the question

Step 3: Scan and Match

6. There is a possible .... between temperature and coral bleaching

~~*Step 1: Assess the answer options*~~ *(not applicable as the question does not have answer options)*

Step 2: Rephrase the question

Step 3: Scan and Match

Answers:
1. A
2. B
3. B
4. D
5. Skeletal growth
6. Correlation

4 Thinking in Synonyms

Up to this point, we have covered some basic strategies that you can use to answer IELTS questions more quickly. These will serve you well for basic and intermediate questions, but when it comes to more advanced material you may find yourself stuck at places.

For example, a frequent observation is that students often come up to us and say that they've used the "Scanning and Matching" technique, except they still end up with the wrong answer. This is usually due to one of the following reasons:

a) The keywords scanned and matched to a sentence in the passage. The student lifted the answer directly from that sentence, but did not perform a check to make sure that the answer was relevant to the question and accurate.

b) The student highlighted keywords in the questions and/or answer options. However, the student was unable to match it to anything within the passage.

If you have faced any of the problems above before, we have a solution for you. It requires practice, but by training your mind to think in the correct way, you will be able to answer these more complex questions. This strategy is what we call "Thinking in Synonyms" and it aims to prepare you for IELTS's implicit test of whether you truly understand and are able to apply the English language.

Simple Steps

1. Think of direct synonyms for the keyword that cannot be matched to the passage
2. Think of examples that can illustrate the meaning of that keyword
3. Scan the passage once more for the items you have thought of in Steps 1 and 2

Elaboration with Examples

Here's the deal. You're not being directly tested on vocabulary in the IELTS, unlike in other standardized tests such as the SAT. There is no set list of words for you to memorize, and that can be a problem for some people who dislike uncertainty.

The Academic Reading Section

Instead, you're expected to understand different variations of sentences that possess the same meaning. Refer to the following example:

Sample passage:

> In most societies and families, a disproportionate amount of attention is spent on physical health. We rack up thousands in doctors' bills, medical check-ups and health supplements every year in a bid to fight off sicknesses and age. But is this the correct approach? An increasing number of doctors have begun to call for raising public awareness on the importance of maintaining mental health as well. Over the past decade, statistics has shown that the number of depression-related cases has nearly tripled. Suicides that have occurred as a result of depression have also been on the rise, even amongst teenagers. In certain examination-oriented societies, the pressure of obtaining good results at school can sometimes be so great that it drives those as young as primary school children to end their own lives.

Based on the passage above, the following statements are true, **except**

A. Maintaining good physical health can be costly
B. Poor mental health can lead to drastic consequences
C. It is important that doctors need to maintain mental health
D. All members of society, regardless of age, need to maintain good mental health

By highlighting the trap word "except," we know that we are supposed to look for the FALSE statement. Next, suppose we apply the "Scanning and Matching" technique, we will begin by underlining keywords in each answer option and matching them to the passage, as follows.

1. **Maintaining good <u>physical health</u> can be <u>costly</u>**

The keyword "physical health" matches to the following sentence within the paragraph:

> In most societies and families, a disproportionate amount of attention is spent on <u>physical health.</u>

So far, so good. But, if the student were to scan the vicinity of the matched sentence for "costly," she wouldn't be able to find it because it's not there. Because of this, the student may incorrectly assume that this statement is false, and hence select it as the answer — only to feel very puzzled when it turns out that answer option A isn't the correct option after all.

What just happened? The key problem is that the student wasn't thinking in synonyms. She wasn't flexible or adaptable enough in her way of thinking. If she couldn't find "costly" in the passage, then the next step would have been to find something that is synonymous to costly. She doesn't necessarily have to spell out each synonym for "costly" one by one, but the least she can do is keep this in mind as she scans the passage. As she evaluates every word, consider whether it could bear the same meaning as "costly."

If she did that, then she would probably have noticed this phrase: thousands in doctors' bills. This is another way of saying that it is "costly" — and therefore answer option A is in fact true. The student could safely rule that out as one of the possible answers.

In short, the *Simple Steps* completed were as follows:

Step 1: Think of direct synonyms for the keyword that cannot be matched to the passage
Step 2: Think of examples that can illustrate the meaning of that keyword
Step 3: Scan the passage once more for the items you have thought of in Steps 1 and 2

Step 1	Step 2	Step 3
Expensive	A lot of money	We rack up thousands in doctors' bills, medical check-ups and health supplements every year in a bid to fight off sicknesses and age

2. **Poor mental health can lead to <u>drastic consequences</u>**

Let's look at another example. In this case, the student attempts to scan and match for the keywords "drastic consequences," but to no avail. This could have the following consequences:

- The student could assume that the statement is false simply because the keywords cannot be matched to the passage
- The student could take a wild guess based on the other answer options available

The Academic Reading Section

Whatever the outcome, it's not going to look good. Both involve guessing, which means that points are not guaranteed.

Instead, if the student were to think in synonyms and look for something that meant "drastic consequences," she would likely have noticed the fact that poor mental health led to drastic consequences. This is not a direct synonym but it is an *example* that implies a similar meaning to "drastic consequences."

Hence, like answer option A, answer option B is true and therefore not the FALSE statement that we are looking for.

Step 1: Think of direct synonyms for the keyword that cannot be matched to the passage
Step 2: Think of examples that can illustrate the meaning of that keyword
Step 3: Scan the passage once more for the items you have thought of in Steps 1 and 2

Step 1	Step 2	Step 3
Terrible results	Death	<u>Suicides</u> that have occurred as a result of depression have also been on the rise, even amongst teenagers

3. It is important that <u>doctors</u> need to maintain mental health

This answer option would make the student feel a little more comfortable. The keyword matches to the passage easily, and the student is led to zoom in onto the following sentence:

> An increasing number of <u>doctors</u> have begun to call for raising public awareness on the importance of maintaining *mental* health as well.

The student may think that it is a good sign. The keyword "doctors" match, and on top of that, there are other similarities as well. For example, the matched sentence and answer option C both include the words "mental health" and "maintain."

Because of this, the student may jump to the conclusion that the statement must be true simply based on the matching keywords and similarities. But is it really true? Take a closer look. Answer option C states that *doctors* need to maintain good mental health. However, the passage says something completely different: that doctors are *calling for* others to maintain good mental health.

Thinking in Synonyms

The variation between the answer option and the passage is relatively minor, but as you can see, the impact is significant. It may cause the student to misinterpret answer option C as a true statement, when it is in fact false.

4. **All members** of society, <u>regardless of age</u>, need to maintain good mental health

Let's look at the last answer option. Here, the student will face a similar problem and that is the keywords do not match the passage. The student may end up facing the same consequences as demonstrated in answer option B, but this can be avoided if she had thought in synonyms.

For example, is there any indicator of age within the passage? There are a couple — the mention of "teenagers" and those "as young as primary school children." Did the doctors mention that only those of a certain age group should maintain good mental health? Not at all. Therefore, the statement is true — the advice is intended for all members of society.

The example above was deliberately tailored to show you the kinds of complications you may face when answering questions in the IELTS, and how thinking in synonyms can help you overcome these challenges. With this in mind, we will guide you through the steps needed to start thinking in synonyms so that you can avoid the mistakes that were done in the examples above.

Step 1: Think of direct synonyms for the keyword that cannot be matched to the passage
Step 2: Think of examples that can illustrate the meaning of that keyword
Step 3: Scan the passage once more for the items you have thought of in Steps 1 and 2

Step 1	Step 2	Step 3
Regardless of age	Young and old	Suicides that have occurred as a result of depression have also been on the rise, even amongst <u>teenagers</u>. In certain examination-oriented societies, the pressure of obtaining good results at school can sometimes be so great that it drives those as <u>young as primary school children</u> to end their own lives.

The Academic Reading Section

IELTS Trainer

*Test your understanding of the strategy outlined in the **Simple Steps** with the following short passages and questions. They have been deliberately designed such that you should think in synonyms. Otherwise you may not be able to arrive at the correct answer.*

The Melamine Milk Scare

Food safety is an important issue that is often overlooked, resulting in health problems such as vomiting and diarrhea. However, in recent years, there have been a number of food safety scandals that involved the deliberate act of tainting food for profit. The most prolific case was that of milk poisoning in China, which was exposed in 2008. This involved the addition of a chemical called melamine, which is derived from coal. The purpose of adding this chemical was to give the dairy processors the impression that the milk possessed a higher level of protein than it actually did. Of course, that translates into letting the processors believe that the milk is of a higher quality, and the irresponsible farmers would then receive more money than they were entitled to. In addition, this also helped conceal the fact that some farmers had added water to milk to increase volume, and needed to hide the watered-down protein levels.

These actions had drastic consequences because the raw milk was used in the production of several types of products, including infant milk formula. Melamine has the effect of causing small crystals to form in the kidneys, which can lead to the formation of kidney stones. These kidney stones can have the adverse effect of blocking urine production. In serious cases, this can lead to kidney failure and subsequently death, especially if left untreated.

In the case of the milk scandal, the effects were particularly shocking because many babies consumed some of the poisoned milk. Because babies have a much more vulnerable immune system and have no way of communicating any physical discomfort or ailment they may feel apart from through crying, a few succumbed to death. As many as 300,000 other babies fell sick, and this caused a global uproar. Many consumers began to doubt local brands of milk, and began flocking to foreign milk instead, as the latter was perceived to have stricter safety controls. As you might imagine, parents were willing to pay the premium as long as they could afford it, as this concerned the lives of their precious children.

Questions:

In boxes 1–10 on your answer sheet, write

> TRUE   if the statement agrees with the claims of the writer
> FALSE   if the statements contradicts the claims of the writer
> NOT GIVEN   if it is impossible to say what the writer thinks about this

1. Nowadays, everyone has very high awareness of why food safety rules need to be adhered to.

Step 1	Step 2	Step 3

2. Most serious food safety issues were caused by carelessness.

Step 1	Step 2	Step 3

3. When tested, milk with melamine may appear to be more nutritious than it is.

Step 1	Step 2	Step 3

4. There are potential additives that can be mixed into milk.

Step 1	Step 2	Step 3

5. Farmers who added melamine to milk were ethical.

Step 1	Step 2	Step 3

6. Few people know about the melamine milk scandal that surfaced in 2008.

Step 1	Step 2	Step 3

7. Raw milk can be used to make different types of items.

Step 1	Step 2	Step 3

8. Those who drink milk that has melamine will die.

Step 1	Step 2	Step 3

9. Chinese milk brands have recovered from the effects of the scandal.

Step 1	Step 2	Step 3

10. The milk poisoning scandal did not surprise anyone.

Step 1	Step 2	Step 3

11. Newborns are at much higher risk of being affected by poisoned milk, as compared to adults.

Step 1	Step 2	Step 3

12. Foreign babies are less likely to be affected by tainted milk.

Step 1	Step 2	Step 3

13. Many babies were affected by the melamine milk scandal.

Step 1	Step 2	Step 3

14. Only the Chinese were concerned about the melamine milk scandal.

Step 1	Step 2	Step 3

15. Parents are very cost-conscious when it comes to buying milk.

Step 1	Step 2	Step 3

Answers:
1. FALSE
2. FALSE
3. TRUE
4. NOT GIVEN
5. FALSE
6. FALSE
7. TRUE
8. FALSE
9. NOT GIVEN
10. FALSE
11. TRUE
12. NOT GIVEN
13. TRUE
14. FALSE
15. FALSE

5 True, False or Not Given?

The IELTS departs from the conventional form of this question, which has binary answer options (true or false). The part that most students stumble on is when differentiating between "false" and "not given." "False" means that the statement is absolutely wrong, whereas "not given" means that the question itself is flawed in the sense that it has asked you for an answer that cannot be found within the passage.

The other challenge with this type of question is that there are often traps embedded within the question itself. If you don't have a sharp enough eye to catch and understand the implications of these "traps," then you could end up giving the incorrect answer (even if you had genuinely understood the passage.) Thus, it is as much a test of whether you can understand the question as whether or not you understand the passage.

Fundamental examples of such "traps" include the usage of "except," which immediately turns a positive statement into a negative one. More subtle instances include the application of "already," which is an indication of a specific moment across a timeline. These small and seemingly insignificant changes have the power to determine whether or not you select the correct answer, so don't underestimate them.

This chapter will take you through the traps you need to recognize when faced with "true, false or not given" questions.

Simple Steps

1. Underline the traps in the question and answer options
2. Rephrase the question to reflect its direct meaning
3. Attempt to prove whether a statement is true or false; "not given" is a last resort

Elaboration with Examples

Step 1: Underline the traps in the question and answer options

Here are broad categories of traps that you should look out for. These are the words that, if overlooked, will change the meaning of the question completely.

Under each category, we will show examples of how these traps can trick you into thinking that the question is something that it is not.

While we will list out all the usual traps that may be used in the IELTS, note that this is not exhaustive and you should still keep a sharp eye out for other traps that may be weaved into the questions.

a) Negations

Negations normally make a statement negative. However, it is also possible for the question to contain double negatives that would make the statement *positive*.

Here is an example of a single-negation:

> The following statements are true, EXCEPT ...

What it means, of course, is that you should look for the *false* statement. The same question rephrased with a double-negation is as follows:

> The following statements are false, EXCEPT ...

As you can see, there are two negations in the question above. The first one is "false," and the second "except." This makes the statement a positive one overall, and you should therefore begin looking for the statement that is *true*. You can imagine how you could easily get this wrong, should you glance over the question much too quickly during the examination and miss the first negation.

No.	Negations	Sample Questions
1	False	Which of the following statements is false?
2	Not	Which of the following statements is not true?
3	Except	The following are all contributors to environmental pollution, except ...
4	Never	Which of the following has never been attempted by the United Nations?

b) Quantifications

Quantifications can appear in two ways. The first manner is in the form of a specific number. For example, "Which of the following has a presence in two countries?" The trap here is the number "two" — select any option that has more or less than that, and you lose the point.

The second manner is in the form of indicating a degree. This is not as specific as providing numbers, but it can change the nature of the question quite significantly. Refer to the following example:

Why did introducing hybrid vehicles have <u>little</u> effect on reducing pollution?

Rephrased, the question above asks why hybrid vehicles were *ineffective* in reducing pollution.

To understand the impact of the word "little," consider the following example of what the exact same question would look like otherwise:

Why did introducing hybrid vehicles have an effect on reducing pollution?

As you can see, just a mere word "little" transformed the meaning of the question into a more positive one. If we were to rephrase the question above, it is equivalent to asking why hybrid vehicles were *effective* in reducing pollution.

Most people think that the positive and negative statements are only influenced by negations as shown in "a) Negations." The examples above, however, show that even quantifications can have the same effect.

Thus, when faced with a "true, false or not given" question, always look out for these "traps." They will help you understand the direct meaning of both the question and the answer options, so that you avoid losing marks due to oversight.

No.	Quantifications	Sample Questions/Answer Options
1	All	All countries have adopted laws on human rights.
2	Some	The police have had some success in eradicating human trafficking.
3	Most	Most people believe that humans evolved from chimpanzees.
4	Few	Few would argue that restricting the sale of sugar is a wise move.
5	Little	There has been little support for the mayor's proposed plan to build a new shopping mall.
6	Minimal	Which of the following have had a minimal effect on the political climate in Brazil?
7	Significant	What was a significant factor in Thomas O'Brien's decision to become a priest?
8	Somewhat	The jury was somewhat undecided in this particular court case.
9	Fully/wholly	The general public has been wholly supportive of the new policies.
10	Major	Did public opinion play a major role in deciding government policy on public smoking?
11	Minor	The complaint was dismissed because it was only a minor issue that was raised.

c) Time

Time is another important aspect that can completely change the meaning of a statement or question. For some students whose native language is not English, this can be even more of an issue because not every language has tenses.

Let's look at some examples to see precisely why time is important:

When Albert Einstein began exploring relativity, what progress had <u>already</u> been achieved in the field of physics?

Now, take a look at a version of the same question, albeit without "already":

When Albert Einstein began exploring relativity, what progress had yet to be achieved in the field of physics?

While the former zooms in on what was in existence *before* Albert Einstein, the latter focuses on what did not yet exist until *after* Albert Einstein's time. You can see how misunderstanding or overlooking the time-markers could cause you to miss the correct answer completely.

Here are some examples of time markers that you should look out for:

No.	Quantifications	Sample Questions/Answer Options
1	During	What did Barack Obama achieve <u>during</u> his presidency?
2	While	What did the victim do <u>while</u> waiting for the police to arrive?
3	In the meantime	The victim hid in the bathroom. <u>In the meantime</u>, she barricaded the door so that the intruder could not get in.
4	Before	<u>Before</u> Churchill became prime minister, what was the political climate like in Britain?
5	Pre	What was the political climate like in Britain <u>pre</u>-Churchill?
6	Prior to	What do lawyers normally do <u>prior</u> to a major trial?
7	Preceding	What was the most significant event <u>preceding</u> the National Day celebrations?
8	Post	What problems did France face <u>post</u>-World War II?
9	After	Why are doctors only able to determine the root cause of mental illnesses only <u>after</u> numerous tests and observations?
10	Following	<u>Following</u> the terrorist attack, many countries imposed stricter immigration rules.
11	Later	It was only <u>later</u> that the doctor realized the patient was suffering from multiple sclerosis.

12	Not yet	France had <u>not yet</u> built nuclear power plants at the time.
13	Already	By the time the government clamped down on the virus outbreak, it was <u>already</u> too late.
14	Pending	The project has stalled and is <u>pending</u> the approval of governmental licenses.

d) Modal verbs

Modal verbs are used to convey varying degrees of doubt or certainty on whether something is going to happen. Common modal verbs include "can," "must," "might" and so on.

In the IELTS, here is how modal verbs can trip you up. Imagine you are given the following two statements in a "true, false or not given" type of question.

> Before participating in a high-risk activity such as sky-diving, you <u>must</u> do thorough research about the risks involved.

> Before participating in a high-risk activity such as sky-diving, you <u>might</u> want to do thorough research about the risks involved.

If you are not familiar with modal verbs, you may skim over these subtle differences without realizing that it can have a significant impact. The first statement (with the word "must") means that researching the risks involved is something that is necessary. The second statement (with the word "might") merely says that doing such research is advisable — you should do it, but if you don't, no one is going to penalize you or prevent you from participating in sky-diving.

In addition, modal verbs can be used to describe ability as well — for example, "He can speak Mandarin." But for the purposes of the "true, false or not given" type of question, understanding the usage of modals in expressing degrees of certainty is still the topmost priority for you.

Here are more examples of modals in action:

No.	Usage	Modal Verb Examples
1	To imply that there is a possibility	May Could Might
2	To imply that there is a probability (more certain than possibility) or to make a recommendation	Should Ought to
3	To imply conditionality or habits	Would
4	To imply that something is definite and will happen	Must Will

Step 2: Rephrase the question to reflect its direct meaning

To avoid confusion, ensure that you rephrase the question to reflect its direct meaning immediately after you have highlighted the traps.

For example, let's take a look at some rephrased questions:

Original: The following happened after Winston Churchill became Prime Minister, except

Rephrased: Which of the following **did not happen after** Winston Churchill became Prime Minister?

OR

Rephrased: Which of the following happened **before** Winston Churchill became Prime Minister?

Based on the example above, you should be able to understand how rephrasing makes life easier for you. If you were to follow the original wording, you would have to bear *two* things in mind while searching for the question: first, you need to remember that you are looking for something that happened after Winston Churchill became Prime Minister. Then, all of a sudden, you have to flip that thought around with an "except." It's tiring and it's confusing. Turn potentially confusing questions into straightforward questions — it'll save you a headache, and some points.

Step 3: Attempt to prove whether a statement is true or false; "not given" is a last resort

Here's the breakdown of logic and how you should approach each statement.

a) FALSE — It is much easier to prove that something is wrong, rather than it is true. You only need one false detail to declare an answer as false.
b) TRUE — On the flip side, to prove that the statement is true, you must ensure that not even the tiniest detail is false. This is why trying to prove something is TRUE should only be your second step.
c) NOT GIVEN — This is the hardest to determine because you have to read the entire passage to ensure that the statement is truly and surely "not given."

For students who find it hard to differentiate between "false" and "not given", here is a simplification of the major differences:

Aspect	FALSE	NOT GIVEN
Definition	The statement can be disproved with information from the passage	There is no information to help you decisively ascertain as to whether the statement is true or false
Sample Passage	For decades, humankind has dreamt of exploring the galaxy and understanding what truly lies beyond us. The question of whether "we are alone" — that is, whether or not aliens exist has remained unanswered despite the incredible advances in modern technology. Curiosity, therefore, is one of the reasons as to why governments have poured billions of dollars into funding space exploration projects. But there is a second reason. Our planet will not be able to sustain us forever, unless we can find a way to control the amount of wastage and pollution that we produce. There are some scientists who believe space exploration is a necessary protection against potential disasters in the future. Should Earth become uninhabitable one day, we can look to the stars to form new colonies in outer space.	
Sample Statement	A false statement is as follows: Curiosity is the only reason as to why governments have funded space exploration projects.	A "not given" statement: China has overtaken the United States in terms of space exploration funding.

| Explanation | You can disprove the above statement by highlighting that the passage raises a second reason: space exploration can also be used as a tool to find other potentially habitable stars and planets. | You cannot disprove or prove the above statement because the passage simply does not mention space exploration funding in such specific terms. |

IELTS Trainer

Answer the questions based on the passage below:

> TRUE   if the statement agrees with the claims of the writer
> FALSE   if the statements contradicts the claims of the writer
> NOT GIVEN if it is impossible to say what the writer thinks about this

From the Modern to the Postmodern: Louis Kahn

The enigma of Louis Kahn can be examined from two angles. Firstly, his position as a key transitional figure between the modern masters of architecture (traditionally associated with the likes of Mies van der Rohe, Le Corbusier, Walter Gropius and J.J.P. Oud) and the subsequent rise of postmodernism. The second and most important point concerns the development of a personal, distinctive architectural style most aptly described by Neil Levine as the "aesthetics of the unfinished." While directly influenced by the architecture's growing interest in simplified abstraction and the works of Mies van der Rohe, Kahn ultimately re-examined and redefined modern architecture through the lens of historical representations that had been largely forgotten over the first half of the twentieth century. One trope in particular would occupy his fascination for the rest of his life: the image of the ruin.

    Kahn's aesthetics of the unfinished is multifaceted and is best explained through examples of his work that possess these elements. One of his earliest commissions, the Yale University Art Gallery (1951–1953) illustrates the renaissance concept of "non-finito", or the "inability or lack of will to bring … work to completion," that had made a resurgence in 19th-century schools of art and architecture as a symbol of the modern. In architecture, non-finito suggests ambiguity, subjectivity, self-consciousness, and the acknowledgement of "the difficult transaction that takes place in art … between abstraction of thought and material demands of brute matter." This open-ended quality is particularly apparent in how the thin horizontal bands of light stone on the front facade wall project out as shallow ledges and run the entire length of the building, only to be terminated by the street. Some Miesian characteristics can be seen in the end wall infill of steel and glass. However, Kahn makes the design his own by having the end wall read as a sectional cut of a building that was never meant to be finished nor ended by the mere street.

Not only that, Kahn's unfinished aesthetic delights in the richness that comes with juxtaposing the new sensibilities of modern architecture and the dated historical image of the ruin. Kahn wholly embraced new materials and methods of construction at the beginning of his career but showed a marked preference for timeless, existential materials such as unpolished concrete and wood later on. He was preoccupied with the notion of the "existence-will" of a building, claiming that "what will be has always been," but it is the architect's duty to factor in the current circumstances in the process of designing. This Neo-Platonic concept came to be known in the terms of "Form and Design," or "Desire and Need." The Library at Philips Exeter Academy (1965–1972), with its load-bearing naked brick walls, reinforced concrete ring and extremely grand central atrium, easily conjures the image of Kahn "wrapping ruins around buildings."

Finally, the "lack" or the want found in Kahn's buildings plays a very significant role in bridging the gap between grandiose historical modes of representation and those of the modern era. To Kahn, it is awareness of this state of incompleteness that adds a layer of phenomenological awareness to one's experience of architecture, and inspires wonder. At his best, Kahn sought to not only challenge the status quo of representation in purely functionalist and materialist terms — unlike his predecessor Mies, but also acknowledge the power of the individual imagination to supply the most elegant solution to this lack of deliberately maintained and exaggerated in all his buildings. The Salk Institute best exemplifies this power: the open, porous meeting place on the central plaza flanked by the various private laboratories widens up to an undiminished view of the Pacific Ocean on the horizon, sky reflected and mirrored in the homogeneous marble slabs of the plaza.

As a conclusion, Kahn's work breaches a new level of self-consciousness, paving the way for multiple readings, individual interpretation and recursive questioning in a field historically dominated by rational logic and universal order. Though there are several inconsistencies in Kahn's vast and confusing terminology, it is his intentional ambiguity that gives his work strength and verisimilitude to withstand the chaos of an era fraught with representational concerns.

Author: Darell Koh

Questions

1. Louis Kahn was a friend of Mies van der Rohe.
2. Louis Kahn made a significant impact on the world of architecture.
3. The Yale University Art Gallery was designed by Louis Kahn.
4. Walter Gropius was obsessed by the image of the ruin.
5. There are some similarities between Louis Kahn and Mies van der Rohe's style of architecture.
6. Louis Kahn had always preferred materials such as unpolished concrete and wood.
7. The concept of "non-finito" was created by Louis Kahn.
8. Many architects today practice Louis Kahn's belief in the notion of the "existence-will" of a building.
9. Mies van der Rohe challenged the status quo of representation in purely functionalist and materialist terms.
10. The Salk Institute is by far the work that Louis Kahn is most proud of.

Answers:

1. NOT GIVEN
2. TRUE
3. TRUE
4. FALSE
5. TRUE
6. FALSE
7. FALSE
8. NOT GIVEN
9. FALSE
10. NOT GIVEN

Academic Reading Practice Examinations

Practice Examination 1

Reading Passage 1

You should spend about 20 minutes on **Questions 1–13**, which are based on Reading Passage 1 below.

"Population Doom" in Japan

Japan has seen a wave of media and scholarly attention describing the impending "population doom." For Economics professor Hiroshi Yoshida, the myriad publications describing Japan's demographic decline were not alarming enough. In April of last year he and his research team used the most recent national statistics to calculate the rate of decrease in the population of children, and created an online population clock that counts down to the last child in Japan. Because the countdown relies on static conditions, it is unreliable. Nevertheless, it is a critical statement of Japan's future prospects, and a reminder of a problem the Japanese government has been actively facing for over fifteen years. Furthermore, it upholds the relevancy of Japan's demographic issue.

Japan is a worthwhile case study for demographers because demographic data presents two extremes: lowest fertility rate and longest life expectancy. Data compiled by the Organization for Economic Cooperation and Development (OECD) shows that Japan is amongst the countries with the lowest fertility rates. Japan's total fertility rate (TFR) fell below replacement level in 1980 to 1.75, and has remained below the population replacement threshold since then, reaching its lowest point in 2005 at 1.26. Since then, the TFR has increased, reaching 2.39 in 2010, but has yet to reach a stable level that would ensure future population growth.

Japan, like most industrialized nations, currently faces the demographic issue of a declining birth rate, but Japan seems to be getting more attention than other countries. Perhaps it is because Japan's life expectancy is the highest in the world, and *this*, combined with low fertility rate, poses a more serious threat to Japan's socio-economic structure than any other low-fertility nation.

Aging in the population through the pyramid results in an inverted pyramid with a heavy top and a narrow bottom. These projections show that a large portion of the population by 2050 will be older than 65. In fact, it is estimated that by 2050 the ratio of working population to those at the retirement age will be nearly 1:1 — down from 3.6:1 in 2000. If we include the portion of the population below working age, it means by 2050 Japan will be facing an unstable dependency ratio in which dependents outnumber those in the working population. In Japan, these demographic issues are described in terms of a new "low birth-aging society" (*shōshika kōrei shakai*).

In response to the "low birth-aging society" (*shōshika kōrei shakai*), the Japanese government developed a series of family-friendly policies (*famirī furendurī seisaku*) that would create an environment conducive to childbearing. For example, reforms to maternity leave laws, and laws targeting the high costs of childrearing in Japan. These policies in 1994 became known as the Angel Plan, which began a wave of five-year plans aimed at increasing the nation's TFR. The first of these Angel Plans was for the period of 1995–2000, and focused on the compatibility of work and childcare and more importantly solidified public support for child support. Nevertheless, finding the right balance of policies to effectively impact demography is an endless challenge for the leading political parties of Japan: Democratic Party of Japan (DPJ) and Liberal Democratic Party of Japan (LDP). Continuing debates on policy details have prevented these rival parties from acting, and it was only recently that they could agree on reforming the Childcare Allowance Act.

The problem with many of the pro-natalist policies is that they have been one-dimensional and were mostly focused on the economics of childrearing. Within the last half century, the field of demography, or population studies, has made significant findings that support the use of varied policy levers to combat declining fertility and population decline. One of the most important contributions to the demographic study of fertility decline was made possible through the Princeton Fertility Project. Ansley J. Coale, one of America's foremost demographers, found that 1960 marked a point in European history in which all countries were on a "continuous and irreversible" path to a decline in childbearing. He further suggested that contemporary adults would limit their births in terms of their own interest, which results in lower fertility rates.

Academic Reading Practice Examinations

This is in contrast to historical controls of birth dictated by social structures conducive to higher levels of childbearing. These were trends that would continue and prevail in all most industrialized countries, and have now led to population decline instead of population growth, which was the heart of demographic studies since Malthus. Since then, there has been extensive research and studies on declining birth rates.

Author: Daniel Velasco

Questions 1-7

Do the following statements agree with the information given in Reading Passage 1?

In boxes 1-7 on your answer sheet, write

    TRUE   if the statement agrees with the claims of the writer
    FALSE   if the statements contradicts the claims of the writer
    NOT GIVEN if it is impossible to say what the writer thinks about this

1. The threat of "population doom" in Japan is a recent trend that has only emerged over the last few years.
2. Ironically, Japan has both the lowest fertility rate and longest life expectancy.
3. Japan is not the only country that is facing the demographic issue of a declining birth rate.
4. In other industrialized nations, a large part of the population will be over 65 years of age by 2050.
5. The Angel Plan was a series of family-friendly policies aimed at decreasing the total fertility rate.
6. The leading political parties of Japan could not decide on a plan to tackle the falling birth rate due to restricted financial resources.
7. Tackling the declining birth rate requires a multi-dimensional approach.

Questions 8–13

Choose the correct letter, **A, B, C or D**.

Write the correct letter in boxes 8–13 on your answer sheet.

8. In 2010, what was Japan's total fertility rate?
    A. 1.75
    B. 1.26
    C. 2.39
    D. 3.6:1

9. According to the passage, which of the following is **not** an implication of Professor Hiroshi Yoshida's work on Japan's demographic decline?
    A. Japan's demographic decline is truly alarming
    B. The Japanese government needs to ensure that the demographic decline is reversed
    C. The countdown relies on static conditions, and is unreliable
    D. Japan's demographic issue remains relevant today

10. Which of the following is **not** a measure that the Japanese government has undertaken to tackle demographic decline?
    A. Reforming maternity leave laws
    B. Targeting the high costs of childbearing in Japan
    C. Focused on the compatibility of work and childcare
    D. Created public awareness campaigns regarding the joys of having children

11. Which of the following statements regarding the Angel Plan is true?
    A. It is a five-year plan aimed at increasing Japan's total fertility rate
    B. Its execution was delayed due to political debate
    C. It has been effective in increasing Japan's total fertility rate
    D. It led to the Childcare Allowance Act

12. According to Ansley J. Coale, what is one of the typical drivers behind demographic decline?
    A. Modern careers would make it difficult for parents to have children
    B. Modern adults would limit their births in terms of their own interest
    C. Social structures became more conducive to higher levels of child bearing
    D. Modern society only uses a one-dimensional approach to tackle demographic decline

Academic Reading Practice Examinations

13. What is the author's general view on Japan's demographic issue?
    A. Most industrialized nations will face similar demographic issues, just like Japan
    B. A multi-dimensional approach is needed to solve the pressing issue of Japan's demographic decline
    C. There needs to be more research and studies on demographic decline
    D. Japan's demographic decline could have been prevented

Answers to Questions 1–13

1. FALSE
2. TRUE
3. TRUE
4. NOT GIVEN
5. FALSE
6. NOT GIVEN
7. TRUE
8. C
9. C
10. D
11. A
12. B
13. B

Reading Passage 2

You should spend about 20 minutes on **Questions 14–26**, which are based on Reading Passage 2 below.

An Account of Detached Macrophytes in South Western Australia

Detached macrophytes are essentially broken-off pieces of plants such as the pieces of seaweed and kelp that you see on the beach. They are commonly seen drifting or beached along some beaches in South Western Australia, and they hold significant value for the marine and nearby ecosystems as well as a few human industries. Additionally, drift may even be of value to some aspects of marine ecological research. However, little study has been done on the topic.

As an exploration into the topic, this article aims to provide an account of the abundance and composition of drift found over a day (14 February 2012), as well as to test a methodical design for future considerations. Beached drift from two parallel bays on opposing shores of Point Peron, Western Australia was collected, identified, separated by species and weighed.

The results were compared for between bay similarities, and analyzed in relation to available hydrological and local ecosystem information. The findings suggest that though some correlations may be inferred, there is little validity due to the constantly fluctuating deposition of detached macrophytes and limited information on the ecosystem. Additionally, the temporal and spatial scales of the correlations are difficult to assess. The potential use of drift information in scientific research exists, but much research needs to be done to further explore the questions of feasibility, methodology and validity.

The decomposition of drift macrophytes is an important step in the nutrient cycle, returning dissolved carbon and other nutrients to the water. Hyndes and Lavery (2005) found that drift is an important source of nutrition for detritivores and thus play a significant role in the near-shore food web as detritivores are preyed upon by secondary consumers. Beached macrophytes play a similar role as a source of nutrition for terrestrial detritivores. Studies conducted in the near-shore shallows of Western Australia found that there is a positive relationship between fish abundance and presence of drift. Because a significant number of the fish sampled were juveniles, Robertson and Lenanton (1984) suggest that drift macrophytes may act as nurseries for some economically significant fish species due to the availability of food such as amphipods. Their results also suggest that these mats provide shelter from avian predators in the daytime.

Apart from its role in the ecosystem, drift is also economically useful. Kirkman and Kendrick (1997) reviewed some of these uses: algae can be used as alginate, agar, fertilizers and feed for cattle and abalone farms; seagrasses can be used as insulating material and fertilizer. Detached macrophytes are harvested both from subtidal drift mats and from the beach, although regulations are still being developed to control harvests due to the importance of drift in the ecosystem.

As studies have shown that near-shore fish fauna are affected by the abundance of drift, it would be interesting to assess if drift may be used as a proxy or indicator for subtidal fauna community. Similarly, drift composition may potentially be used as a proxy for living macrophyte communities offshore because drift is detached from living reefs and beds. Coupled with data on living offshore floral communities, another possible use of data on drift is to aid in studies of hydrology as drift is transported by water currents and wind. Although such information is potentially informative, the composition and abundance of drift has scarcely been studied.

The study sites are two parallel bays along Point Peron, Western Australia. Shoalwater Bay (SHW) is a stretch of beach about 500 m long on the southwest face of the point, while Mangles Bay (MNG) is approximately 2 km long on the northeast face. Most of the terrain up to 5 km off the shore of SHW consists of sandy bottoms with some limestone platforms. The limestone platforms from Warnbro Sound up to SHW are dominated by brown algae of the genus *Sargassum* and *Ecklonia* as well as a variety of red algae, while the sandy flats are predominantly beds of *Posidonia* and *Amphibolis*. The marine flora around MNG is similarly dominated by seagrass beds of *Posidonia*. Within Cockburn Sound there are species of *Ecklonia, Sargassum, Ulva, Cladophora* and red algae around the eastern flats.

Overall, drift density was much higher at SHW than at MNG and there was only 20% similarity in species densities between the bays. However, similarity between the two bays was estimated to be higher at approximately 50% when looking at average contribution of species to total density. *Ecklonia radiata, Sargassum sp.* and *Posidonia sp.* were found in high densities at both bays. Though not found in great abundance, the number of red algal species was double that of brown algae.

The difference in drift density between the bays might be explained by the area's hydrology and winds. As studies have shown, water circulation is primarily wind-driven around Point Peron and circulation in Cockburn Sound is predominantly from the north. However, due to the Garden Island causeway, the stretch of MNG in this study probably receives mass transport most from the west. A Southwest wind is capable of driving water up round the tip of Point Peron and into the study site of MNG, but the waves generated would be much weaker than if the site was directly exposed to Southwest winds.

The composition data from this study agrees to some extent with expectations, given the information about the living macrophyte communities around Point Peron; these communities were dominated by *Ecklonia, Sargassum, Posidonia, Amphibolis* and red algae in previous studies. There seems to be some support for the feasibility of using drift or beached macrophytes as a proxy for living offshore macrophytes. However, the accuracy of such a proxy will require much more extensive studying of drift composition coupled with surveys of live seabed flora. Additionally, hydrology and wind will have to be taken into account.

Author: Flora Wong

Questions 14–21

Classify the following roles that macrophytes play or could play in relation to

- A. The ecosystem
- B. Economics
- C. As a proxy in further research

Write the correct letter, **A, B or C**, in boxes 14–21 on your answer sheet

14. Return dissolved carbon and other nutrients to the water
15. Used as feed for cattle and abalone farms
16. Source of nutrition for terrestrial detritivores
17. Used as an indicator to assess the subtidal fauna community
18. Act as nurseries for certain fish
19. Provide shelter to fish from avian predators
20. Aid in hydrology studies
21. Produce insulating material and fertilizers

Questions 22–26

Complete the sentences below.

Write **NO MORE THAN TWO WORDS** from the passage for each answer.

Write your answers in boxes 23–26 on your answer sheet.

22. The decomposition of drift macrophytes is an important step in the ....
23. Regulations are being developed to control the .... of drift macrophytes due to its importance in the ecosystem.
24. The limestone platforms of Warnbro Sound up to Shoalwater Bay are dominated by .... as well as red algae.
25. Around Point Peron, water circulation is primarily driven by......... ....
26. Between Sholwater Bay and Mangles Bay, there was only a 20% similarity in ....

Answers for Questions 14–26

14. A
15. B
16. A
17. C
18. A
19. A
20. C
21. B
22. Nutrient cycle
23. Harvest
24. Brown algae
25. Wind
26. Species densities

Reading Passage 3

You should spend about 20 minutes on **Questions 27–40**, which are based on Reading Passage 3 below.

Theater in Victorian London

A. Sir William Schwenck Gilbert (1836-1911) and Sir Arthur Seymour Sullivan (1842-1900) are to this day synonymous with founding British comic opera (now called an operetta), an original musical genre entwining elements of classical European opera with witty British playwriting. Their Savoy operas, as the Gilbert and Sullivan comic operas are now called, eventually changed the course of performing arts history, since modern-day musical theater is soundly grounded in the theatrical innovations that arose from the original Savoy productions. The Savoy operas also gave Victorian actresses — British, American, and European — social respectability as well as vibrant characters to aspire to and to one day perform.

B. Before the emergence of the Gilbert and Sullivan canon, theater in Victorian London was frequently amateurish, unprofessional, and severely limited in theatrical opportunity. While there was a significant Pantomime theater scene, these productions were written and produced for the lower classes; middle- and upper-class citizens had limited entertainment, which was primarily composed of imported European operas. In pre-Gilbertian British culture, going out to see a theatrical production was considered disgraceful; actors were deemed vagabonds and actresses were assumed to be prostitutes.

C. Victorian theatrical productions had also mainly been about special effects rather than plot, and formal European operas concentrated on vocal display rather than strong acting. Gilbert and Sullivan changed this; through their collaboration, the dialogue and plot became *as important* as the theatrical effects and musical score. Before Gilbert and Sullivan there was also no English music theater; the only reputable musical entertainments were foreign operas like Mozart's *The Magic Flute* (1791) and Donizetti's *Don Pasquale* (1843). The closest endeavors to English musical entertainment were vocal renditions of Henry Russell's *The Far West, or The Emigrant's Progress from the Old World to the New* (1845) and his songs like "There's a Good Time Coming, Boys" (1846). English pub songs were also popular with the less-educated masses, yet upper-class citizens would not have dared to be seen at these performances. British society now needed respectable and witty *theatrical* entertainment, and this was the void that the Gilbert and Sullivan comic operas filled. The Savoy operas were the middle ground between low burlesque and formal European operas, making theater accessible and respectable for all.

D. Mr. Richard D'Oyly Carte (1844–1901) directly addressed this budding need for new entertainment. Already a well-known theater manager, Carte became the frontrunner and manager of the D'Oyly Carte Opera Company, which later produced all of the Savoy operas. In the late 1860s, Carte saw an opportunity to simultaneously educate the masses *and* cultivate a new musical following via theater. Because of his efforts and unique vision, the seeds of British comic opera were sown. This vision gave middle- and upper-class patrons — who had increasing amounts of leisure time and a disposable income — a kind of spectacle that was simultaneously witty and entertaining as well as respectable.

E. The first time Sullivan wrote music for comedic theater was in 1867, when he composed for the one-act opera libretto *Cox and Box* and the two-act comic opera libretto *Contrabandista*; in *Cox and Box* a musical theme emerges that is later seen in the Savoy operas, namely, that the finale has three verses and ends triumphantly at the top of the musical scale. Between 1869 and 1871 (the premiere of the Gilbert and Sullivan short comic opera *Thespis*), both Gilbert and Sullivan continued to gain widespread acclaim in their respective fields. In 1869, Sullivan composed "The Prodigal Son," again propelling him to fame, and became a professor at the Royal Academy of Music in London.

F. Gilbert established himself as a producer and playwright of both serious and comic works, prospering financially and reviving the energy of the Victorian stage. Unlike other Victorian playwrights, Gilbert had a say in how actors presented his words and how they interpreted his characters; Gilbert's rehearsals became notorious throughout London for being much longer and more detailed than those run by his contemporaries. Gilbert was also in charge of all technical and production aspects, tasks that were usually allotted to a stage manager. Like Gilbert, Sullivan also prospered financially and occupationally; Queen Victoria herself asked him to revise Prince Albert's amateur musical works. By 1871, both Gilbert and Sullivan were among the most famous in their respective occupational fields.

G. Performers had long been chastised, condemned, and mistrusted in British society, and it was largely through the creation of the Gilbert and Sullivan operas that this reputation changed. Importantly, the Gilbert and Sullivan tradition made actresses respectable with all social classes and with both female *and* male theatergoers. The Savoy operas also gave actresses an unexpected level of respectability and income. These women no longer needed to make a living as courtesans or prostitutes, or had to depend on a man to support them financially; the ladies of the Savoy Theater made a handsome income in recognition of their performance skills and professionalism, paving the way for women's economic independence in a professional career. Gilbert often wrote female characters with a particular actress in mind, and thus, the original actresses live on in today's revivals of the Gilbert and Sullivan tradition.

H. The Gilbert and Sullivan comic operas continue to be exceptionally popular, making modern audiences laugh and cry whether we see the satire or not, and Gilbert's implicit criticism making us continually re-interested in their works.

Author: Elizabeth Anne Biddle

Questions 27–31

Reading Passage 3 has eight paragraphs, **A–H**.

Which paragraph contains the following information?

Write the correct letter, **A–H**, in boxes 27–31 on your answer sheet.

27. Gilbert and Sullivan comic operas fulfilled British society's need for respectable and witty theatrical entertainment.
28. The Savoy Theater succeeded in empowering women, allowing them to have an exceptional level of respectability and income.
29. British culture used to view going out to see a theatrical production as a disgraceful act.
30. Queen Victoria asked Sir Arthur Sullivan to revise Prince Albert's amateur musical works.
31. "The Prodigal Son" helped boost Sir William Gilbert to fame.

Questions 32–35

Do the following statements agree with the information given in Reading Passage 3?

In boxes 32–35 on your answer sheet, write

        TRUE   if the statement agrees with the claims of the writer
        FALSE   if the statements contradicts the claims of the writer
        NOT GIVEN if it is impossible to say what the writer thinks about this

32. Sir William Gilbert's rehearsals were known to be much longer and detailed than his contemporaries.
33. Despite being collaborators, Sir William Gilbert and Sir Arthur Sullivan were competitive, and were sometimes jealous of each other's achievements.
34. Sir William Gilbert's female characters were often based on real women.
35. English pub songs were very popular amongst upper-class British citizens.

Questions 36–40

Complete the summary below.

Choose **NO MORE THAN TWO WORDS** from the passage for each answer.

Write your answers in boxes 36–40 on your answer sheet.

Gilbert and Sullivan's comic operas are also known as **36** ………………… and merged **37** ……………………… opera with witty British playwriting. Mr. Richard D'Oyly Carte was a famous **38** …………………… that produced all of the Savoy operas. Gilbert and Sullivan quickly gained widespread fame, and received personal requests even from monarchs such as **39** ………………….. Sir Thomas Sullivan was also appointed as a **40** ………………… in the Royal Academy of Music in London.

Answers to Questions 27–40

27. C
28. G
29. B
30. F
31. E
32. TRUE
33. NOT GIVEN
34. TRUE
35. FALSE
36. Savoy operas
37. Classical European
38. Theatre manager
39. Queen Victoria
40. Professor

Practice Examination 2

Reading Passage 1

You should spend about 20 minutes on **Questions 1–11**, which are based on Reading Passage 1 below.

Seeing Me, Seeing You

A. In conventional theater, the actors in a play act according to a script. Everyone on stage knows who is supposed to be doing what, and what their underlying intentions are. However, in the theater of everyday life, the absence of a pre-determined script forces us to use other tools to try to understand the motives of other people. In order to communicate our intentions, we translate them into bodily actions so that other people can understand them as well. This works when there is a shared experience between the actor and the audience, as they both agree to the meaning of the act. When you tell me something, I understand you because we both share an understanding of the language and connotations that accompany the words that are used. However, it is more often the case that we encounter actions or situations of others which we have never personally experienced before. Variances in age, experience, upbringing, culture and other personal factors ensure that when we meet another person, our paradigms will invariably differ in some way or another. As a result of the difference of our paradigms with that of others, misunderstandings can occur.

B. Of course, we may think that this applies to people that we have never met before, or people from different cultures. However, misunderstandings can occur just as often in close familial relationships. In Martha Manning's *The Common Thread: Mothers, Daughters, and the Power of Empathy*, she details many such instances where conflicts between mother and daughter arise as a result of different viewpoints. One such instance is when the author took her daughter to see *Bambi*, thinking of it as a classic Disney movie. However, she forgot that while movies like *Bambi* are sentimental Disney classics to adults, they are akin to disaster flicks for young children. Her daughter gets upset after Bambi's mother gets shot and is traumatized at Bambi's mother getting killed, and insists that they leave straightaway. Hence, the difference in one's experiential structure in terms of age is just one of the many reasons for the occurrence of misunderstandings, even between close family members.

C. The common perception about empathy is that it is only about understanding others, and nothing else. This is flawed, as empathy is more than that. Empathy is not only about understanding others; it is also about understanding oneself to understand others. By being more aware of ourselves, we are able to gain better insight into the situations of others through empathy. In terms of performance, this means that the audience should not only rely on the actor to convey his intended meaning correctly — they should also try to understand how they interpret the actor's actions, and by doing so they gain a better capability to understand the actor and his actions.

D. To see how understanding others requires an understanding of oneself, one should also realize that empathy does, in a sense, *evolve* with time — that our empathic capabilities increase and change as we grow older. The corollary to this is the fact that empathy requires that we survey our past and understand how we felt about ourselves or the general situation before we can understand others. For example, in the case of mother–daughter relationships, being able to introspectively go back to *then* helps because we tend to take our experience for granted — things that seem trivial to a mother might be seen in a different light by her daughter. Hence, by realizing one's past, one is able to see through the veil of experience and time to gain a better capability of empathizing with someone who was in the same situation before.

E. However, just as empathy allows us to glimpse both sides of the coin (ourselves and others), so must we look at both the positive and negative aspects of empathy. Although many people may view empathy as something that is essential in everyday interaction, with some even considering it a mark of humanity, there are downsides to empathy as well. A noticeable part of this is when empathy is used under the pretense that an exact understanding of the feelings other person is gained. Empathy does not provide such other understandings, but rather a feeling that correlates to the situation of the other person. However, when one assumes that one knows exactly what the other person is going through, then such "empathy" can actually pose as a barrier to communication rather than as a tool. For example, "I know exactly how you feel" is a lie, and such assertions often result in the decision to say nothing — the exact opposite of communication.

F. Another downside to empathy is that it can come in many layers, and these layers can interfere with each other such that the true significance of an event is concealed from a person. As people in a relationship spend more time getting to know each other, they get more attuned to each other's habits and thoughts, and an empathic bond forms between them. However, the emotional link that sustains such a bond can make a person oblivious to the larger meaning of an event, as his emotions cause him to empathize with the person but not with the actual motivations behind that person's actions. Ironically, the closer we are to a person, the more likely such inconsistencies are to happen because we have become *too* familiar with them in terms of our paradigms. As a Chinese proverb goes, "He who is in the mountain knows less about the shape of the mountain than he who observes the mountain from afar."

G. In the theater of everyday life, we try to find meaning in the actions of others through empathy. But what if we tried to find meaning in that very action of empathizing with someone? Although we may not realize it, the subconscious process of empathy that we use in everyday life is more introspective than we think. We may think that we understand ourselves best, and that may be so relative to other people, but when we try to take a look inside, we may find that we may not know that much after all.

Author: Jee Ian Tam

Questions 1–5

Reading Passage 1 has seven paragraphs, **A–G**.

Which paragraph contains the following information?

Write the correct letter, **A–G**, in boxes 1–5 on your answer sheet.

1. Age can be one of the reasons behind misunderstandings, even between close family members.
2. Empathy can become a barrier to communication if one side assumes that they know exactly how the other feels.

3. The common belief is that empathy is only about understanding others, which is not accurate.
4. Occasionally, too much empathy can prevent us from being able to see the bigger picture.
5. Our empathic capabilities develops with time.

Questions 6–11

Choose the correct letter, **A, B, C or D**.

Write the correct letter in boxes 6–12 on your answer sheet.

6. Why did Martha Manning daughter become upset while watching *Bambi*?
   A. Misunderstanding can occur just as often in close family relationships
   B. Moves like *Bambi* are akin to disaster flicks for children
   C. She became traumatized after watching Bambi's mother get killed
   D. Conflicts between the mother and daughter arose

7. Under what situations can empathy be a barrier to communication?
   A. When both sides' experiential structures differ in terms of age
   B. When one side pretends to completely understand the other
   C. When one grows older and encounters different experiences
   D. When we try to find meaning in the actions of others through empathy

8. What is the difference between conventional theater and the theater of everyday life?
   A. Actors possess a script in conventional theater, whereas the theater of everyday life does not come with fixed instructions
   B. Actors in conventional theater do not possess empathy, whereas one develops empathy through the theater of everyday life
   C. There are never any misunderstandings in conventional theater, whereas misunderstandings occur frequently in the theater of everyday life
   D. The theater of everyday life is more meaningful than conventional theater

9. According to the passage, what is empathy?
   A. Empathy is about emotional links between people
   B. Empathy is essential in everyday life

C. Empathy is about a shared experience between the actor and the audience
D. Empathy is about understanding others, and understanding oneself in order to understand others

10. Which of the following is an example of pretending to completely understand another person?
    A. Interpreting another person's actions in order to gain a better understanding of who they are
    B. Becoming too familiar with another person, to the point where you can only empathize with their personal self and not the motivation behind their actions
    C. Telling someone that you know exactly how they feel
    D. Bringing someone to watch a movie that you think they would enjoy

11. Based on the passage, which of the following is not a way in which people view empathy?
    A. A tool to gain economic benefit
    B. A mark of humanity
    C. A necessary component of everyday interaction
    D. A way to form emotional bonds with others

Answers for Questions 1–11
1. B
2. E
3. C
4. F
5. D
6. C
7. B
8. A
9. D
10. C
11. A

Reading Passage 2

You should spend about 20 minutes on **Questions 12–26**, which are based on Reading Passage 2 below.

Good Governance Reforms

Good Governance Reforms (GGRs) are a specific group of policies advocated and implemented by the International Financial Institutions (IFIs) from the mid-1990s onwards. These reforms were a reaction to the failings and consequent criticism of the Washington Consensus.

The Consensus emerged during the late 1970s and early 1980s from the IFIs and attempted to apply neoclassical economic principles, such as market equilibrium and individual rational self-maximization, to the policy recommendations advocated and enforced by the IFIs in lesser-developed countries (LDCs).

In practice the Washington Consensus meant a liberalization of markets, rolling back of state, removal of barriers to trade and a number of other measures to encourage the market to work unfettered by state interference. The perceived failure of these policies was underlined by a lack of sustained growth and even recession in countries where the IFIs implemented their Structural Adjustment Programs. Alongside these failed policies in LDCs, the Washington Consensus also lost influence as a result of its inability to explain the economic success of the East Asian countries, whose economic policies were at odds with the Consensus.

A need to explain both the theoretical and policy failings of the Washington Consensus led to the emergence of the Post-Washington Consensus, or New-Institutionalism, characterized by GGRs. New institutionalists argued that institutions such as property rights could help overcome these market failures and make the market work better, leading to economic growth. GGRs were the policy manifestation of new institutionalism and aimed to improve the institutions of LDCs, with areas targeted including an improvement in the rule of law and property rights, and a reduction in corruption and expropriation. These reforms sometimes expanded much further than this, with democratization, accountability, and legal reform addressed.

One of the main arguments against GGRs is that there is no strong empirical evidence linking them to sustained economic growth in LDCs. The main dataset available on governance indicators (which broadly reflect the GGRs of the IFIs) comes from the World Bank. The World Bank measures governance through control of corruption, government effectiveness, political stability and absence of violence/terrorism, regulatory quality, and voice and accountability. This data suffers from a number of different problems — that the data has only been collected since 1996, the collection method and the indicators selected.

Also central to the question is the issue of sustained growth, with Rodrik (2003) arguing that kick-starting economic growth is far simpler than sustaining it, which historical evidence supports. While historically many LDCs, such as Mexico and Brazil, have achieved short-term spurts in growth, it is rare that this is translated into sustained growth. In cases where this has been achieved, such as East Asian countries (which can no longer be considered LDCs), including China, Malaysia and South Korea, or those from other regions such as Botswana, it cannot be attributed to a specific set of reforms that can be reproduced. Both the Washington Consensus and the Post-Washington Consensus suffer from the assumption that a specific set of policies can be applied in a variety of different LDCs with hugely different institutional, political and economic backgrounds. While China achieved sustained growth through its dual-track agricultural approach, and its Township and Village Enterprise interpretation of property rights, these reforms are not replicable elsewhere.

A fundamental barrier that most LDCs face in implementing GGRs is one of resources. Many of the countries where the IFIs have attempted to implement these reforms do not have the capacity and resources to implement the Structural Adjustment Programs. The GGRs represent an extension of these programs, as the Post-Washington Consensus is not a significant ideological or theoretical break from the Washington Consensus. These reforms simply meant an expanding list of requirements that the IFIs could enforce in LDCs, without consideration for their operational feasibility or context suitability. The feasibility argument has resulted in many people advocating "good enough governance" where only necessary interventions are targeted.

The GGRs of the World Bank and the IMF are neither feasible nor necessary to promote sustained economic growth in LDCs, and can, in the worst case, lead to conflict through disruption of an unstable power balance. However, institutional change and reforms are possible if the political and institutional capabilities of the country in which GCRs are being implemented are taken into account, if the reforms are carried out at an appropriate pace that complements rather than predates economic development, and if the reforms do not destabilize an already fragile country through disruption of power networks.

Author: Lydia Levy

Questions 12–18

Do the following statements agree with the information given in Reading Passage 2?

In boxes 12–18 on your answer sheet, write

> TRUE if the statement agrees with the claims of the writer
> FALSE if the statements contradicts the claims of the writer
> NOT GIVEN if it is impossible to say what the writer thinks about this

12. The Good Governance Reforms were a reaction to the successes of the Washington Consensus.
13. The Washington Consensus lost credibility because it was unable to explain the economic successes of East Asian countries.
14. The Washington Consensus studied and adapted lessons from the successes of East Asian countries.
15. Malaysia and South Korea are considered LDCs.
16. Botswana achieved sustained growth through a dual-track agricultural approach.
17. Good Governance Reforms are challenging to adopt due to a lack of resources.
18. The World Bank is looking to revise the Good Governance Reforms, and to ensure that LDCs can adopt them in the future.

Questions 19–26

Match the following descriptions to the relevant party or concept

> A. The World Bank
> B. Washington Consensus
> C. Post-Washington Consensus

Write the correct letter, **A, B or C**, in boxes 19–26 on your answer sheet

19. Emerged during the late 1970s and early 1980s
20. Provides the main data set available on governance indicators
21. Applied by the International Financial Institutions from the mid-1990s onwards
22. Emerged due to the failings of the Washington Consensus
23. Also known as New Institutionalism

24. Measures governance through a range of factors, including control of corruption and government effectiveness
25. Involved the implementation of the Good Governance Reforms
26. Adopted economic policies that were contrary to those implemented in East Asian countries

Answers to Questions 12–26

12. FALSE
13. TRUE
14. NOT GIVEN
15. FALSE
16. FALSE
17. TRUE
18. NOT GIVEN
19. B
20. A
21. B
22. C
23. C
24. A
25. C
26. B

Reading Passage 3

You should spend about 20 minutes on **Questions 27–40**, which are based on Reading Passage 3 below.

The French Welfare System

To begin with, the target of initial social policies in France was different. While many other nations' welfare policy was for the purpose of "equalizing" gendered labor division by providing monetary rewards for unpaid labor (childcare and elderly care), French policies first and foremost targeted the wellbeing of children. In "Gender and Welfare Regimes," Jane Lewis explains that French welfare policies did not focus on deconstructing gender norms, but instead originated as tools for "horizontal redistribution of wealth" based on family size — the more the children, the higher the benefits in the early twentieth century. The provision of child benefits, she states, indirectly benefited women by providing them with the financial benefits that could be considered as wages for their unpaid labor as caregivers. Furthermore, women continued to participate as fulltime workers, which she attributes to the lack of attempts to push women out of the labor market. This system continued up until the late 1930s.

French welfare policy remained relatively focused on the horizontal redistribution of wealth until the latter half of the twentieth century when it shifted towards a vertical redistribution from high-income homes to low-income homes. Previous polices — *frais de garde* (care expenses) and *mere au foyer* (women at home raising children) — were combined into the *complément familial* (family income supplement). Nonetheless, continued changes to French welfare policy show the continued emphasis on larger families. Since 1921, families of three children or more have been offered the *carte de famille nombreuse* (big family card), which offers discounts with partner businesses in addition to discounts on tickets via the national railroad system — the discounted percentage increases with the number of children. Moreover, policy reforms have now created an "advantage" through tax cuts that lower taxes regardless of income level, and, for families of moderate income, will essentially be tax-free. These tax cuts for larger families are different from the previous distribution of wealth via benefit payments that defined initial French welfare policies. Additionally, French laws outlining paternity and maternity leave are quite diverse.

Social acceptance and support of women's participation in the labor force and childcare was essential for the maintaining a stable total fertility rate in France. Early intervention by the French government focused on taking responsibility for child welfare and helped women remain in the labor force rather than obliging women to leave the labor force. At the same time, it is important to note that despite the high levels of government support and vast financial subsidies made available to French women there is very little gender equality. Women are still the ones assuming most, if not all, of the responsibilities associated with household management and child rearing. An evaluation of domestic work using the French National Institute of Statistics and Economic Research's (INSEE) statistical data concluded that unpaid "home production" could be estimated to be 33% of the national gross domestic product, and women do 64% of total home production. In fact, these conditions significantly lowered France's rank in the World Economic Forum's Gender Gap Report. According to this annual report, France's rank went down due to the decreased number of female politicians and a poor score on the perceived wage equality indicator.

In terms of parental leave, France is also very supportive. Maternity leave was initially introduced in 1909 and guaranteed mothers 100 percent of their salary for six weeks prior to childbirth and an additional 10 weeks after. In 1997, unpaid parental leave with job security was granted for up to three years of leave, and could be taken by either the mother or the father, but not both — paternity leave was not legally outlined until 2002 and only for a period of 11 days at full pay.

On the surface, these policies appear to be completely supportive of women in the workforce, but they maintain the double burden for women — work life and a full load of domestic responsibilities. Nevertheless, French policy did take a comprehensive approach in its child welfare policy by establishing an array of childcare services, while also providing child allowances.

Author: Daniel Velasco

Questions 27–33

Complete the sentences below.

Write **NO MORE THAN TWO WORDS** from the passage for each answer.

Write your answers in boxes 27–33 on your answer sheet.

27. The provision of .... indirectly benefited mothers by providing them with financial compensation that could be considered as wages for unpaid labor.
28. Until the latter half of the 20th century, French welfare policy was focused on the .... of wealth.
29. French families that have the "big family card" enjoy increased............ .... with the number of children.

30. Policy reforms introduced tax cuts that lower taxes regardless of………
……………………..
31. Accepting and supporting women's participation in the ………… ……………… was essential for maintaining a stable total fertility rate in France.
32. ………………….. assume most of the responsibilities related to household management and child rearing.
33. Despite a significant amount of government support and financial subsidies for French women, ……………………… remains a challenge.

Questions 34–40

Choose the correct letter, **A, B, C or D.**

Write the correct letter in boxes 34–40 on your answer sheet.

34. What was a key similarity between initial French welfare policies and that of other nations?
    A. To equalize gendered labor division by providing monetary compensation for unpaid domestic labor
    B. To ensure that women remained within the labor force
    C. To provide fully-paid maternity *and* paternity leave
    D. To increase the number of children within each family

35. Which of the following is a measure linked to the earlier "horizontal redistribution" French welfare policy?
    A. Care expenses
    B. Big family card
    C. Family income supplement
    D. All of the above

36. Which of the following statements is **not** true?
    A. The larger the family, the more discounts they received
    B. It is estimated that women do 33% of home production
    C. French welfare policy aimed to keep women within the labor force
    D. Women can still receive pay even if they take leave to give birth

37. Why did France's rank drop in the World Economic Forum's Gender Gap Report?
    A. The judges concluded the ranking based on outdated information
    B. There was a decreased number of female politicians
    C. The amount of paid maternity leave that a woman could take was too low
    D. Women were encouraged to remain within the labor force

38. According to the passage, in total, how many weeks of paid maternity leave could women receive?
    A. 6
    B. 10
    C. 16
    D. 11 days

39. Which of the following is **not** a measure that French welfare policy has implemented?
    A. Special awards for women who give birth to a large number of children
    B. Tax cuts for families with children
    C. Special discounts for families with children
    D. Implementation of both maternity and paternity leave

40. What does the writer conclude about the effect that French welfare policy had on women?
    A. It has allowed women to develop their careers and gain more financial independence
    B. An increasing number of fathers are beginning to take on work related to home production
    C. The number of female politicians has decreased
    D. There have been improvements, but women still have the double burden of professional work and domestic responsibilities

Answers for Questions 27–40
27. Child benefits
28. Horizontal distribution

Academic Reading Practice Examinations

29. Discount percentages
30. Income level
31. Labor force
32. Women
33. Gender equality
34. A
35. A
36. B
37. B
38. C
39. A
40. D

Practice Examination 3

Reading Passage 1

You should spend about 20 minutes on **Questions 1-15**, which are based on Reading Passage 1 below.

Child Mortality Rate Differentials across Populations

A. The study of mortality differentials within populations has been, and still is an interesting subject of study. Populations are fluid and ever changing, due to social, economic and environmental reasons that make current observations rather different from those that came before. Changes in demographic data often reflect changes in a community, and mortality data can provide telling information about a population. For example, a country that has enjoyed peace and experienced improvements in the economy and infrastructure is likely to have a lower mortality rate compared to a war-torn, impoverished country even if both countries are located in the same region or continent.

B. Waldron's (1998) article on infant and child mortality described possible biological factors for sex differences in infant and child mortality. She mentions congenital anomalies, increased susceptibility to infectious disease and perinatal conditions, e.g., prematurity and immature lungs, as possible biological causes of increased male vulnerability leading to mortality during infancy. This can be hypothesized as a purely biological phenomenon as the data given shows a trend for increased male infant mortality in all populations.

C. However, once infants become young children, sex differentials in mortality start to differ between populations. Different researchers have explored the question of why child mortality differs between males and females, depending on the population studied. Waldron (1998) puts forward different biological causes of mortality contributing towards sex differentials. For example, boys tend to have more active lifestyles (a possible effect of testosterone on their brains) and thus are subject to greater risk of injury-related mortality; girls in some societies have higher measles related mortality possibly due to being more vulnerable to high doses of the measles virus.

D. Despite her trying to outline biological causes of sex differentials in child mortality, Waldron (1998) does admit that social factors are deeply involved with these differences. Factors such as maternal education, social status and household wealth also play an important role. Educated mothers tend to have fewer children, but their children have a significantly lowered mortality risk as educated women are more likely to be part of high-status, higher-income households, which means more resources are available for the children. An educated mother is also more likely to seek medical care for her children and understand certain healthcare procedures. As a result of what we would normally call "good childcare," there is a lowered risk of mortality from infectious disease, malnutrition and injury among the offspring of educated women.

E. High-status households with high income have increased child survival overall, as the clan could afford to care for all offspring without neglecting children otherwise assumed to be unwanted or less useful in other households. In fact, in these families, all children seem to be useful to the family in some way. Levine (1987) illustrates the example of a wealthy Tibetan household where the general consensus was that sons could manage and inherit the family assets, and daughters could be married off to other upper-class families, thus making beneficial social connections for the clan. Perhaps, being able to provide for many children of both genders could be seen as a status symbol, and a large family often means better social support and childcare.

F. As a country develops and becomes more modern, interventions from the government, non-governmental organizations (NGOs) and local economic growth tend to have the effect of reducing overall child mortality. Usually development results in the building of better-quality homes; education; improved sanitation, utilities and healthcare; more resources being available; and changing attitudes to childcare.

G. Interventions from governments and NGOs have changed child mortality patterns in certain regions, particularly in developing countries. Governments and NGOs aim to reduce overall mortality by raising the standards of infrastructure and provision of healthcare, supplying clean water and adequate sanitation, encouraging parents to provide better nourishment for their children, and implementing oral rehydration therapy guidelines where diarrhea-related diseases are endemic and nationwide vaccination programs, all part of what is called development from a Western perspective. Often interveners try to change people's behavior on a community-based level through education, healthcare or aid provided by donations. All these efforts usually result in a reduction in child mortality within developing countries.

H. These changes decrease child mortality by improving child health, but are all interventions beneficial? Nearly all these interventions follow the activist model proposed by Cassidy (1987), where interveners intend to bring forth change in the communities they work in. However, these changes might be detrimental to the very people they are trying to help. Cassidy (1987) states that often there are situations where the interests of the community and the interveners are very different, resulting in less than optimal results. She gives an example of mortality reduction among unwanted daughters in India, where the mothers of these children have been encouraged by interveners to provide better nutrition to all their children even though cultural discrimination against girls was still present. However, this resulted in more surviving girls who are unwanted by their families (Cassidy, 1987). Another similar and harmful situation could be an eventual dramatic rise in population caused by reduced mortality among children who would not have survived if not for interventions, leading to greater competition for limited resources and rise in unemployment levels (Cassidy, 1987).

I. Despite the presence of models that make it easier to identify reasons for mortality differentials, the factors contributing to child mortality are all enmeshed in the complex network we call society and nearly always do not act independently to produce specific mortality patterns.

Author: Shuen-Yi Long

Questions 1–12

Do the following statements agree with the information given in Reading Passage 1?

In boxes 1-6 on your answer sheet, write

TRUE   if the statement agrees with the claims of the writer
FALSE   if the statements contradicts the claims of the writer
NOT GIVEN   if it is impossible to say what the writer thinks about this

1. Child mortality rates are different depending on the gender of the child.
2. Girls have a higher mortality rate because the higher level of testosterone within their bodies lead to more active lifestyles.
3. Educated mothers tend to have more daughters than sons.
4. Economic development usually results in lower child mortality rates.
5. In Tibetan households, child mortality rates tend to be lower.
6. Supplying clean water is one method that can help increase child mortality rates.

Questions 7–15

Reading Passage 1 has nine paragraphs **A–I**.

Choose the correct heading for each paragraph from the list of headings below:

i. Not all intervention may be beneficial
ii. The importance of demographic data and mortality differentials
iii. Introducing interventions in developing countries
iv. Methods of intervention
v. Household status
vi. Social factors
vii. Biological factors
viii. Gender difference
ix. Complex web

7. Paragraph A: ……
8. Paragraph B: ……
9. Paragraph C: ……
10. Paragraph D: ……

11. Paragraph E: ......
12. Paragraph F: ......
13. Paragraph G: ......
14. Paragraph H: ......
15. Paragraph I: ......

Answers for Questions 1–15
1. TRUE
2. FALSE
3. NOT GIVEN
4. TRUE
5. NOT GIVEN
6. FALSE
7. ii
8. vii
9. viii
10. vi
11. v
12. iii
13. iv
14. i
15. ix

Reading Passage 2

You should spend about 20 minutes on **Questions 16–27**, which are based on Reading Passage 2 below.

Violence, Conflict and Development

Violence does not always undermine the prospects of democracy, and has in fact played a central role in the formation and maintenance of many states. The prospects of democracy are much improved by secure property rights, effective land reform, and a system of taxation. Violence has historically been integral in the formation of these three institutional factors, and the implicit threat of violence is essential in the maintenance of them.

The role of violence in state formation and in progress has been well documented. Charles Tilly (1985) offers a persuasive analysis of why historically violence and war helped to create most of the institutions we value today, such as democracy and the rule of law. For Tilly, war-making, extraction and capital accumulation all interacted to create European nation states. To achieve these three processes, a ruler first had to establish a monopoly of violence. The professionalization of the military in order to centralize and monopolize power and later the establishment of police forces were both violent processes in themselves, and established law and order through the implicit threat of violence, something that clearly remains today in most nation states. By monopolizing violence the state also took control of protection, for which they could demand payment in the form of taxes. Law and order translated into secure property rights, which alongside taxation are central to the success of a nation state.

The monopolization and professionalization of violence made leaders more powerful, but was also motivated by the ever-present threat of war with neighboring states. The taxation that leaders could demand in exchange for protection was essential for funding these interstate wars, with war-making also offering an opportunity and justification for the expansion of this taxation. The return to peacetime rarely brought a reduction in these taxes, further concentrating power in the hands of the monarch or the central elite. Alongside taxation, Britain's access to credit can also be seen as central in its success in financing war-making.

The third key component in improving the prospects of democracy was effective land reform, which usually resulted in a shift to commercial agriculture. Land Reform in England, known as the Enclosure Movement, is a key component of Karl Marx's *Capital*, and of his theory of Primitive Accumulation.

For Marx, human progress is seen as something violent but essential, with land reform leading to capitalism, and capitalism to the emergence of class consciousness among the working class. The Enclosure Movement, a process that spanned around 70 years during the 15th and 16th centuries, involved the forcible eviction of peasants from the land they used for subsistence agriculture, and the enclosure of this public land into larger commercial farms. It was a brutal process that severed peasants from the land (means of production), and forced them into the towns in search of jobs (wage labor). The Enclosure Movement played a major part in the Agrarian Revolution and created the boom in the British wool trade. This led to the Industrial Revolution, and the emergence of Britain as the greatest power in the world. Alongside its role in the emergence of capitalism, land reform in Britain also helped to reinforce property rights. While Marx saw the emergence of capitalism as instrumental rather than an end in itself, this does not change the common interpretation of violence as something integral to state formation and human progress.

The vast majority of land reform was very violent itself or followed a violent upheaval, such as a civil war. In the wake of the Korean War, the United States pushed South Korea to carry out significant land reforms, which redistributed land, removed major landowners and encouraged industry, partly as a method of undermining communist support. This produced a growth in the industrial working class in a similar way to the Enclosure Movement. Taiwan, itself created out of a conflict, also went through a similar process of land reform.

Many countries, particularly those in South America such as Colombia, never experienced land reform on the same scale and this can help us to understand the divergent paths we see in terms of state formation and democracy. There is clearly a degree to which the three factors emphasized in this essay are interdependent. Land reform is not possible without a monopoly of violence. Although it often violates the property rights of either large landowners or peasants, it is meaningless without secure property rights for encouraging future investment and a system of taxation to maintain it.

Violence was integral in the formation of systems of taxation, secure property rights, and in land reform. All of these three factors encouraged the emergence of capitalism, with land reform weakening large landowners and creating a workforce of former peasants to drive industrialization. Taxation helped to establish and secure the state, and property rights encouraged investment.

Author: Lydia Levy

Questions 16–21

Choose the correct letter, **A, B, C or D**.

Write the correct letter in boxes 16–21 on your answer sheet.

16. Based on the passage above, which of the following is **not** an aspect that will improve the prospects of democracy?
    A. Secure property rights
    B. Effective land reform
    C. A system of taxation
    D. The maintenance of many states

17. What does Charles Tilly mean by the "monopoly of violence"?
    A. War making, extraction and capital accumulation all interacted to create European nation states
    B. The professionalization of the military in order to centralize power and maintain law and order through the implicit threat of violence
    C. Making leaders more powerful, and also motivated by the ever-present threat of war with neighboring states
    D. Demanding taxation in exchange for protection

18. Which of the following statements about the Enclosure Movement is not true?
    A. Occurred for a duration of about seven decades
    B. Involved the forced eviction of peasants from agricultural lands
    C. Forced peasants into the towns in search of jobs
    D. It was a well-organized and gentle process that received widespread public support

19. What is the link between the Enclosure Movement and the British wool trade?
    A. The Enclosure Movement played a significant role in the Agrarian Revolution that created the boom in British wool trade
    B. The peasants became part of the labor force for the British wool trade
    C. The agricultural lands were transformed into wool-production facilities to boost the wool trade
    D. Led to the emergence of capitalism and the enforcement of property rights

20. The following countries experienced some degree of violence in land reform or occurred after a violent upheaval, except
    A. Britain
    B. Taiwan
    C. South Korea
    D. Colombia

21. What is the writer's central argument?
    A. We should embrace and encourage violence in society
    B. Violence undermines the prospect of democracy
    C. Violence is integral to the process of state formation and human progress
    D. It is natural to expect some degree of violence in our lives

Questions 22–27

Complete the summary below.

Choose **NO MORE THAN TWO WORDS** from the passage for each answer.

Write your answers in boxes 22–27 on your answer sheet.

Contrary to what most people might believe, violence **22** .... always undermine the prospects of democracy. Rather, historically, it has played an integral role in key processes including taxation, secure property rights and effective **23** .... Land reform usually results in a shift to **24** .... A significant number of land reforms involved violent transitions or happened after violent upheavals. For example, land reforms occurred in South Korea after the **25** .... These land reforms had the consequence of weakening large landowners, and generating a labor force of former peasants to drive **26** .... This led to the emergence of **27** ...., which Karl Marx thought was instrumental rather than an end in itself.

Answers for Questions 16–27

16. D
17. B
18. D
19. A
20. D

21. C
22. Does not
23. Land reform
24. Commercial agriculture
25. Korean War
26. Industrialization
27. Capitalism

Reading Passage 3

You should spend about 20 minutes on **Questions 28–40**, which are based on Reading Passage 3 below.

Sultan Abdülhamid II: Educational Policies and Reforms

The 19th century presented a difficult situation for the Ottoman Empire. Military defeat and economic crises led to the perception of the empire as a declining power both by foreigners and by Ottoman subjects. During Sultan Abdülhamid II's reign education was seen as one of the main solutions to the empire's problems, particularly as the concept of nationalism was one of the biggest threats to the unity of a multi-ethnic, multi-religious, and multi-linguistic empire such as the Ottoman Empire.

As with many other aspects of the Hamidian period of the Ottoman Empire, education has been and continues to be under the scrutiny of scholars. Among the scholars that have approached the subject of the Hamidian educational system, Benjamin Fortna, Selim Deringil, Selçuk Akşin Somel, and Emine Evered have presented analyses that show both similarities and differences. There are several aspects that affect this outcome, one of which is the complex nature of the subject of education and the number of factors that need to be taken into consideration when studying and analyzing such a subject. However, the different areas of focus that each of these scholars has chosen addresses an issue that can only add to our understanding of the Hamidian educational system.

The Hamidian educational policies and reforms were an important aspect of Sultan Abdülhamid II's reign. Somel, Fortna and Evered are all in agreement that the Hamidian reforms continued the policies set forth by the Public Education Act of 1869, but with significant modifications because, they claim, many of the provisions of the Education Act could not be implemented until the 1880s. The task of executing the plans fell to Abdülhamid II. In addition to building a large number of much-needed schools, thus extending the scant network of primary schools available throughout the empire, certain changes were made to the curriculum of these schools. More emphasis was placed on moral education, and the Islamic factor of the educational system was increased. Somel goes as far as saying that there was not only a strong emphasis on religious values, but also on authoritarian ones.

Although there seems to be a consensus among these four scholars on the religious aspect of the Hamidian educational system, there is a difference in the way Somel and Fortna approach the subject. On one hand, Somel takes a much more pessimistic view of the Hamidian educational system than Fortna does. He characterizes certain aspects of the educational system as "authoritarian" and he sees it as fraught with clashes which led to the failure of the system to create a synthesis of the different values it promoted, such as traditional religious values, and modernization and progress.

Fortna, on the other hand, casts a more positive light on the educational reforms. Whereas Somel briefly mentions some similarities to other educational systems, Fortna takes the time to place the Hamidian educational system into a wider context, drawing parallels to educational reforms undertaken by governments all over the world. He mentions the moral agenda of the American educational system in the 19th century, the fact that "secular" schools in Russia taught that religion was at the base of the Russian state system, and several other examples, such as China, Japan and France in which moral and religious instruction played an important role. Thus, although he admits that the Hamidian educational bureaucracy also played a role in attempting to control that what was taught in the classroom was applied in practice, thus reaching a certain level of control, he places it in a context in which this was considered standard practice to a large extent. By placing the Hamidian educational system in a wider context, Fortna creates a new platform from which to view it. In this way, Fortna and Somel differ in their views on the Hamidian educational system because of the starting point from which they each choose to analyze the Hamidian educational reforms. This is significant because an analysis of the Hamidian educational system as an isolated system may very well lead to a conclusion such as Somel's in which the system is a tool used to indoctrinate and keep the population under control.

The role that the Ottoman statesmen played in the educational reforms of the Hamidian era is an important one. They helped shape and support these reforms and the attitude that they had towards them is telling of their perception of the time. Benjamin Fortna presents the idea that the Ottoman statesmen were pessimistic about the present situation of the empire but viewed education as the ultimate solution to the problems of the empire. He claims that the Ottoman statesmen placed great faith in education as an agent of change. Similarly, Evered states that the opposition of the religious establishment to the Ottoman Empire's centralizing reforms of the nineteenth century led to their depiction by the new leaders of the state as antimodernist and reactionary. Thus, in an effort to improve the Ottoman state's image both abroad and within the empire, it defined itself as against the "backward" religious establishment and by taking over the role of provider of primary education it tried to depict itself as "progressive."

There is a similarity between the views of Fortna and Evered in that they both say that the Ottoman statesmen viewed education as the way forward. However, Fortna focuses on their belief in the potential of educational reforms whereas Evered's analysis places more emphasis on the idea that the Ottoman statesmen were using these reforms in order to improve the state's image, thereby placing its legitimacy on its abilities to modernize as opposed to basing it on religious and dynastic grounds. The essence of the difference between Fortna's analysis of the attitude Ottoman statesmen had towards education and Evered's analysis is that Fortna advocates the sincerity of the statesmen's belief in the possibilities for change educational reform would create, whereas Evered expresses the view that these reforms were a political tool used to reconsolidate the state's image and therefore its grounds for legitimacy.

The different conclusions that the abovementioned scholars have drawn in relation to the outcome of the Hamidian educational system are heavily reliant on the focus they each place on the many aspects of the system. They drew different conclusions because there were many factors at play in the way the Hamidian educational reforms were received by the population. The context is a complex one that often seems to be simplified in order to emphasize a particular aspect as being the main cause of what is generally seen as the failure of the Hamidian educational system and its reforms. However, when analyzed side by side it becomes clear that these studies complement each other, fill different gaps in the academic field and address different issues, creating a much broader picture of the Hamidian period as a whole and the place of education within this context.

Author: Marilu Lucescu

Questions 28–33

Complete the sentences below.

Write **NO MORE THAN TWO WORDS** from the passage for each answer.

Write your answers in boxes 27–33 on your answer sheet.

28. During Sultan Abdülhamid II's reign, ... was a threat to the unity of the highly diverse Ottoman Empire.
29. Hamidian reforms continued the policies set forth by the Public Education Act of 1869, albeit with ....
30. Many of the .... within the Education Act could not be implemented until the 1880s.
31. Hamidian educational policies increased the number of .... in the country.
32. When compared against other countries, the inclusion of some degree of religion or moral agenda within education is actually ....
33. According to the passage, Benjamin Fortna suggests that .... saw education as an agent of change.

Questions 34–40

Match the following arguments to the relevant scholars/academics

    A. Benjamin Fortna
    B. Selcuk Somel
    C. Emine Evered

Write the correct letter, **A, B or C**, in boxes 34–40 on your answer sheet

34. Characterized certain aspects of the Hamidian educational system as "authoritarian"
35. Hamidian bureaucracy's attempt to control the population via education was largely standard practice when compared against the rest of the world
36. The opposition of the religious establishment to the reforms of the nineteenth century led to their depiction by the new leaders of the state as antimodernist and reactionary
37. Advocates the sincerity of the statesmen's belief in the possibilities for change educational reform would create
38. These reforms were a political tool used to reconsolidate the state's image
39. The system is a tool used to indoctrinate and keep the population under control
40. Ottoman statesmen were pessimistic about the present situation of the empire but viewed education as the ultimate solution

Answers for Questions 28–40

28. Nationalism
29. Significant modifications
30. Policies
31. Schools
32. Standard practice
33. Ottoman statesmen
34. B
35. A
36. C
37. A
38. C
39. B
40. A

Practice Examination 4

Reading Passage 1

You should spend about 20 minutes on **Questions 1–15**, which are based on Reading Passage 1 below.

Modern "Frankenstein"

In 1818, a novel entitled *Frankenstein* was published by Mary Shelley. It tells the grotesque tale of how an alchemist by the name of Victor Frankenstein managed to create new life in his laboratory. Frankenstein had intended his creation to be one of beauty, but because he found it challenging to recreate the smaller and more delicate parts of the human body, the creation ended up being much larger, at eight feet tall. The creature gained consciousness and felt saddened at being rejected by human society because of his looks. Out of anger and rage, it murdered several people who were close to Victor Frankenstein. In the end, out of misery, the creature also decided to kill himself.

The tale of *Frankenstein* might seem like science fiction and indeed it was hailed as one of the first true examples of the genre. But, recent events have shown that creating life through science may not be fictional for much longer. For the past century, scientists have been experimenting with "full body" or "head" transplants, where one organism's brain is transplanted to another organism's body. The most infamous of these experiments was one conducted by Dr. Robert White, a neurosurgeon who managed to transplant one monkey's head to another's body. The monkey survived the surgery, but died eight days later after the body rejected the new head. It was also unable to breathe and move because the spinal cords were incorrectly connected. Now, in 2015, Italian surgeon Dr. Sergio Canavero has announced that a head transplant would be performed on a human being in as little as two years' time.

Such procedures may seem grotesque and many have spoken out against the ethics of doing so. Similar to the theme of Mary Shelley's *Frankenstein*, there is the fear that it may be too overwhelming for someone to accept an entirely new body. Arthur Caplan, director of medical ethics at New York University's Langone Medical Center is of the view that those who undergo such a procedure "would end up being overwhelmed with different pathways and chemistry than they are used to and they'd go crazy."

Society's reaction to the result of such a transplant may also be negative. Would society be able to accept a person who now controls a "donated" body? Would there be any discrimination, backlash or even fear towards those who have undergone such transplants?

Indeed, the question of "full body" or "head" transplants touches upon many sensitive bioethical issues. Meddling too much with nature, it is feared, would cause more harm than good. Yet, there are still those who would want to voluntarily opt for the procedure simply because they are terminally ill and this transplant offers them the only hope of survival. According to Dr. Sergio Canavero, many have approached him with interest in a head transplant. From among those who have expressed interest, Dr. Canavero selected a 30-year-old computer scientist called Valery Spiridonov who suffers from Werdnig-Hoffman disease. Werdnig-Hoffman disease is a severe muscular disorder that can make it difficult for patients to perform even simple actions such as breathing, sucking and swallowing. Quality of life is reduced as the patient's limbs begin to weaken, rendering him or her able to only perform basic actions such as maneuvering a mouse. Survival rates are not high, as patients may succumb to muscle-related issues such as respiratory problems.

For Spiridonov, therefore, Dr. Sergio Canavero's head transplant procedure is the rational choice. Despite what others may say about the procedure, Spiridonov is willing to bear the risks at the chance of having a better life. Given other organ transplant procedures that commonly take place these days, which includes heart, kidney and even face transplants, it may seem harsh to dismiss head transplants outright. These transplants could be the only hope for many others like Spiridonov. And, after all, he has chosen this option knowing very well that there are considerable risks involved. There are a million things that could go wrong during the surgery, and the body may even reject the new head. Complications may also occur during the recovery period, and it is impossible to say whether chemical reactions between the head and its new body may lead to further consequences for the patient. At the end of the day, the patient has the right to decide. We may not agree with it, but it is ultimately difficult to judge without being in their shoes.

Questions 1–7

Complete the sentences below.
Write **NO MORE THAN TWO WORDS** from the passage for each answer.
Write your answers in boxes 1–7 on your answer sheet.

1. *Frankenstein* was considered to be a very new type of novel, because it was one of first few examples of …………………………..
2. Dr. Robert White experimented with head transplants by using……………………………
3. Dr. Arthur Caplan is concerned that a head transplant may cause the patient to go ………………..
4. Those who are interested in head transplants tend to be those who are …………………..
5. The reason why society may not be able to accept head transplants is over the …………………… involved.
6. Those with Werdnig-Hoffman disease have low …………………….
7. During the ………………….., head transplant patients may face even more complications stemming from chemical reactions between the head and the new body.

Questions 8–12

Match the following perspectives or statements to the relevant individuals

A. Sergio Canavero
B. Arthur Caplan
C. Valery Spiridinov

Write the correct letter, **A, B or C**, in boxes 8–12 on your answer sheet

8. A head transplant is the only hope for survival
9. Patients could go insane as a result of the head transplant procedure
10. Human beings could undergo head transplants in as little as two years' time
11. Many patients are interested in head transplants

Answers for Questions 1–12

34. Science fiction
35. Monkeys
36. Terminally ill
37. Crazy

38. Bioethical issues
39. Survival rates
40. Recovery period
41. C
42. B
43. A
44. A

Reading Passage 2

You should spend about 20 minutes on **Questions 12-26**, which are based on Reading Passage 2 below.

The Credit Card Conundrum

With convenient electronic payment systems such as Paypal, Alipay and mobile payments, credit cards may be on the verge of fading into history. In a century's time, it is possible that we may live in a wholly digital world where you can pay for shopping without even having to open your wallet. After all, credit cards have only been around for about 60 years, and already their dominant position is being threatened by upcoming alternatives.

When credit cards were first introduced, you would not have imagined that they would evolve into what they are today. One of the very first credit cards that operated under the brand "Diners' Club" actually began as a piece of cardboard back in the 1950s. Those who held Diners' Club credit cards could eat at selected restaurants without having to pay in cash. Customers only had to pay up when Diners' Club billed them at the end of the month. Technically, at the beginning at least, Diners' Club was a charge card although it later evolved into becoming a credit card.

The key difference between a charge card and credit card is that while customers are obliged to pay the bill in full for the former, they can opt to pay only a minimum balance for the former. The outstanding amount on the credit card bill is then rolled over onto the following month, and interest is charged. Because the credit card providers are able to charge high interest rates, the credit card business as a whole has become increasingly lucrative. Apart from interest charges, credit card issuers can earn from charging annual fees to consumers. Merchants also have to cough up a small percentage of their revenue in order to be able to process credit card transactions, without which they may lose many customers who are less inclined to use cash for big-ticket purchases. The *Wall Street Journal* estimates that for 2014, American card-issuers will rake in about US$158.6 billion in revenue.

Whether or not mobile payment tools will eventually replace credit cards is yet to be seen. Today's credit cards are sophisticated and rely on several levers to attract subscribers as well as encourage higher consumer spending. A common way is by offering points or rewards in exchange for higher spending. Consumers who pay with credit cards feel that they are gaining something in return for using the card, making the purchase seem like less of a burden than it is.

The second way is by offering readily available unsecured credit. Consumers do not have to go through the lengthy and sometimes tedious process of applying for a loan before receiving funds. Instead, they can simply swipe their card and receive the goods on the spot — instant gratification. The third aspect relates to the trust that consumers still hold in physical banks today. Even though many transactions can be done via online banking, many consumers still end up frequenting bank branches and prefer speaking face-to-face with a bank officer.

Mobile payments still have a way to go in terms of gaining enough traction and market share to be able to profit enough from the business in order to incentivize consumers to move away from credit cards. The relatively low penetration of consumers holding phones that can process payments easily may also be a barrier. Furthermore, consumers have yet to grow used to the idea of paying via mobiles. From a technical perspective, mobile payments may be as safe as or even safer than credit cards, but what ultimately matters most is how consumers perceive this method of payment. Mobile payment systems may also find it challenging to replicate the branding that comes with owning certain credit cards. For example, those who earn a high income or who are members of elite society gain a certain degree of utility from being able to flash credit cards that are reflective of their status.

For mobile payments to succeed, it has to emulate the attractiveness of credit cards and also pounce where credit cards are weak. The increasing regulatory scrutiny from central banks and financial regulators may offer one such opportunity. Fearful of rising debt and potential credit defaults, regulators in certain countries have been tightening the law pertaining to credit cards. This is done by imposing a minimum income requirement, additional scrutiny before issuing cards and even attempting to cap the profit made by issuers so as to reduce the number of incentives that encourage consumers to spend.

Questions 12–19

Complete the summary below.

Choose **NO MORE THAN TWO WORDS** from the passage for each answer.
Write your answers in boxes 12–19 on your answer sheet.

Electronic payment systems and **12** ………………….. have emerged as modern-day competitors to credit cards. Credit cards have had a long history stretching back many decades. One of the first credit cards was actually made out of **13** ………………….. However, many people are still confused about the differences between credit cards and **14** ………………….. The key difference is that you can roll over the balance for the former, whereas you must pay in full for the latter. Credit card issuers earn a profit from charging customers **15** ………………….. and they also charge merchants for processing credit card **16** ………………….. Furthermore, credit card issuers charge high **17** ………………….. on any unpaid balances. Despite the higher financing costs, consumers may prefer borrowing on credit cards as opposed to taking out a personal loan because applying for a loan is a lengthy and **18** ………………….. process. Mobile payments have a long way to go before they can replace credit cards, but could begin by focusing on where credit cards have weaknesses. One such weakness is the increasing **19** ………………….. from central banks and regulators.

Questions 20–26

Choose the correct letter, **A, B, C or D.**

Write the correct letter in boxes 20–26 on your answer sheet.

20. Based on the passage above, which of the following is **not** a way in which credit card issuers earn profit?
    A. Charging interest rates on unpaid balances
    B. Annual fees
    C. Loan application fees
    D. Transaction fees
21. Why do credit card issuers offer points or rewards to credit card users?
    A. To encourage users to spend more
    B. To gain more profit
    C. To gain more users
    D. To improve the credit card's branding

22. Why would merchants be willing to pay a transaction fee in order to process credit card payments from customers?
    A. The fee is a very small percentage of the actual sale
    B. Merchants want instant gratification
    C. Some customers prefer using credit cards for large purchases
    D. The credit card issuers will split the profit with the merchants
23. Which of the following is **not** a barrier to increased mobile payments usage?
    A. Relatively lower number of users with mobile phones
    B. Safety of using mobile payments
    C. Users still find mobile payments strange and foreign to them
    D. Branding of elite credit cards
24. What does the passage mean by the importance of "the branding that comes with owning certain credit cards"?
    A. Consumers still believe in the brand and reputation of physical banks
    B. The reputation of mobile payments is not as good as that of credit cards
    C. Consumers see credit cards as part of their personal branding
    D. Consumers see credit cards as a way to show off their elite status
25. Which of the following is a reason as to why regulators are tightening the laws on the credit card industry?
    A. Credit card issuers are earning too much profit
    B. The fear of rising debt and potential credit defaults
    C. Oversaturation of credit cards in the market
    D. Uncontrolled spending
26. What is **not** an example of how tightening regulations can affect the credit card industry?
    A. Screening credit card issuers more thoroughly
    B. Imposing a cap on the profit that can be made by credit card issuers
    C. Requiring more scrutiny before credit cards can be issued to consumers
    D. Imposing a minimum income requirement

Answers for Questions 12–26
12. Mobile payments
13. Cardboard
14. Charge cards
15. Annual fees
16. Transactions

17. Interest rates
18. Tedious
19. Regulatory scrutiny
20. C
21. A
22. C
23. B
24. D
25. B
26. A

Reading Passage 3

You should spend about 20 minutes on **Questions 27–40**, which are based on Reading Passage 3 below.

Wine through the Ages

A. Given that not every ancient civilization left written records detailing their way of life, it can be difficult for archaeologists and historians to pinpoint the exact beginning of any one event. It is even more complicated to trace the history of wine, which is one of the world's oldest beverages. The reason for this is because wine leaves very few unique chemical markers for archaeologists to definitively identify and differentiate from other forms of produce. However, according to estimates, the cultivation of the grapevine stretches back at least 9,000 years, in the area around Turkey and Iran.

B. It is said that humans first discovered wine after observing and wondering why birds were obsessed with feasting on fermented fruit. That began the process of exploring and experimenting, which eventually led to the mass-scale production of wine. Contrary to popular belief, wine is not made exclusively with grapes. It can be produced by fermenting various types of produce, including rice, plums and even dandelions. Different cultures and ethnic groups have their own traditional versions of wine. In Europe, grape wine is the most prevalent. In Asia, rice wine is more common, ranging from simple everyday cooking wine to luxury brands such as "Kweichou Moutai." At one point, a single bottle of 1985 Moutai was auctioned off for the price of 1.45 million yuan.

C. The wine industry today has evolved dramatically over the years. China, surprisingly, is now one of the largest "new-world" wine producers, taking second place after the United States with an annual production of about 150 million cases of wine in 2012. In fact, Chinese wine consumption has overtaken the United Kingdom and may even surpass Italy in the near future.

D. However, the single largest producer and consumer of wine is still France. There are many famous wine-producing regions within France, such as Burgundy, Bordeaux and the Loire valley. Wines are sometimes referred to by the region they came from in France. Champagne, for example, refers to a region in France and there are laws that restrict the usage of the term "champagne" in order to prevent misuse. Within France itself, there is a strict wine quality classification system to help consumers differentiate between the numerous types of wine available. This classification system officially began in 1935 and had four main categories. In ascending order of stringency, these categories were: Vin de Table, Vin de Pays, Vin Délimité de Qualité Supérieure (VDQS) and Appellation d'Origine Contrôlée (AOC). In 2012, this system was simplified to reflect only three categories: Vin de France, Indication Geographique Protegee (IGP) and Appellation d'Origine Protegee (AOP). This effectively removed the VDQS category, but the law also introduced new labels for organic and biodynamic wines as well to keep up with modern times.

E. One of the reasons as to why France emerged as a key wine producer is due to its geographical advantages. Different wine regions in France boast a variety of combinations that have contributed to the fine wine produced. Vineyards in Champagne, the Loire Valley and Burgundy all benefit from a mix of limestone and marl. Limestone consists mainly of fossilized seashells, whereas marl has a mix of various clays in addition to the calcium and magnesium carbonates from fossilized shells. These fossilized shells provide important nutrition for the vineyards. However, growing good wine grapes is not just about nutrition. Temperature can play an important role as well. For example, in Chateauneuf-du-Pape, smooth, oval-shaped stones that were formed after centuries of floodwaters help to absorb the sun's heat. In the evenings, this heat is then radiated back onto the vines. The end product is wine that is relatively spicier, richer and higher in alcoholic content — something that one may not have easily deduced simply by observing the presence of the oval-shaped stones in the soil.

F. Today, these vineyards play a significant role not only in producing wine but also generating tourism revenue. In France's Saint-Emilion, which is now a UNESCO World Heritage Site, it receives at least an estimated 1 million tourists a year. These tourists are willing to pay entrance fees and wine-tasting fees just to get a glimpse of what a real French vineyard looks like. Some vineyards even offer accommodation, wine-tasting courses and horse rides — and the prices quoted are far from cheap. The boost provided by tourism has encouraged vineyard owners such as Jean-Francois Janoueix and Jean-Michel Cazes to heavily invest in reviving old villages to suit tourists' tastes. In fact, Janoueix has personally invested in Sarpe, a village just outside his vineyard, and strives to create a rustic atmosphere despite the higher costs incurred. While some may protest that recreating the rustic vineyard look just to cater to tourists' taste will not truly help to preserve the spirit of the area, this may be the only way to save traditional vineyards from complete demolition into modernized factories.

G. Regardless of how the wine is made, the beverage itself is clearly here to stay. It has survived at least the past few thousand years, and remains a firm classic on many dining tables throughout the world. For now at least, that appears to be the status quo for the years to come.

Questions 27–34

Reading Passage 1 has seven paragraphs **A–G**.
Choose the correct heading for each paragraph from the list of headings below:
  i. Wine will certainly remain a classic drink for the years to come
  ii. The success of French wine can be attributed to its geographical advantages
  iii. The wine industry has gone through rapid development and changes
  iv. Vineyards can also generate tourism revenue
  v. It is challenging to correctly estimate the precise origin of wine
  vi. How wine was discovered, and its cultural variations
  vii. Background to French wine
  27. Paragraph A: ……
  28. Paragraph B: ……
  29. Paragraph C: ……
  30. Paragraph D: ……
  31. Paragraph E: ……

32. Paragraph F: ……
33. Paragraph G: ……

Questions 34–40

Do the following statements agree with the information given in Reading Passage 3?
In boxes 34–40 on your answer sheet, write

    TRUE   if the statement agrees with the claims of the writer
    FALSE   if the statements contradicts the claims of the writer
    NOT GIVEN if it is impossible to say what the writer thinks about this

34. A bottle of 1920 Moutai can cost more than a million yuan.
35. There are four main categories in the French classification system.
36. Fossilized shells are the single most important contributor to the quality of French wine.
37. Wine produced in Chateauneuf-du-Pape is relatively spicier, richer and higher in alcoholic content.
38. Selling wine is not the only way in which vineyards can generate revenue.
39. Some believe that the cost of maintaining the wine villages' rustic atmosphere can be justified by potential tourism revenue.
40. It is possible to stay at a vineyard as a tourist.

Answers for Questions 27–40

27. v
28. vi
29. iii
30. vii
31. ii
32. iv
33. i
34. NOT GIVEN
35. FALSE
36. FALSE
37. TRUE
38. TRUE
39. TRUE
40. TRUE

Practice Examination 5

Reading Passage 1

You should spend about 20 minutes on **Questions 1-13**, which are based on Reading Passage 1 below.

Sugar without Calories

There probably isn't a single person in this world who has not tasted sugar, and the majority of us likely cannot live without this sweet substance. Imagine how bitter your chocolate cake would be if it were made purely with cocoa, or how your plain coffee would taste like without sugar. In the United Kingdom, each person consumes on average 96.5 grams of sugar per day whereas this figure is slightly higher at 117 grams per day in the United States. That amounts to at least eight tablespoons of sugar per day. It is likely that we would all like to eat even more of it were it not for the negative health impact that excessive sugar can have. For one, eating too much sugar can cause excessive weight-gain, which leads to other problems such as heart disease and diabetes.

The idea of a calorie-free sugar that will not make you gain weight or cause any other health problems is one of the holy grails within the food and beverage industry. Globally, the production of sugar now exceeds 165 million tons a year. Based on findings from BCC Research, the global sugar market size is set to hit US$97 billion by 2017. You can imagine therefore why a calorie-free sugar would make an attractive investment, as it has the potential to generate as much as US$97 billion in revenue.

In many ancient civilizations such as Persia, honey was used as the main natural sweetener. However, in 510 B.C., the Persian Emperor Darius arrived in the Indian sub-continent where he discovered that people were using sugarcane as a sweetener instead. Surprised by this new finding, the ancient Persians called the sugarcane "the reed which gives honey without bees." The Persians brought sugarcane back with them, but it was not until 710 A.D. that Egypt developed the technology required to process, refine and crystallize sugar cane into sugar.

Today, we consume sugar not just in the form of crystallized sugar but also syrup, sugar cubes and powder. We also consume a wide range of sugar substitutes and artificial sweeteners, especially those that are low in calories. Common artificial sweeteners that you may have heard of are aspartame, saccharin and cyclamate. Most people associate artificial sweeteners with "low calorie," but the truth is that natural sweeteners can also be low in calories. Stevia, for example, has made headlines in recent years for being 250–300 times sweeter than conventional sugar — without the calories. Like honey, the stevia plant has been around for centuries and is native to Paraguay. In fact, stevia has become so popular that it has fuelled the rise of companies such as PureCircle, which focuses primarily on the development and production of high-purity stevia. Raw stevia on its own may have unpleasant aftertastes, and PureCircle focuses primarily on extracting only the stevia glycosides that contribute to stevia's sweetness.

The main reason why natural low-calorie sweeteners has made the world excited is because while artificial low-calorie sweeteners have been around for a long time, consumers in general have a negative perception of such sweeteners. Though it has not been officially proven, certain studies have linked artificial sweeteners to health problems such as cancer. It began in the early 1970s, when studies on laboratory rats showed that saccharin (a type of artificial sweetener) was linked to bladder cancer. This led the American Congress to mandate a warning label on saccharin-containing food, but studies did not show concrete evidence that saccharin could cause cancer in humans. Nonetheless, the negative perception has prevailed. You can imagine, therefore, why a natural and healthy low-calorie sweetener would appeal to the general market. This is especially if companies like PureCircle are able to completely remove the bitter aftertaste that comes with stevia. It would be like being able to consume nearly unlimited amounts of sugar without any of the consequences.

As a result, beverage companies that have suffered from growing awareness that high sugar consumption is not good for health are pouncing on the possibility of low-calorie natural sweeteners. Both Coca-Cola and Pepsi have announced that they will begin producing cola drinks sweetened with stevia. In 2014, Coca-Cola launched "Coca-Cola Life," which has a third fewer calories than regular Coca-Cola and comes in green packaging. Pepsi has also opted for green packaging under the name "Pepsi Next."

More research and development, as well as public education, is required before natural low-calorie sweeteners can replace traditional sugar. The biggest challenge is to produce sweeteners that taste exactly like conventional sugar at an affordable price. The first company that is able to do that and also protect its intellectual property will have significant rewards in store, given the vast global market.

Questions 1–13

Complete the sentences below.
Write **NO MORE THAN TWO WORDS** from the passage for each answer.
Write your answers in boxes 1–7 on your answer sheet.

1. In ancient times before sugarcane was discovered and commercialized, ... was used as a natural sweetener.
2. Ancient Egyptians developed early methods to .... sugarcane into sugar.
3. .... is an example of natural low-calorie sweetener.
4. People became worried about artificial sweeteners because it was shown that these sweeteners could cause .... in laboratory rats.
5. One of the downsides of stevia is that it has a ....
6. Both Coca-Cola Life and Pepsi Next can be easily recognized by its ....

Questions 7–13

Do the following statements agree with the information given in Reading Passage 1? In boxes 7–13 on your answer sheet, write

TRUE   if the statement agrees with the claims of the writer
FALSE   if the statements contradicts the claims of the writer
NOT GIVEN   if it is impossible to say what the writer thinks about this

7. On average, people in the United Kingdom consume more sugar than people in the United States.
8. Eating too much sugar can cause bladder cancer in laboratory rats.
9. The ancient Persians also used stevia as a natural sweetener.
10. In general, people still have a negative perception of artificial low-calorie sweeteners.
11. Aspartame is a type of artificial sweetener.
12. Both Coca-Cola and Pepsi purchased stevia sweeteners from PureCircle.
13. Coca-Cola Life has fewer calories than regular Coca-Cola.

Answers to Questions 1–13

1. Honey
2. Crystallize
3. Stevia

4. Bladder cancer
5. Bitter aftertaste
6. Green packaging
7. FALSE
8. FALSE
9. NOT GIVEN
10. TRUE
11. TRUE
12. NOT GIVEN
13. TRUE

Reading Passage 2

You should spend about 20 minutes on **Questions 14–25**, which are based on Reading Passage 2 below.

Den-Sharing in Mountain Brushtail Possums

A. Social behavior can change dynamically in response to severe alterations in the environment such as a sudden loss of resources. Under such circumstances, altruism may evolve if sharing with kin would increase inclusive fitness. This has been demonstrated in the mountain brushtail possum (*Trichosurus cunninghami*), a species of marsupials endemic to southeastern Australia. They are nocturnal generalist herbivores that den in tree hollows during the day. Although mostly solitary, mountain brushtail possums sometimes share dens, especially during mating season when they form mating pairs. With the decline of forest stands and consequently hollow-bearing trees, mountain brushtail possum populations were expected to dwindle due to the loss of daytime shelter. However, their numbers remained stable.

B. Banks *et al.* (2011a) hypothesized and investigated how the brushtail possums might have adapted their social behavior in response to the loss of hollow-bearing trees. They fitted a sample of mountain brushtail possums with radio collars so they could locate which dens were being used. The device also measured the proximity between individuals which was an indicator of interaction (i.e., den-sharing). Genetic tests of seven microsatellites were used to identify the degree of relatedness between individuals. Additionally, Banks *et al.* (2011a) surveyed the study site for hollow-bearing trees. Mountain brushtail possums were found to stay in a den the entire day, and may move to a different den only at night before the next day.

C. Banks *et al.* (2011a) measured the per day probability of den-sharing between individuals, and compared it to their relatedness and the availability of hollow-bearing trees. They found that as the number of available tree hollows decreased and competition for dens was high, mountain brushtail possums shared dens less often with non-relatives and more with relatives. By doing so an individual can increase its kin's chances of survival, thus increasing the inclusive fitness of the sharing individual.

D. In another similar study, Banks *et al.* (2011b) investigated how a wild fire might affect hollow-bearing tree availability and social interactions between mountain brushtail possums. The wild fire drove many mountain brushtail possums to an unburnt patch of forest, though some remained at the burnt habitat. This increased the population density and competition for dens in the unburnt habitat. The wildfire also increased competition in the burnt habitat because the number of available dens was reduced. Consequently, Banks *et al.* (2011b) observed an increase in kin-biased den-sharing in both burnt and unburnt areas.

E. Furthermore, both these studies show that only under certain conditions do mountain brushtail possums preferably share dens with kin. In the first study, i.e., Banks *et al.* 2011a, the probability of den-sharing with non-relatives can be much higher when hollow tree availability was high. Similarly, Banks *et al.* (2011b) found that even when competition for dens was high, mountain brushtail possums have a tendency to share with non-relatives during mating season. This evidence suggests that the cost of sharing with relatives would be higher when resources are abundant and when it is mating season.

F. Banks *et al.* (2011a) proposed two reasons for why the cost of sharing may be higher: inbreeding depression and pathogen susceptibility. Kin may share genetic susceptibility to certain pathogens, thus making transmission of diseases among kin more efficient. This together with inbreeding depression can incur great costs to fitness and should be selected against. Therefore, when resources are abundant or when it is mating season, mountain brushtail possums prefer to share dens with non-relatives. This is consistent with Hamilton's rule, whereby kin-biased behavior is only observed when benefits are higher than its costs.

Author: Flora Wong

Questions 14–19

Choose the correct letter, **A, B, C or D**.
Write the correct letter in boxes 14–19 on your answer sheet.

14. What is the main question that the passage seeks to answer?
    A. Why mountain brushtail possums share dens
    B. Why mountain brushtail possum numbers have remained stable despite the loss of daytime shelter
    C. How a wild fire might affect whether mountain brushtail possums share dens
    D. Social interactions between mountain brushtail possums and its impact on den-sharing

15. How did Banks *et al.* manage to locate which dens were being used by the mountain brushtail possums?
    A. Observing the possums' social behavior
    B. Measuring the proximity between each possum
    C. Radio collars
    D. Inducing fires

16. Under what circumstances would mountain brushtail possums share dens more often with relatives?
    A. During mating season
    B. When the number of available tree hollows decrease
    C. When tree hollow availability is high
    D. When resources are abundant

17. Which of the following statements is false?
    A. Mountain brushtail possums are used to sharing dens
    B. Banks *et al.* used genetic tests to determine "relatedness"
    C. The wildfire resulted in fewer dens
    D. Most of the possums fled due to the wildfire

18. Which of the following is a reason as to why mountain brushtail possums might **not** want to share dens with relatives?
    A. Competition for resources
    B. To increase chances of survival
    C. The mountain brushtail possums are largely solitary creatures
    D. To avoid transmission of certain pathogens

19. What is the key argument of the passage?
    A. The population of mountain brushtail possums have remained stable despite the loss of daytime shelter

B. Social behavior can alter drastically if there is a significant change in the environment
C. The possums avoid sharing dens with relatives due to inbreeding depression and pathogen susceptibility
D. Mountain brushtail possums prefer sharing dens with relatives

Questions 20–25

Reading Passage 2 has six paragraphs **A–F**.
Choose the correct heading for each paragraph from the list of headings below:

i. Two reasons for preferring to share dens with non-relatives
ii. Great changes in the environment may cause a shift in social behavior
iii. How the natural experiment was set up
iv. Conditions under which the possums prefer sharing dens with kin
v. Measurement and analysis
vi. The impact of a wildfire

34. Paragraph A: ……
35. Paragraph B: ……
36. Paragraph C: ……
37. Paragraph D: ……
38. Paragraph E: ……

Answers to Questions 14–25

14. B
15. C
16. B
17. A
18. D
19. B
20. ii
21. iii
22. v
23. vi
24. iv
25. i

Reading Passage 3

You should spend about 20 minutes on **Questions 26–40**, which are based on Reading Passage 3 below.

Leishamaniasis

Leishamaniasis is categorized as a "neglected tropical disease" and has been targeted for elimination. There are three forms of leishmaniasis: cutaneous, mucocutaneous and visceral. These are caused by protozoan parasites that are passed onto humans through the bites of infected female phlebotomine sandflies. This article will focus on visceral leishmaniases (VL) — also known as kala-azar — which is caused by the parasite *Leishmania donovani (L. donovani)*. VL is the most life-threatening of the three forms of leishmaniasis, as it attacks the body's vital organs. Symptoms include fever, significant weight loss, swollen spleen and liver, and anemia. If left untreated, patients may succumb to VL in as little as two years.

It is not still clear that origin of Leishmania was Paleoartic or Neoartic. However, ancient Leishmania could not be responsible for spreading leishmania between old world and new world, since sandflies have short life cycle and could not migrate. The most accepted theory is that mammals, such as infected rodents, spread leishmania through Bering Straits during the Miocene. A study of skulls in Chile revealed presence of *L. donovani* before migration of Europeans to America. Up to now, there is no evidence of how *L. donovani* was brought to the new world.

Today, VL occurs primarily in East Africa (Sudan, Ethiopia, Kenya, Somalia) and South Asia (India, Bangladesh and Nepal), and is also found in South America in Brazil, Argentina, Columbia and Venezuela. While the scope of disease is broad, distribution is clustered in areas of severe poverty and high population density. Individuals of all ages are susceptible to clinical infection. In regions with sustained endemic transmission, acquired immunity may cause a decrease in susceptibility with age. However, other studies suggest that susceptibility can increase with age, while some strains are particularly likely to infect children, such as *L. donovani infantum*.

L. donovani is also an opportunistic parasite, and individuals that are immunocompromised (many of whom are elderly) are more susceptible to infection, perhaps skewing statistics regarding age-related immunity to clinical infection by *L. donovani*. The mechanism may be specifically connected to *L. donovani*'s preference for immune systems with lowered T-cell concentrations, which has been shown to occur in the elderly. There is also some observational evidence to suggest men are more likely to contract clinical infections than women, although it is unclear if this is due to genetic differences between genders or lifestyle factors, especially in socio-economic regions where men may travel more often. For example, in one study it was found in one region where women and children would typically fish on a river bank where vectors were more common while men performed other tasks, that women and children were the most likely to become clinically infected.

As humans are the only reservoirs for *L. donovani*, effective diagnosis and treatment is important not only to reduce mortality and morbidity due to VL, it is essential in reducing transmission. The most common first-line treatment of VL is antimonials. These are effective and are believed to act in restricting glycolysis and metabolic pathways, thereby killing off *L. donovani*. However, some disadvantages of antimonial treatment are: three to four weeks of hospital admittance for intramuscular administration, toxic effects, cardiotoxicity risk in higher-dose long-term usage, and variability in quality and costs of these drugs.

The last decade has seen the emergence of new drugs, such as the orally administered Miltefosine, which has shown high efficacy, although there are major concerns about its long half-life which may allow resistance to emerge more easily. Amphotericin-B is used in second-line treatment and rarely have relapse and unresponsiveness been observed except in HIV co-infected hosts. Similar to antimonials, amphotericin-B has prolonged treatment and adverse side effects. Its lipid formulations have been found to be effective, more selective, safer and faster — but unaffordable to most.

Recent studies are pointing toward developing treatment regimes with a combination of pre-existing drugs, such as miltefosine and paromomycin. This type of treatment is expected to have enhanced efficacy over shorter treatment regimes. Expected lower toxicity and reduced costs should improve compliance — thus the reduced likelihood of resistance emergence. Furthermore, alternative treatment options need to be studied for HIV-*leishmania* co-infections, because these patients in general display have lower prognosis, higher toxicity and fatality rates compared to patients with intact immune systems. One possibility could be the combination of allopurinol and azole, which has been shown to be more effective in some immuno-suppressed patients, though more thorough studies are necessary.

A major implication of studies on control efficacy and drug resistance over the decades is the importance of a drug-use policy. India provides the perfect case study, indicating how a lack of regulation could quickly lead to antimonial-resistant strains of *L. donovani*. The availability of miltefosine over the counter in India is raising concerns that the same will soon happen for this new drug.

Overall, a complete prevention and control program will require all effective diagnosis, treatment and vector control. It will be crucial to develop a policy to ensure the continued efficacy of treatment and vector control programs.

Author: Flora Wong

Questions 26–32

Complete the summary below.
Choose **NO MORE THAN TWO WORDS** from the passage for each answer.
Write your answers in boxes 26–32 on your answer sheet.

Leishamaniasis is caused by **26** .... and visceral leishamaniasis is the most **27** .... form of the disease. Those with a weak immune system, especially the elderly, are more **28** .... to this illness. Antimonial treatment can fight off leishamaniasis by restricting glycolysis and blocking **29** .... In recent years, new drugs have been invented to combat leishamaniasis. For example, Miltefosine is a popular choice but its downsides include a relatively long half-life that can allow **30** .... to develop. Amphotericin-B is another effective option, but its higher price may render it **31** .... to most patients. To properly eliminate the disease, not only are accurate and diagnoses and cures needed but also an effective **32** .... program that will help prevent transmission of the disease in the first place.

Questions 33–40

Choose the correct letter, **A, B, C or D**.
Write the correct letter in boxes 33–40 on your answer sheet.

Practice Examination 5

33. Which of the following is **not** a symptom of leishamaniasis?
    A. Sandfly bites
    B. Fever
    C. Swollen spleen
    D. Swollen liver
34. How do we know that the Europeans did not bring leishamaniasis to America?
    A. Sandflies have short life cycle and could not migrate
    B. Mammals, such as infected rodents spread leishmania through Bering Straits during the Miocene
    C. A study of skulls in Chile revealed presence of *L. donovani* before migration of Europeans to America
    D. Up to now, there is no evidence of how *L. donovani* was brought to the new world
35. Where are you most likely to find cases of leishamaniasis?
    A. Areas with teenagers
    B. Areas with rampant poverty
    C. Rivers
    D. The Bering Straits
36. Which of the following statements is true?
    A. Antimonial treatment can have toxic effects
    B. Patients with HIV-leishmania co-infections have better chances of recovery
    C. A combination of allopurinol and azole is much more effective than antimonial treatment
    D. Miltefosine is not available widely in India
37. Which of the following is **not** a potential downside of antimonial treatment?
    A. Toxic effects
    B. Cardiotoxicity risks
    C. Resistance
    D. A longer half-life
38. Why are alternative treatments needed for patients with HIV-leishmania co-infections?
    A. These patients are not able to afford the expensive treatment needed to cure leishmaniasis
    B. Antimonial treatment is ineffective when it comes to this type of patient

C. HIV-leishmania co-infections are more aggressive than visceral leishmaniasis
D. These patients have a weaker immune system and are more likely to succumb to the disease

39. Why is the passage concerned about the availability of miltefosine over the counter in India?
   A. It may lead to antimonial-resistant strains of the *L. donovani*
   B. It may allow pharmaceutical companies to profit too much at the expense of patients
   C. Miltefosine has many dangerous side effects
   D. Miltefosine is not the best type of treatment available

40. Why does the passage emphasize the importance of vector control?
   A. To enhance scientific research on leishmaniasis
   B. Transmission needs to be eliminated to stamp out the disease
   C. Vector control plays an important role in any tropical disease
   D. Sandflies, which are the vectors for *L. donovani*, can easily spread the disease all over the world

Answers to Questions 26–40

26. Protozoan parasites
27. Life-threatening
28. Susceptible
29. Metabolic pathways
30. Resistance
31. Unaffordable
32. Vector control
33. A
34. C
35. B
36. A
37. D
38. D
39. A
40. B

The Academic Writing Section

Introduction

The academic writing section consists of two tasks. Most students think that the most important goal is to write English that is grammatically correct. This is wrong. Just imagine, you could write an essay that has sentences with not more than four words each:

> Dogs exist nearly everywhere. Dogs are nice. Many people have dogs. Most dogs are pets. People like their company. They are loyal companions.

As you can see, the example above is grammatically correct. But it is also very dry and unstructured. It is not clear what insights the reader can obtain from the essay, nor why it was written at all.

And so, the IELTS requires more than just correct English. It also requires you to:

1) Be able to analyze basic data
2) Be able to use English to explain your analysis (this also means acquiring the vocabulary necessary for such writing)
3) Apply the correct formal tone in English writing
4) Structure essays clearly with an argument that is supported by specific points
5) Display maturity in making arguments by also being able to consider and also counter alternate viewpoints

Task 1 (20 minutes)

The first writing task usually consists of some form of graphic stimulus, such as some charts and graphs. You will be asked to summarize information and present an analysis of the data in writing. This is something unique to the IELTS — you would not, for example, find this kind of writing task in the TOEFL.

Many students find this task challenging because they do not know how to interpret the data given and they lack the appropriate vocabulary needed to present their analysis. Words such as "percentage," "year-on-year increase" and "incremental" may not come naturally to everyone.

Furthermore, the recommended time for this section is a mere 20 minutes. This means that you must ensure that you have the required vocabulary and thought processes on hand so that you can complete the analysis in this very short period of time.

Task 2 (40 minutes)

The second writing task will present a scenario to you and you will have to pick a viewpoint. More importantly, you will have to justify why you chose that viewpoint. Most students think that they can justify their viewpoint solely based on how they see it. But, what the IELTS is also looking for — and what you can observe from the model answers provided — is the ability to anticipate and give justified responses to those who hold the opposing view.

In contrast to Task 1, Task 2 focuses more on your ability to create nuanced arguments. You may think that this is easier, given that you don't have to memorize analytical vocabulary like you did for Task 1, but there are certain techniques you must acquire before you can do it well.

In summary, the abilities that will be tested via the two tasks are as follows:

	Task 1: Data Analysis	Task 2: Argument
Analyze basic data	√	
Explain data analysis	√	
Structure essays	√	√
Formal tone	√	√
Anticipate and counter alternative viewpoints		√

As you can see from the above, there are some skills that are more important for Task 1, and there are others that are more relevant for Task 2. On top of that, there are skills that are universal to both tasks, such as having a solid structure and applying a formal academic tone to the writing.

Bearing this in mind, the Writing Section is structured as follows:
1) Structure
    a) Drawing a Blueprint
    b) Introductions
    c) Connecting Paragraphs
    d) Concise Conclusions

The Academic Writing Section

2) Tone
   a) Formal Writing
3) Data Analysis Skills
   a) Analytic Vocabulary
   b) Generating Insights
4) Argumentative Skills
   a) Forming a Viewpoint
   b) Countering Arguments

1a Drawing a Blueprint

Introduction

A blueprint is something that construction companies must prepare before building a house or any other building. In a way, writing is a lot like building a house. You need to make sure you have a clear idea of what you want to convey, and how you want to do this effectively.

The essay below is an example of an essay that suffers from poor structure. This was written by a student preparing for the IELTS, whom we will call "Student A" for now.

Essay Question: Some people say that advertising is such a key factor in driving consumption that sales figures are more of a reflection of effective advertising rather than a genuine need for the product.

To what extent do you agree or disagree with this opinion?

Give reasons for your answer and include any relevant examples from your own knowledge or experience.

Write at least 250 words.

[Poor Structure]:

Advertisements are shown everywhere to persuade people to buy products. Some people think that the high sales of popular consumer goods reflect the power of advertising and not the real needs of the society in which they are sold. I do not agree with this claim.

Comment: In the introduction, the student stated that she does not agree that the high sales of goods reflect the power of advertising.

However, just take a look below at the first paragraph of the main body. The student strongly states: "it is true that advertisements can promote manufacturers' sales." This immediately confuses the reader, who will begin to wonder whether the student agrees or disagrees with the statement. When you have confusion over a basic detail such as this, then it is very likely your grade will take a hit.

The Academic Writing Section

As we can see, it is true that advertisements can promote manufacturers' sales. Manufacturers will invest quite a large amount of money to design amazing product introduction videos or pictures so that people can remember their products at first sight. Furthermore, good quality products advertisements that are shown on television or in magazines can make people buy products compulsively. They can also inform consumers about the advertised products. Although costumers do not really need the products, they will sometimes follow the trends.

On the other hand, it is the people's decision whether or not to buy a product. People have a wide range of options from which they can select which product they want to buy. They will combine different factors such as price, quality, manufacturer and brand. Advertisement are only one part of the equation.

Moreover, people have budgets, which influence their decisions. It is not easy for manufacturers to influence one's mind with advertising in just a few minutes. In my country, people usually buy products that meet their real needs even if they have high disposable income. **Therefore, I regard high sales of popular consumer goods as the reflection of the real needs of society.**

Comment: In paragraphs 3 and 4, the student attempts to respond to the counter-arguments by explaining why high sales do not reflect the real needs of society. However, this seems to come only as an afterthought. The student only emphasizes this in the last sentence of paragraph 4. If the student had written a solid structure to begin with, she would have known to emphasize this point much earlier.

In conclusion, people have the free will to choose products. Though people do love to watch advertisements because they are creative and entertaining, it is fairly difficult to say that advertising sways everyone.

Drawing a Blueprint

Comment: The conclusion does not reflect the key points made in the main body. If the student had structured the key points properly, she could have written a better conclusion. We'll look into conclusions in greater detail later on in the book.

Now, let's take a look at how this essay could have been improved if the student had bothered to work on structure in the first place. Let's just focus purely on structure for now.

[Good Structure]:
Suppose the student had spent just a few minutes on writing a proper essay structure. It could have looked like this:

1) Introduction — Disagree with the statement
2) Main Point 1 — People factor in many considerations into their buying decisions, and advertisements are only one of many factors
   a. There are many options to begin with
   b. They will consider price, quality, manufacturer and brand as well
3) Counter-Argument 1 — However, it is true that consumers will sometimes follow trends blindly
   a. Manufacturers invest a large amount of money to design amazing videos or pictures
   b. Good advertisements can push people to buy things compulsively
4) Main Point 2 — Despite Counter-Argument 1, people have financial budgets and no amount of advertising can persuade someone to buy something they cannot afford
   a. You would still have to buy necessities first before buying discretionary goods
5) Conclusion — Because advertisements cannot ultimately dictate consumer decisions, this means that high sales could instead reflect other phenomena such as the growing income of consumers. Therefore, I disagree with the claim

The Academic Writing Section

Revised Essay:

> Advertisements are shown everywhere to persuade people to buy products. Some people think that the high sales of popular consumer goods reflect the power of advertising and not the real needs of the society in which they are sold. I do not agree with this claim.
>
> Consumers have free will and it is the people's decision whether or not to buy a product. People have a wide range of options from which they can select which product they want to buy. They will combine different factors such as price, quality, manufacturer and brand. Advertisements are only one part of the equation.
>
> However, to a certain extent, it is true that advertisements can affect a consumer's decision. Manufacturers will invest quite a large amount of money to design amazing product introduction videos or pictures so that people can remember their products at first sight. Furthermore, good quality products advertisements that are shown on television or in magazines can make people buy products compulsively. They can also inform consumers about the advertised products. Although costumers do not really need the products, they will sometimes follow the trends.
>
> Nonetheless, the power of advertisements is limited by a fundamental factor — financial budgets. No amount of advertising can persuade someone to buy something they cannot afford. People still have to buy necessities first, before considering other items like discretionary goods. In my country, people usually buy products that meet their real needs even if they have high disposable income.
>
> Because advertisements cannot ultimately dictate consumer decisions, this means that high sales could instead reflect other phenomena such as the growing income of consumers. Therefore, I disagree with the claim.

We focused mainly on moving the points around and restructuring the essay such that it made better logical sense. As you can see, this simple yet powerful act transformed a mediocre and somewhat confused essay into a much more convincing and well-articulated argument.

While there is still room for improvement, it's important you realize what structuring can do for you and your essay. Now, let's move onto the **Simple Steps** that you need to complete before you can structure an essay well.

Simple Steps

1. Calculate paragraphs and allocate word count
2. Determine the key point of each paragraph
3. Determine supporting points for each key point highlighted in Step 2

Elaboration with Examples

Step 1: Calculate paragraphs and allocate word count

This step is crucial because if you've noticed, Task 1 and Task 2 have very different word count expectations. Task 1 requires at least 150 words, whereas Task 2 asks for at least 250 words. Because of the difference in word count, the structures for Task 1 and 2 will also differ slightly.

How do you determine the number of words that should be allocated for each paragraph? There is no fixed formula, but as a general rule, the structure of an essay often looks like this:

15%	Introduction
70%	Main body (distributed evenly across the key points)
15%	Conclusion

This means that in the context of Tasks 1 and 2, the word count allocation looks something like the following:

	Task 1	Task 2
Introduction	22	38
Main body	105	175
Conclusion	22	38

Note: The IELTS does not require you to write *exactly* 150 or 250 words. Therefore, the numbers above are for reference only, and you can certainly write more than that. The best way to determine the ideal essay length for yourself would be to give yourself several timed written examinations. Count the number of words you are able to write in the amount of time allotted by the IELTS — that should be your target. You don't want to overstretch and spend too much time structuring an essay that you could never fully develop. At the same time, you don't want to write too little, and weaken the foundations of your essay.

The Academic Writing Section

Task 1 — Ideally 3 key points

Based on the calculation above, you can see that rationally, you won't be able to allocate more than three paragraphs to the main body of Task 1. Imagine, if you allocated four paragraphs, for example, you would have only about 26 words per paragraph, which is hardly enough to hammer in a key point along with supporting points.

In addition, consider how Task 1 is always accompanied by two charts or tables. The ideal number of key points should therefore be two or three — you could spend a paragraph each on each chart or table provided. The third paragraph can be an analysis of both charts and can also be enmeshed with the conclusion.

Therefore, don't let your mind wander and don't try to squeeze in every single point you can think of just for quantity's sake. Distil your thoughts and come up with two or three very good points. That would make your essay much more powerful than a confusing 200-word essay with 10 points scattered around.

Task 2 — Ideally 3-4 key points

For Task 2, a more eloquent and developed argument is needed. Because of this, you need a longer introduction to give an overview of your essay. In addition, your key points are likely to be more complex. It is a very different method of writing from Task 1, which tests your ability to read and analyze facts. Task 2 is more abstract. You're supposed to generate your own points (without any prompts, such as a bar chart) and at the same time, you must be able to explain why your viewpoint is better than the opposing stance. Having 3-4 key points would leave you with about 43-58 words per paragraph.

Step 2: Determine the key point of each paragraph

This is one of the most important aspects of every essay — the key points. Key points to an essay are what your brain is to your body. If the key points don't make sense, it doesn't matter how well-written the rest of your essay is — you're going to get a low grade.

How do you determine your key points? From this aspect, Task 1 is a lot more straightforward than Task 2. The general formula goes like this:

Task 1

1) Introduction — Describe the data presented in general terms
2) Main Point 1 — Describe the first chart or table

3) Main Point 2 — Describe the second chart or table
4) Conclusive Point — Analyze both charts or tables side by side, and generate some insights

Task 2

As mentioned earlier, Task 2 is more complex because it requires a more refined argument. It is a test of your logical skills as well as your ability to write coherently. Here's a checklist that you should go through before setting your pen to paper:

1) Have you repeated a similar point within your list of key points? If so, can you merge the similar points together?

Many students tend to be in such a rush to write their essays that they don't plan their key points well enough. As a result, there tends to be repetition at times.

Let's look at Student A's original essay once more to see this in action:

> On the other hand, it is the people's decision whether or not to buy a product. People have a wide range of options from which they can select which product they want to buy. They will combine different factors such as price, quality, manufacturer and brand. Advertisements are only one part of the equation.
>
> Moreover, people have budgets, which influences their decisions. It is not easy for manufacturers to influence one's mind with advertising in just a few minutes. In my country, people usually buy products that meet their real needs even if they have high disposable income. Therefore, I regard high sales of popular consumer goods as the reflection of the real needs of society.

Now, Student A has very neatly written two paragraphs that *seem to reflect two different key points altogether*. But are these really two different points? Think carefully. The first point says that people have the ultimate decision as to whether or not to buy a product, and they will consider multiple factors. The second point states that financial budgets are a strong factor that influences decisions, and this cannot be swayed by advertising.

This is an example of repetition because financial budgets are the same as the factor that the student raised in the first point — price. This makes the second point more of an elaboration rather than a new key point, and weakens the essay in terms of logical structure. Imagine that your entire essay is just an in-depth discussion of all the various factors that go into a consumer's decision. At best, the reader would think you are being long-winded. At worst, the reader may think that you have no better points to raise and you may get points taken off for a weak argument.

2) Would someone be able to say something against your point? (This is what we call a "counter-argument")

You can't have a strong argument without being aware of what others may say against your points.

3) Is your point based on fact, not on unverifiable feelings or opinions?

This may be hard to visualize, so let's take another look at Student A's essay. She had a lot of great fact-based points in it, but there were also some feelings mixed in, which weakened the logical strength of the rest of her essay:

> Nonetheless, the power of advertisements is limited by a fundamental factor — financial budgets. No amount of advertising can persuade someone to buy something they cannot afford. People still have to buy necessities first, before considering other items like discretionary goods. In my country, people usually buy products that meet their real needs even if they have high disposable income.

Take a close look at the last sentence in the paragraph above: "In my country, people usually buy products that meet their real needs even if they have high disposable income."

The problem with including unverifiable feelings or opinions is that it's just that — an opinion. It's not based on fact nor reasoning, making it less persuasive. Someone else could easily come along and say, "But in *my* country, people don't buy products that meet their real needs even if they have high disposable income." Who is right and who is wrong?

The answer is no one, because there are no facts to back this claim up. If you were writing a research paper, you could use available surveys and data to provide support for your claim. For example, perhaps you read a research paper that stated 80% of high-income consumers in your country still prefer buying necessities over discretionary goods. But in the IELTS, you don't have access to such data.

Nonetheless, if you wanted to still make this point, you *can* do it. You just have to use more facts and reasoning to convey your point. Here's one way of doing it:

Regardless of the perception created by the media, basic necessities are still the key concern of consumers. This is evident from the public backlash whenever the government removes subsidies for key goods such as fuel, or when there is a shortage of certain foods such as meat. However, you would very rarely — if never — see people rioting or protesting because there is a shortage of Coca-Cola, for example.

As you can see, the approach above is very different. We are using factual examples that show why necessities are important and why they drive consumer spending much more than discretionary goods.

4) Is your point redundant? In other words, are you stating the obvious?

The last question you must ask yourself is whether or not your key point is redundant. A redundant point is something that everyone knows and agrees on. No one would dispute this point and hence it is redundant because an argument cannot exist if everyone agrees.

Here are some examples of redundant points:

- All humans have two legs
- We need to breathe in order to survive
- Doing exercise can be tiring

Now, when looking at the examples above, you may think that you would never ever make redundant points. But, it happens more frequently that you may think. Let's take a look again at Student A:

In my country, people usually buy products that meet their real needs even if they have high disposable income.

Is it surprising to hear that people usually buy products that meet their real needs even if they are wealthy? Not really. Does Student A need to go out of her way to mention that she has observed this in her country? Not really, either.

These are the kinds of redundant points that all students should try to avoid. It won't hurt you as much if you do this for the supporting points or elaboration. In fact, when it comes to introductions and giving the reader some background information, "redundant" sentences are sometimes used because there is no way of knowing how much prior knowledge the reader actually has.

The Academic Writing Section

However, try to link these "redundant" points with analysis, so that your essay gains greater depth. Here's an example of how you can do so:

- All humans have two legs → All humans have two legs, which reinforces Charles Darwin's theory that humans evolved from chimpanzees.
- We need to breathe in order to survive → Reducing air pollution is of utmost importance because we need to breathe in order to survive.
- Doing exercise can be tiring → Doing exercise can be tiring, which is why the fitness industry has grown to include energy drinks and even sports massage centers.

In terms of seeing how all this works in an actual IELTS essay, let's take a look at a sample question and sample structure of key points.

> Essay Question: Some people say that fast food has caused a sharp rise in obesity cases and other health issues. Therefore, the sale of fast food should be strictly controlled.
> To what extent do you agree or disagree with this opinion?
> Give reasons for your answer and include any relevant examples from your own knowledge or experience.
> Write at least 250 words.

1) Introduction — Agree that fast food can cause obesity but disagree that fast food should be strictly controlled, because there are many other factors that also contribute to obesity
2) Main Point 1 — Even if you restrict fast food, there are so many other causes that will lead to higher obesity
   a. For example, those who can no longer eat fast food may turn to junk food and sugary drinks
   b. It is not feasible to ban every single food and drink on the planet that is "unhealthy"
   c. Therefore, the problem of obesity would still remain
3) Main Point 2 — Taking this step would infringe on the free will of people
   a. If we impose this restriction, we may as well also force everyone to exercise
   b. This is a slippery slope, as it can lead to the imposition of all sorts of other measures

4) Main Point 3 — Instead, we should focus on educating people about proper dietary habits and encouraging them to maintain a healthier lifestyle
   a. If executed properly, this will be better than banning fast food altogether, as people will control their eating on their own
   b. It would also avoid the problem of potentially infringing on free will
5) Conclusion — While fast food is bad, there are more sustainable and effective ways to combat obesity

Step 3: Determine supporting points for each key point highlighted in Step 2

Think of supporting points like moves in a chess game. Before you can reach the ultimate checkmate, you must first make certain moves and out-maneuver your opponent. If you do not have strong supporting points, you won't be able to write a good essay even if you have good main points.

Here are some tips that you can use when developing supporting points of your own, with examples to illustrate how they can be applied.

1) Action and reaction

One way you can solidify your main point is to show what would happen if your suggestion is *not* implemented. Conversely, you can show what would happen if your suggestion *is* implemented.

You can also use this to explain why counter-arguments won't work. Show that if the counter-argument is accepted, there would be undesirable consequences.

How does this work in practice? Let's use some examples from above and break it down:

> Main Point 1 — Even if you restrict fast food, there are so many other causes that will lead to higher obesity
>   a. For example, those who can no longer eat fast food may turn to junk food and sugary drinks
>   b. It is not feasible to ban every single food and drink on the planet that is "unhealthy"
>   c. Therefore, the problem of obesity would still remain

Action: Restrict fast food
Reaction: Obesity would still remain because there are so many other causes that also lead to this problem

Immediately, you can see why restricting fast food is a bad idea. Using the action-and-reaction technique helps the reader understand why certain choices are better than others.

Let's take a look at another example:

Main Point 2 — Taking this step would infringe on the free will of people
a. If we impose this restriction, we may as well also force everyone to exercise
b. This is a slippery slope, as it can lead to the imposition of all sorts of other measures

Action: Restrict fast food
Reaction: Infringes on the free will of people and is a slippery slope that can lead to the imposition of all sorts of other measures

Main Point 2 reinforces Main Point 1, making the restriction of fast food seem more and more undesirable.

Main Point 3 — Instead, we should focus on educating people about proper dietary habits and encouraging them to maintain a healthier lifestyle
a. If executed properly, this will be better than banning fast food altogether, as people will control their eating on their own
b. It would also avoid the problem of potentially infringing on free will

Action: Educating people about proper dietary habits and encouraging them to maintain a healthier lifestyle
Reaction: People may control their eating on their own, and this avoids the problem of potentially infringing on free will

Finally, Main Point 3 presents an alternative to restricting fast food. This makes your argument even more convincing as you have shown the negative consequences of the proposed action. Even better, you generated your own alternative and showed why this alternative is more effective than the initial proposal.

2) Examples and illustration

Another very helpful way to support and build on your main point is to provide some examples and illustrations. This can come in the form of anecdotal evidence and if you read the IELTS questions carefully, this is encouraged. In Task 2, the question will almost always conclude with these instructions:

> Give reasons for your answer and **include any relevant examples from your own knowledge or experience.**

Examples are crucial because often the main point can seem very abstract. Examples help to make the main points concrete. Let's see how this works:

> Main Point 1 — Even if you restrict fast food, there are so many other causes that will lead to higher obesity
> a. **For example, those who can no longer eat fast food may turn to junk food and sugary drinks**
> b. It is not feasible to ban every single food and drink on the planet that is "unhealthy"
> c. Therefore, the problem of obesity would still remain

The main point only states that there are "so many other causes that will lead to higher obesity." In order to show the examiner that you truly understand what you mean by "many other causes," and also to persuade the examiner of your point, you need to provide examples. By giving junk food as an example of something people can turn to even if fast food is banned, you effectively show that there are indeed more factors than just fast food.

Think about how you like to learn and how you best absorb information. Often, when you start learning new concepts, you would want to see examples of how these concepts apply in practice so you can visualize it better. The same goes for essays.

3) Connecting the dots

Another strategy that can effectively bolster your main point is to connect the dots. What does this mean? It means to connect seemingly separate ideas together, like a mind map. This gives a strong boost to your essay, as it shows that you are able to think in an analytical fashion that goes beyond just churning out points.

Let's take a look at another example, unrelated to the essay above.

The Academic Writing Section

> Essay Question: Some people believe that experience is the best teacher, and that it is more valuable for college students to do internships during the holidays as opposed to taking on some extra classes.
>
> To what extent do you agree or disagree with this opinion?
>
> Give reasons for your answer and include any relevant examples from your own knowledge or experience.
>
> Write at least 250 words.

1) Introduction — Work experience is indeed very valuable and students should try their best to do internships during the holidays
2) Main Point 1 — Learning knowledge and applying knowledge are different things altogether. We can learn knowledge from textbooks, but we can only know how to apply the knowledge if we have experience
   a. For example, you can learn a great deal of mathematics, but you would not know in what way this knowledge can be useful unless you have some work experience and understand the needs of a company or organization
   b. In the same way knowledge in the classroom is imparted by teachers, students also need work mentors who can teach them how to adapt to work life; this can only be done by learning from colleagues
3) Main Point 2 — Students can learn skills that they cannot learn in the classroom
   a. For example, students can learn business presentation, networking and teamwork skills
   b. All this is done under a working environment, where students will be under greater pressure to perform
   c. Challenges help people grow, and the new challenges at the workplace will certainly help students go further
4) Main Point 3 — For most students, the ultimate goal is to graduate and get a job
   a. Having work experience will make you a better candidate for jobs
   b. In addition, you will be better prepared and more ready to handle the transition between college and working life
   c. Having experience can also help you decide which industry or job you are suitable for. For example, many students often find out that the dream job they thought they wanted turned out to be unsuitable for them
   d. It is better to find out sooner rather than later

5) Conclusion — Students should definitely try to obtain work experience if possible, as they have nothing to lose and all to gain

Let's zoom in onto the first point to see how the dots were connected:

Main Point 1 — Learning knowledge and applying knowledge are both different things altogether. We can learn knowledge from textbooks, but we can only know how to apply the knowledge if we have experience

a. For example, you can learn a great deal of mathematics, but you would not know in what way this knowledge can be useful unless you have some work experience and understand the needs of a company or organization

b. **In the same way knowledge in the classroom is imparted by teachers, students also need work mentors who can teach them how to adapt to work life;** this can only be done by learning from colleagues

The way ideas were connected in the bolded section above is through a method called drawing parallels between student and work life. An idea that is held to be true for student life (knowledge is imparted by teachers) is applied to work life (students need work mentors).

This helps to persuade those who may be against your argument, because you are connecting a concept from student life to work life. It makes it harder to argue against you, because arguing against you would first require unravelling why the concept from student life is incorrect. It also demonstrates to the examiner that you are capable of more complicated logical thinking.

Here's another fine example of connecting the dots:

Main Point 3 — For most students, the ultimate goal is to graduate and get a job

a. Having work experience will make you a better candidate for jobs
b. In addition, you will be better prepared and more ready to handle the transition between college and working life
c. Having experience can also help you decide which industry or job you are suitable for. For example, many students often find out that the dream job they thought they wanted turned out to be unsuitable for them
d. It is better to find out sooner rather than later

This point is derived by connecting work experience to a student's ultimate goal. The claim that students would be better off spending their vacations taking on extra classes is premised on the thought that they are students, therefore it is better to spend time studying. By connecting the dots, you can flip this around to show that having work experience *is* linked to what a student is supposed to do — that is, to find a job upon graduation.

IELTS Trainer

Write a blueprint or structure for the following essay topics. You may do so in bullet point or point form.

1. Some states still maintain capital punishment or the death penalty as a punishment for serious crimes. However, some believe that such a punishment is too harsh and inhumane, and should therefore be abolished. To what extent do you agree or disagree with this opinion? Give reasons for your answer and include any relevant examples from your own knowledge or experience.
2. The Internet has made it very easy for the general public to express their views online especially via social media platforms. However, some believe that the Internet should be more strictly regulated, as there are members of the public who might abuse these platforms. To what extent do you agree or disagree with this opinion? Give reasons for your answer and include any relevant examples from your own knowledge or experience.
3. There are some who believe that gambling should be banned altogether. However, there are others who believe that gambling plays a critical role in boosting the economy, and therefore should be allowed albeit regulated. To what extent do you agree or disagree with this opinion? Give reasons for your answer and include any relevant examples from your own knowledge or experience.
4. There are some who believe that fee-paying schools should not exist, as those who attend such schools may have an unfair advantage over other students who attend government-funded schools. Others believe that parents should be given the freedom to choose where their children should go to school. To what extent do you agree or disagree with this opinion? Give reasons for your answer and include any relevant examples from your own knowledge or experience.
5. Some countries do not make it mandatory for school children to learn foreign languages, as they believe it is unnecessary. Others believe that it

is important for a child to learn foreign languages, especially international languages. To what extent do you agree or disagree with this opinion? Give reasons for your answer and include any relevant examples from your own knowledge or experience.
6. Deciding on a career is often a challenging process because many are torn between chasing a passion that may not pay much and stable jobs that may not be their passion. Which do you think is more important? Give reasons for your answer and include any relevant examples from your own knowledge or experience.
7. Electronic books are far better than physical books, as they are cheaper and more environmentally friendly. Some, however, believe that physical books have benefits that cannot be replaced by electronics. To what extent do you agree or disagree with this opinion? Give reasons for your answer and include any relevant examples from your own knowledge or experience.
8. Mothers who give up their careers to care for their children are as accomplished as any other successful woman leader or businesswoman there is. To what extent do you agree or disagree with this opinion? Give reasons for your answer and include any relevant examples from your own knowledge or experience.

Answers:

1.

Introduction — The death penalty is a necessary punishment for those who have committed serious crimes and is needed in order to promote social stability.

Main Point 1 — Criminal law requires serious punishments in order to restrict people from committing serious crimes.
- a. Most people would not hurt or kill someone just for fun because they know that will also risk their own life.
- b. The impact of the death penalty is to make the punishment serious enough in order to prevent the public from committing serious crimes.

Main Point 2 — There are not enough prison resources for the growing number of convicts that is on the rise due to high population growth.
- a. If a state decides to abolish the death penalty, that means it needs to build more prisons to hold prisoners.

- b. Serious crimes usually come with prison sentences of more than 25 years, which will definitely translate to high government cost and expenditure of resources.
- c. Those who commit serious crimes may even require more stringent security measures, which once again leads to even higher cost.

Main Point 3 — The death penalty is beneficial for those who need organ transplants.
- a. As we know, most countries have shortage problem of organ donors and death-row convicts' organs are a significant contributor to the organ donation program.
- b. Some countries around the world, in particular developing countries such as China and Iran, support this practice.

Conclusion — Though some people think death penalty is harsh and inhumane, it is an important punishment for the legal system and has its benefits.

2.

Introduction — Internet is good for exchanging information and sharing personal views but due to some specific reasons such as personal information security, it is better for the government to regulate it.

Main Point 1 — People are free to express their own opinions on social media platforms, but some of these views are rumors that can cause social panic.
- a. Right after the Japanese nuclear explosion in 2011, some Chinese Internet users released information that the nuclear radiation would definitely pollute salt. This caused panic-buying of salt even though the news was false.
- b. Free speech does not mean you can say anything without thinking about the possible consequences.
- c. The government has a duty to regulate these social media platforms to preserve social stability.

Main Point 2 — With the Internet, each individual's privacy is at risk.
- a. More and more people interact online and place a large amount of personal information online as well.

    b. It is dangerous if private information is exposed to everyone. It can lead to many unwanted consequences, such as identity theft, unfair defamation and even stalking.
    c. These kinds of personal abuse and cyber crimes should not be tolerated.

Main Point 3 — There are some who abuse social media platforms to make huge profits through unlawful methods.
    a. Though some websites ensure they will protect your personal details, hackers can find other ways to steal all the information and sell it to others or even use it for their personal gain.
    b. The recent case of how some hackers stole and published private information from Sony Pictures, causing a large amount of losses, is a good case study of why the Internet should be regulated.

Conclusion — The government should definitely regulate the Internet strictly if possible to help build a safer Internet environment for all.

3.

Introduction — Gambling is one of the economic sectors that generate significant revenue for the country. Though this may be the case, it needs a strict regulatory regime to prevent possible negative consequences that could arise from the business.

Main Point 1 — The government can use the revenue raised from gambling to build more public goods for the benefit of the society.
    a. In most regions that allow gambling, taxes on gambling profits and licensing fees for new facilities make up the bulk of government revenues.
    b. These funds can be used to build public goods such as schools and hospitals.
    c. For example, gambling can also improve the development of the tourism industry such as that has been done in Las Vegas, Macao and Monte Carlo.

Main Point 2 — Gambling business can provide jobs and reduce unemployment.
    a. In my opinion, casino jobs contribute more to the economy than tax revenue.
    b. Furthermore, the other industries that are supported by the gambling business can also create more jobs to help cut the unemployment rate.

Main Point 3 — Though gambling is a dangerous business that might cause unsatisfactory consequences, the government can enforce laws to minimize these possible negative consequences.
    a. For example, only people above eighteen years old can take part in gambling.
    b. The government implements various methods to strengthen the supervision of this business, including making laws and regulations.
    c. All the same, people will find other ways to gamble together. If the government bans legal gambling, many illegal gambling operations will emerge and the situation will worsen.

Conclusion — As long as the government regulates gambling strictly, this industry can play an important role in the development of the economy.

4.
Introduction — Both fee-paying schools and government-funded schools have their own advantages and disadvantages. It is better for parents to choose where their children should go.

Main Point 1 — Establishing more fee-paying schools is the development trend of national education system.
    a. Most countries do not have sufficient funds to support all the students to go to government-funded schools.
    b. Having some children in fee-paying schools helps reduce the burden on government-funded schools.
    c. The competition between fee-paying schools and government-funded schools can encourage improvements in both types of institutions.

Main Point 2 — In my opinion, each school has its own features and there is no school that is better or worse than the other.
    a. Fee-paying schools have strong financial resources to provide better education facilities and teaching resources.
    b. Most government-funded schools have more teaching experience because they have been around for a much longer time. The government keeps tuition fees low and makes schools accessible to more students.
    c. These schools are all committed to cultivating good students.
    d. Anybody can achieve the same grades, regardless of where they come from, by hard work and determination.

Main Point 3 — Parents are willing to pay the price in order to choose the school that their children will go to.
- a. Parents in a middle-class family will sometimes try their best to send their children to fee-paying schools because in their mind, children might receive better education.
- b. There are some rich people who are able to afford fee-paying schools but would like to choose government-funded schools nonetheless due to the schools' good reputations.
- c. Parents have different opinions on these schools and the decisions are not so easy to make.

Conclusion — Fee-paying schools play an important role in national education system, but this is not to say that government-funded schools are necessarily worse. Parents should be allowed to make the decision as to where their children should go.

5.
Introduction — Schools need to set foreign language courses as compulsory subjects in order to help students receive a more well-rounded education.

Main Point 1 — Learning foreign languages is one of the most important ways for children to acquire and exchange information.
- a. For example, if students have to research British history, it will be better for them to read English history books and browse English websites independently.
- b. Besides becoming more familiar with other cultures, students can communicate with more people coming from all over the world and make new friends.
- c. We regard a foreign language as a useful tool to widen our horizons, acquire information and news from other countries.

Main Point 2 — Learning foreign languages can improve one's general abilities.
- a. Some studies suggest that those who are able to speak two or more languages are able to focus better and learn more quickly.
- b. It can help people enhance their memorization skills, which is important for gaining new knowledge.
- c. It is necessary for schools to offer mandatory foreign language courses.

Main Point 3 — Younger people are able to pick up languages more easily than older people.
- a. Babies have an innate ability to distinguish between various language pronunciations and this ability begins to decline with age.
- b. If one is to learn a foreign language, it is best to begin from a young age.
- c. School children have more time and energy than older people when it comes to learning foreign languages.

Conclusion — Students should definitely learn a foreign language, especially international languages if possible, as they have nothing to lose and all to gain.

1b Introductions

After writing a blueprint, you can start on your introduction. This is the best time to do so, because while writing your blueprint, you'll still be thinking of the different viewpoints and you may not have made up your mind entirely.

Writing a good introduction for the IELTS can be simple and straightforward if you know the correct steps. For Task 1, it is easier, as you only have to describe the data given in general terms. For Task 2, apart from rephrasing the question, you will have to state your stance. This will also be easy given that you have already written a blueprint.

Simple Steps

1. Underline keywords in the question or prompt given
2. Paraphrase the question using the keywords
3. Add your own layer of analysis
   a. For Task 1, this means describing the data given in more specific terms
   b. For Task 2, this means stating your stance on the given topic

Elaboration with Examples

Step 1: Underline keywords in the question or prompt given

Always understand the essay topic or data given. Your introduction is a demonstration of that, and it also helps you to avoid going out of topic. A keyword means a significant word that acts as a reference point or is an important component of a description.

Generally, if you want to decide whether or not a certain word or phrase is "key," you can ask yourself this:

- If you take this word or phrase out of the sentence, could you still grasp the original meaning?

The Academic Writing Section

Refer to the following example:

> Essay topic: Some people argue that <u>unpaid voluntary work</u> should be made <u>mandatory</u> for <u>high school students.</u> This could be in the form of working for a charitable organization or giving free tuition to younger children from underprivileged backgrounds.
> To what extent do you agree or disagree?
> Give reasons for your answer and include any relevant examples from your own knowledge or experience.
> Write at least 250 words.

Notice that we have tried to keep it as brief as possible, and this means excluding the example given, which is an elaboration based on the first sentence. This is because one can still understand the essential meaning of the question without even referring to the example.

Step 2: Paraphrase the question using the keywords

Next, use these keywords as crutches for you to paraphrase the question. Focus on restating the question as well as the debate that it has presented to you. But, remember, paraphrasing isn't just about using different words, but can also come in the form of varying sentence structure.

If you cannot think of any alternative vocabulary or if you feel unsure about some options you have in mind, *don't use them*. You could do yourself more harm than good if you apply new words in the wrong way.

Let's take a look at a student who made this mistake in her attempt to paraphrase the introduction:

There is an argument that whether unpaid voluntary work should be a mandatory part of high school. For instance, students can work for a charity or teach underprivileged children. Concerning about the **study mission,** my suggestion is that school can encourage its students to take part in unpaid community service **instead of constraining them.**

There are two major problems here:

 a) Usage of wrong vocabulary — In an attempt to use different words from the essay topic given, the student used the wrong vocabulary. There is no mention about a "study mission" but the student decided to use it anyway.

She probably meant to say something similar to the "objective of education," not knowing that "study mission" can refer to an educational trip that aims to spread Christianity to non-believers.

b) Misunderstanding the question — The student misunderstood the question by assuming things that are neither true nor applicable. She states that schools can encourage students to volunteer "instead of constraining them." However, the question never said that schools are constraining students from volunteering. Because the student did not stick to the keywords in the essay topic as a guide, she has veered off course and made a logical error. This is a pity because normally, choosing a stance is the easiest thing you can do: either you agree, or you disagree. In this case, the student chose the wrong stance because she had misinterpreted the question completely.

Step 3(a): Add your own layer of analysis — Describe the data given in more specific terms

Let's take a look at a sample question for Task 1:

> Essay topic: The graphs below give information about smartphone ownership as a percentage of the population between 2008 and 2012, and by level of income for the same time period.
>
> Summarize the information by selecting and reporting the main features, and make comparisons where relevant.

Here's what a basic understanding of the topic looks like:

> The bar charts show data about smartphone ownership as a percentage of population.

It sticks to the bare bones of whatever you can glean from the essay topic. However, to add another layer of analysis and to make the introduction a bit more complete, you can make the following move:

> The bar charts show data about smartphone ownership as a percentage of population, with a further classification by level of income, from 2002 to 2010.

By highlighting that you are aware that the data is divided first in terms of smartphone ownership and second in terms of income, you already demonstrate greater mastery of the information at hand. The reader knows that he or she should expect some analysis that relates smartphone ownership with income. In this way, the second introduction, which is more analytical, is better.

Step 3(b): Add your own layer of analysis — State your stance on the given topic

We looked at the example of the student who misinterpreted the question in Step 2. How could she have done it better?

Let's refer once more to the original essay topic and the keywords.

Essay topic: Some people argue that <u>unpaid voluntary work</u> should be made <u>mandatory</u> for <u>high school students.</u> This could be in the form of working for a charitable organization or giving free tuition to younger children from underprivileged backgrounds.

To what extent do you agree or disagree?

Give reasons for your answer and include any relevant examples from your own knowledge or experience.

Write at least 250 words.

First, she could have stated her stance more clearly. By this, we mean answering the question. Does she agree or disagree that unpaid voluntary work should be made mandatory for high school students?

Second, she could zoom in onto the keywords and *dispute* those keywords, rather than create an assumption that is not true at all (that schools currently constrain students from voluntary work). This can be done for each keyword that is highlighted:

a) Unpaid voluntary work — Should the students be paid for their work, or receive some sort of benefit in return such as certification or extra credit?

b) Mandatory — Should it be made voluntary, and should students merely be strongly encouraged to perform voluntary work? There are different degrees to this, and many different ways in which you can argue this point.

c) High school students — Even if you disagree that high school students should do mandatory work, do you perhaps agree that this rule should apply to college students instead? Or, perhaps you may think that this is such a good idea that even primary school students can be taken along on charitable trips?

You can pick any of the above and the best part is that you will not only remain within topic, but also be able to create a more sophisticated argument in the sense that you go beyond just saying "Yes, I agree" or "No, I disagree." You go a step further in offering a different suggestion or alternative solution based on whatever points you decide to make.

To conclude, there is a certain way to write introductions for Task 2 and following the steps will help prepare you to write *any* sort of introduction you wish. To help you on your way, we want to leave you with a formula for introductions. Note that this is applicable *only* for Task 2 introductions:

[Restate the debate surrounding the situation] + [State your stance] + [State the general reason for your stance]

See how it works in practice:

> The question raises the issue of whether there should be compulsory unpaid voluntary work for high school students. This essay will argue that high school students should indeed go for compulsory unpaid voluntary work, as the benefits of doing so far outweigh the costs.

It is simple yet effective. From this paragraph, the reader not only knows where you stand on the issue, but also gets a general sense of *how* you are going to make the argument — and that is by focusing on the benefits of compulsory unpaid voluntary work. At the same time, you also inform the reader that you are not completely biased, and that you are *well aware there are some costs to unpaid voluntary work* but that your reasons for supporting the move are compelling enough to regard these costs as worthwhile.

To make it even easier for you, here are some handy phrases that you can memorize and apply in your essay in order to successfully execute the formula above.

How to restate the debate surrounding the situation:

> Some people argue that …
> The question raises the issue of …
> There is some debate concerning …
> There are different viewpoints regarding …

How to introduce your stance on the debate:

> However, in my opinion …
> I believe that …

The Academic Writing Section

This essay will argue that ...
It is my belief that ...
I would like to argue that ...

IELTS Trainer

Use the *Simple Steps* to write an introduction for the following essay questions. Begin with questions for Task 1 before moving onto Task 2.

Task 1

1. The charts below give information on the consumption of various caffeinated drinks in 1994 and 2014. Summarize the information by selecting and reporting the main features, and make comparisons where relevant.

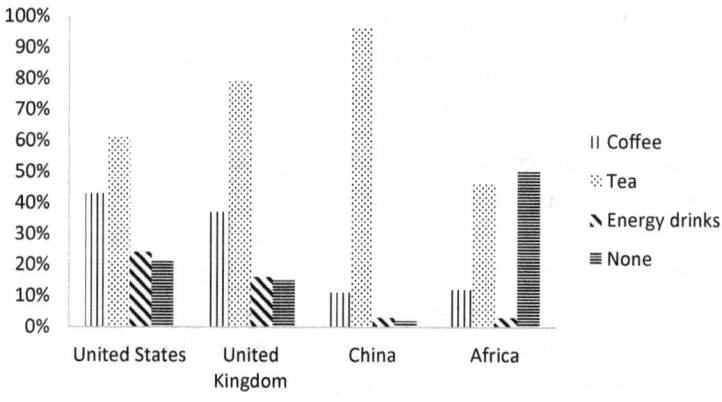

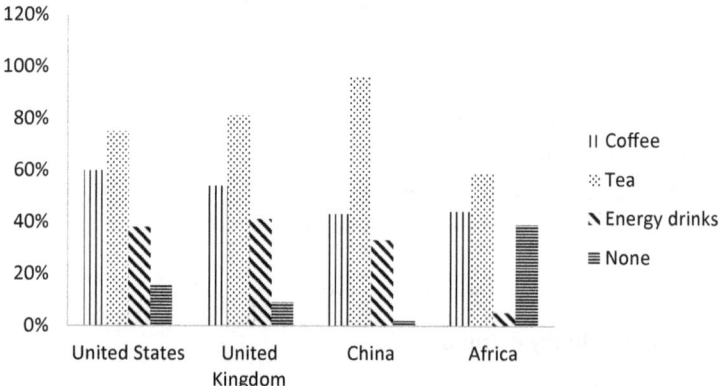

Step 1:

Step 2:

Step 3:

2. The charts below give information on the consumption of sugar as well as obesity rates from 2010 to 2013. Summarize the information by selecting and reporting the main features, and make comparisons where relevant.

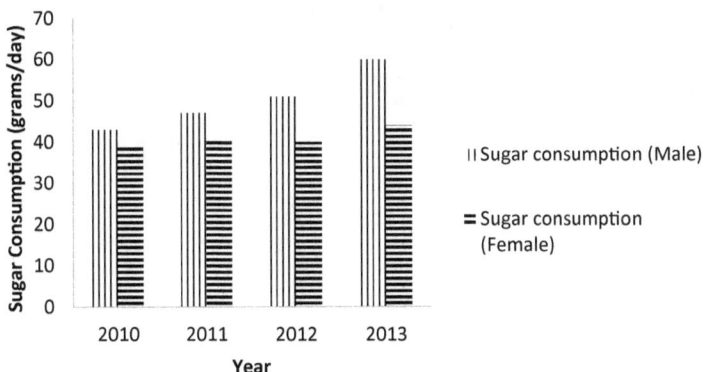

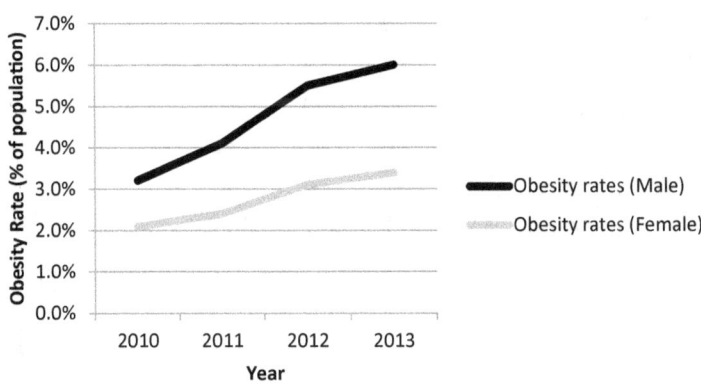

Step 1:

Step 2:

Step 3:

3. The charts below give information about the usage of electronic gadgets as well as average income. Summarize the information by selecting and reporting the main features, and make comparisons where relevant.

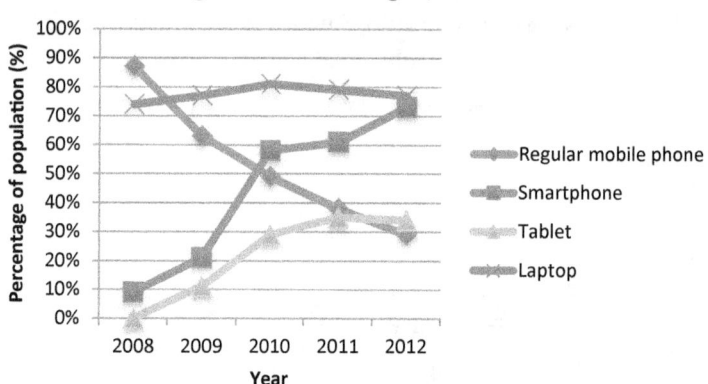

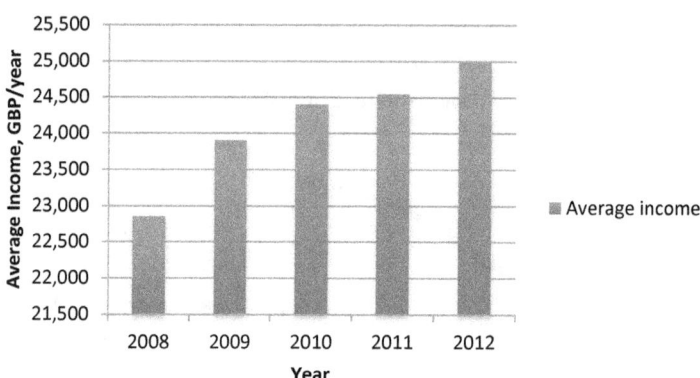

Step 1:

Step 2:

Step 3:

Task 2

4. Every now and then, some cultural traditions die out. Some parties believe that this is not significant because cultural traditions are not beneficial. To what extent do you agree or disagree with this opinion?

Step 1:

Step 2:

Step 3:

5. Some believe that encouraging people to eat healthily is a good way to improve the overall health condition of the public. Others believe that healthy eating alone is not enough. Discuss these views and provide your own opinion on this issue.

Step 1:

Step 2:

Step 3:

6. When choosing a leader, some believe that age is the most important consideration, as a leader needs to be experienced and knowledgeable. Others think that a young person can also be a leader, as long as he or she is capable. Discuss both these views and provide your own opinion.

Step 1:

Step 2:

Step 3:

7. Nowadays, nearly everyone has a smartphone. Some parents even buy smartphones for children as young as seven or eight years old. However, there are some who believe that it is not good for primary school children to own smartphones. Discuss these views and provide your opinion on this issue.

The Academic Writing Section

Step 1:

Step 2:

Step 3:

Answers:
1.
Step 1:
The charts below give information on the <u>consumption of various caffeinated drinks</u> in <u>1994 and 2014.</u>

Step 2:
The charts provide information about the consumption of different caffeinated drinks in 1994 and 2014.

Step 3:
The charts provide snapshots of the consumption of different caffeinated drinks in 1994, as well as the same data from a decade later in 2004.

2.
Step 1:
The charts below give information on the <u>consumption of sugar</u> as well as <u>obesity rates</u> from <u>2010 to 2013.</u>

Step 2:
The charts provide information regarding sugar consumption and obesity rates from 2010 to 2013.

Step 3:
The charts provide information regarding sugar consumption, with relevant information about the trend of obesity rates from 2010 to 2013.

3.
Step 1:
The charts below give information about the usage of <u>electronic gadgets</u> as well as <u>average income.</u>

Introductions

Step 2:
The charts provide some data about the usage of electronic gadgets and average income in the United Kingdom from 2008 to 2012.

Step 3:
The charts provide some data about the usage of electronic gadgets in the United Kingdom, with relevant information on average income from 2008 to 2012.

4.
Step 1:
Every now and then, some <u>cultural traditions</u> <u>die out.</u> Some parties believe that this is <u>not significant</u> because cultural traditions are <u>not beneficial.</u>

Step 2:
Some cultural traditions die out from time to time. Some people argue that this is not important because these cultural traditions are not useful.

Step 3:
Some cultural traditions die out from time to time. Some people argue that this is not important because these cultural traditions are not useful. It is my belief that cultural traditions are the invaluable representations of a country's history and should be protected.

5.
Step 1:
Some believe that encouraging people to <u>eat healthily</u> is a good way to <u>improve the overall health condition of the public.</u> Others believe that <u>healthy eating alone</u> is <u>not enough.</u>

Step 2:
There is some debate over whether people should be encouraged to eat healthily in order to improve the overall health condition of the public or whether healthy eating alone is not enough.

Step 3:
There is some debate concerning people should be encouraged to eat healthily in order to improve the overall health condition of the public or only healthy

eating is not enough. I believe that while maintaining a healthier diet is one key factor, physical exercise also plays an important role.

6.
Step 1:
When choosing a leader, some believe that age is the most important consideration, as a leader needs to be experienced and knowledgeable. Others think that a young person can also be a leader, as long as he or she is capable.

Step 2:
The question raises the issue of whether age is the most significant consideration for choosing a leader because a leader needs to be experienced and knowledgeable. There are some who believe that a young person can also be chosen, as long as he or she is capable.

Step 3:
The question raises the issue of whether age is the most significant consideration for choosing a leader because a leader needs to be experienced and knowledgeable. There are some who believe that a young person can also be chosen, as long as he or she is capable. In my opinion, when choosing a leader, age is only one factor to be considered. If there are young people who are also capable, they deserve to assume leadership as well.

7.
Step 1:
Nowadays, nearly everyone has a smartphone. Some parents even buy smartphones for children as young as seven or eight years old. However, there are some who believe that it is not good for primary school children to own smartphones.

Step 2:
Almost everyone has a smartphone now. Some parents even give smartphones their children who are as young as seven or eight years old. This raises the question of whether or not it is good for primary school children to have smartphones.

Step 3:
Almost everyone has a smartphone now. Some parents even give smartphones their children who are as young as seven or eight years old. This raises the question of whether or not it is good for primary school children to have smartphones. I would like to argue it is fine for primary school children to own smartphones, as long as they use it for communicating with their parents and for educational purposes, as opposed to playing games.

1c Connecting Paragraphs

After you have written a good introduction for your essay, the next challenge is to connect the paragraphs well. Good logical structure doesn't always automatically translate to a logical essay because some writers find it hard to link ideas together.

The key to doing this is to write good topic sentences for each paragraph. You can think of a topic sentence as something that sets the scene for a particular paragraph. If your topic sentences are written well enough, a reader could read only the topic sentences of every paragraph and still come to a fairly decent understanding of your essay.

Apart from understanding the concept of a topic sentence, you will also need to familiarize yourself with the vocabulary needed to transition from one paragraph to the next. This will also be covered in this chapter.

Let's first take a look at an essay excerpt written by an actual student. While some awkward sentences and grammar mistakes remain, let us focus solely on topic sentences and transition:

Three main paragraphs will introduce the information about fossil fuels (petrol and oil, coal), natural gas and new energy resources (nuclear, solar/wind and hydropower) respectively.

Comment: Take a look at the way the student introduces the essay: "Three main paragraphs will introduce …". This is a redundant and weak statement because it is obvious that the whole purpose of the essay is to introduce information relating to the data provided. It would be like saying, "These words will teach you how to excel in the IELTS."

Therein lies the first lesson that you need to know about topic sentences. They must be informative, and ideally it should be a very concise summary of whatever you are going to write in that particular paragraph. Now, in this example, the student has only written one sentence per paragraph, but you can imagine that this will rarely be the case since you need far more than a sentence per paragraph to write a decent essay.

In light of the graph, we can see petrol and oil emerge at a pace that is quite consistent with coal.

> **Comment:** Here's another mistake — the wrong usage of transition words. The student had probably memorized the phrase "in light of" but did not know how to use it properly. This is a risky move because it relies on luck. A more suitable phrase would have been "According to the data provided," "Based on the given information," or "An analysis of the graph shows that." It may not be as fancy-sounding as "in light of," but it is accurate and most importantly appropriate.
>
> We'll cover transition vocabulary in this chapter, but remember, if you aren't really sure of how to use the word, then you are essentially taking a risk. In this case, the student took a risk that didn't pay off well.

Natural gas generated a drop at first and then firmed up in the next 15 years. The projection shows that it will be exceeded by coal.

Three kinds of new energy resources had flattened growth in the past and sustainable development in the future.

> **Comment:** The paragraphs above are simply weak because they do not have any topic sentence at all that pre-empts and prepares the reader for what you are going to say. Pre-empting is very important. Think about any book that you have read — it usually starts with some form of introduction that introduces you to the situation, character and plot. If the author leapt straight into the details, you would be highly confused. Similarly, you should also bear this in mind and prepare your reader by writing topic sentences that can pre-empt them about what you are going to say.

Simple Steps

It boils down, once again, to a few simple steps. If you follow these steps, you should be able to transition between your paragraphs effortlessly in no time.

1. Write a concise mini-introduction to each paragraph, preferably in a single sentence (this is also known as a "topic sentence")

2. Identify the type of move you are making in each paragraph
3. Apply the appropriate transition word(s)

Elaboration with Examples

Here is where you will see precisely why writing a structure is so important. If you have completed a good structure, you will realize that transitioning well between paragraphs will become a much simpler job.

Step 1: Write a concise mini-introduction to each paragraph, preferably in a single sentence

You may hear people advising you to write concisely, but what does that mean? To turn this abstract concept into something more tangible for you, we have developed a framework:

1) What — What do you want to argue? What is the main point of this paragraph? This is the most basic component of your topic sentence, and if you have written a good structure, you should be able to obtain it directly from there.
2) How — How are you going to convince the reader that your main point is true? For example, which factors or perspectives will you examine or consider? Here's an example of what a topic sentence looks like, if it only answers the "What" aspect:

> "Children should not be allowed to drink coffee."

On the other hand, here's an example of a topic sentence that also answers the "Why" aspect:

> "By considering the possible detrimental effects coffee could have on children, children should not be allowed to drink coffee."

As you can see, the second example is much more compelling. It immediately tells the reader which aspect you will consider and the logical thought process that you will apply. It also shows the reader that you think clearly, and that you have the whole paragraph planned out even before you wrote it — it's a mark of a good writer.

3) **Why is it important** — Why do you want to make this point? Why is it important for the reader to understand this point? Remember, the point must not only be valid but also important for it to support your argument. By "important," we mean that it must answer the original essay question somehow.

It is perfectly possible for your point to be valid, but unimportant. Don't assume that answering the "How" aspect will immediately render your point important. Suppose the essay topic is about whether or not children should be allowed to have smartphones. A point that is valid, but unimportant would be: "Smartphones are very expensive." You could elaborate on the "how" of this point by observing how even the cheapest smartphone costs at least a few hundred dollars. No one would disagree that smartphones are very expensive, but why should this point be of interest to anyone? It simply doesn't answer the question.

Let's look at a point that is valid and also important. Instead of merely arguing that smartphones are very expensive, you can say that: "Smartphones are very expensive, and it would be a waste to let children have them as children may break them easily." Here, you have clearly linked the fact that smartphones are very expensive to the original essay topic by using this to argue that children should not be allowed to have smartphones.

Step 2: Identify the type of move you are making in each paragraph

When writing argumentative essays, there are **four** key moves that every writer will make. Under each key move, there are sub-categories. The first step is to understand the key purpose of the category itself, and to familiarize yourself with the words within each category.

Step 3: Apply the appropriate transition word(s)

However, learning is one thing, and application is another. Memorization is useless unless you can use the words correctly in an essay. To help you achieve this, this section includes example sentences for you to see how the words are used in real essays. This follows immediately after the explanation about how to use each writing move, so that you can instantly see how these transition words can be applied without having to flip back and forth within this book.

We have condensed them as follows:

Writing Move 1: Introducing Basic Ideas

The most basic of writing moves involves introducing basic ideas. You will always have to first let the reader be aware of your most basic thought before moving onto more complex, analytical moves. Think of it as a game of chess. You can't start without first moving your pawn. Similarly, in writing, you can't start before your reader understands the basis of your argument.

Writing Move 1.1: Giving Examples

In the IELTS writing tasks, you are explicitly asked to give examples from your own country or experience. You may also have to highlight examples from the data or charts given as well. Knowing these transition words will help you introduce your examples more smoothly.

No.	Writing Move 1.1: Giving Examples	Application in Essays
1	Such as	Some people would believe that some professions need certain talents such as painting, music-playing and writing.
2	For example	Motivation is a key consideration in any crime. For example, a man who murdered someone due to anger and a man who killed someone because of self-defense are two different cases altogether.
3	For instance	Employers usually ask graduates whether they have some useful skills and knowledge in interviews. For instance, they may ask law school students if they know how to write legal research reports.
4	Particularly	People who have talent will usually excel more quickly, particularly in music and sport.
5	In particular	It had become clear that readers, in particular the young, were getting much of their news online.
6	Notably	A judgment of a crime is an indicator for each country's legal environment, notably for the cases that have significant impact to the society.
7	Like	The younger generations like advanced gadgets, like smartphones, tablets and even smart-watches.

8	Especially	The people who attended the court, <u>especially</u> the family members of the parties involved, would like to see the judge take motivation and circumstance into account when deciding on the punishment.
9	Including	There are some important aspects to be considered when making the final judgement of a crime, <u>including</u> the motivation, the circumstance and the result.
10	By way of example	<u>By way of example,</u> according to criminal law in China, people will be put into prison for at least 10 years if convicted of intentional homicide.
11	As an illustration	<u>As an illustration,</u> a director of the company may want each of his employers to treat other colleagues with mutual respect in order to build a strong culture of teamwork.
12	To illustrate	Some people who are born with certain talents can become very successful. <u>To illustrate this point,</u> let us consider the famous basketball player Michel Jordan.
13	To demonstrate	<u>To demonstrate</u> the view about there should be fixed punishments for each type of crime, we can use the civil law system as a case study.
14	As a demonstration	I am not using Michael Jordan's example to argue that hard work is not important, but only <u>as a demonstration</u> that talent can help people improve faster at a young age.
15	Namely	There are many factors to success, <u>namely</u> talent, hard work and also a bit of luck.
16	As a case in point	Knowledge and skills needed in the workplace should be gained in the university. <u>As a case in point,</u> employers will usually ask interviewees to complete some case studies or logical exercises to show what they have learned from school.
17	Consider (insert example)	<u>Consider</u> the example of an average high school student's daily time schedule. Most would include some time for extra-curricular activities, and this can also include unpaid voluntary work.

Writing Move 1.2: Additions

You're not just going to have one main point to make in your writing tasks. This means that you are definitely going to have to introduce a new idea or key point, and maybe even two or three times.

Some students go for the numerical method: Firstly, Secondly, Thirdly etc. But that method is not only dry, but also shows that you have not yet mastered the English language well enough to diversify your vocabulary.

Using the words below will not only help you transition more smoothly, but will also make your essay more elegant.

No.	Writing Move 1.2: Additions	Application in Essays
1	Indeed	Fixed rules about punishments will help to simplify judges' decisions about how to make judgments in court. <u>Indeed</u>, people will also restrain their behavior because they know the punishments they will receive if they commit crimes.
2	Also	When doing an internship, students do not only learn knowledge but <u>also</u> social skills and team work.
3	Or	<u>Or</u>, one can consider an alternative and that is to include unpaid voluntary work in the education syllabus.
4	Too	The court should consider the motivation and other key factors in specific cases, <u>too</u>.
5	Nor	Though Ms. Zhang was disabled since birth, she never felt frustrated, <u>nor</u> did she give in to any difficulty.
6	Further	Students can learn how to apply the theoretical knowledge they have acquired from college when they do internships. <u>Further</u>, they will be able to better understand the industry they are in and gain a more holistic understanding of the career path they have chosen.
7	Furthermore	Though I applied to both Durham University and Hong Kong University for further studies, I prefer Hong Kong more because of its proximity to Shanghai. <u>Furthermore</u>, England seems unfamiliar to me and I suppose it will take me a long time to adapt to the life there.
8	In fact	He had not been famous at all in his entire life; <u>in fact</u> he had considered himself as a failure.

The Academic Writing Section

9	Moreover	Students should exercise to make sure they stay physically fit. <u>Moreover,</u> students must maintain healthy sleeping habits to make sure they have enough energy for the next day.
10	Alternatively	To help develop a child's creative skills, parents may enroll their children in painting classes. <u>Alternatively,</u> music lessons are also a good choice.
11	As well	Older people are well informed due to their vast experience. Younger members of the public may lack experience but they are still increasingly well informed <u>as well</u> because of the resources available on the Internet.
12	In addition	Doing unpaid community service will not take up too much of a student's time. <u>In addition,</u> it can help students release stress and contribute to society as well.
13	Additionally	Children can learn a foreign language more quickly than adults. <u>Additionally,</u> children can also pick up musical instruments relatively easily.
14	On the other hand	On one hand, some people believe that exercise alone can help one to reduce weight. <u>On the other hand,</u> there are others who believe that a combination of exercise and a healthier diet is needed to lose weight effectively.
15	Either	Some have said that China's real estate industry is going to crash, which is yet to happen. Many have also said that China's economic growth would slow down, but that has not been proven to be true <u>either.</u>
16	Neither	Apple is not going to pre-announce their products, and <u>neither</u> will any of its suppliers.
17	As a matter of fact	While it may seem as though children do not care about their parents' feelings, <u>as a matter of fact,</u> they do think highly of it.
18	Besides (this)	Although the taxes levied on foreign companies in China has been rising, the prices of raw materials have fallen. <u>Besides,</u> companies will not find it easy to move their business out of China.
19	Not only ... but also	Learning a foreign language will <u>not only</u> make you feel more confident when communicating with foreigners, <u>but also</u> allow you to know understand another country's culture more deeply.
20	Not to mention	Students may find it interesting to take part in community service, <u>not to mention</u> they can also use it as a platform to meet more friends.

21	Coupled with	Over-grazing, <u>coupled with</u> deforestation, has led to serious land degradation for the country.
22	To add (onto the previous point)	<u>To add,</u> it is important for judges to set standards for specific situations that have not been detailed in the law.
23	To expand (this thought further)	Universities are responsible for teaching students about knowledge. <u>To expand</u> on this point, it is more essential for students to know how to gain new knowledge by themselves.
24	Apart from	<u>Apart from</u> the motivation and circumstance, the method in which the suspect carried out the crime should also be taken into account when deciding on the punishment.

Writing Move 1.3: Making References

There are times when, if you want to connect the dots for example, you will have to remind the reader of a point you have made before or a point that can be found in the visual stimulus provided. This is what we mean by making references — you need to orient the reader and let them know what you are referring to, so that they don't get lost.

No.	Writing Move 1.3: Making References	Application in Essays
1	With regards to	<u>With regards to</u> learning a foreign language, I would suggest children begin learning at primary school rather than secondary school.
2	With reference to	<u>With reference to</u> the average house price in Shanghai, we can see that it will be difficult for the next generation to own property in the future.
3	According to	<u>According to</u> some psychological experts' suggestions, schools could hold some community service activities to help students reduce study stress.
4	Based on	<u>Based on</u> the length of the project, I think regular communication should be done at least once every few days.
5	Speaking about	<u>Speaking about</u> crimes, I believe many criminals committed crimes because they did not have any other alternative.

The Academic Writing Section

6	Considering	<u>Considering</u> the excellent quality of the product, the price is quite reasonable.
7	Concerning	<u>Concerning</u> the essay topic at hand, my suggestion is that school can encourage its students to take part in unpaid community service instead of constraining them.
8	As for	<u>As for</u> farming, it is quite clear that it is one of the most important industries today.
9	Regarding	<u>Regarding</u> the time that spent on community service, I think students can carve out enough time while also maintaining balancing their academic commitments.
10	With attention to	We can interview some head hunters about what they look for in each candidate, <u>with attention to</u> the knowledge, experience and skills.
11	Noting	<u>Noting</u> historical precedents, it is clear that judges often do consider the circumstances of the suspect before meting out punishments.
12	Former	Both academics and sports are important for students. The <u>former</u> helps the student expand their knowledge, whereas the latter helps them maintain good physical health.
13	Latter	Both academics and sports are important for students. The former helps the student expand their knowledge, whereas the <u>latter</u> helps them maintain good physical health.
14	Respectively	The consumption of apples and oranges is going up and stagnating, <u>respectively.</u>

Writing Move 1.4: Drawing Similar Ideas

As part of your analysis, you may want to show that there are similar ideas or supporting points to bolster your argument. To do this, you must make it clear to the reader that what you are going to highlight next is something *similar* to a point you have just made. These words help you let the reader immediately know that this is the case.

No.	Writing Move 1.4: Drawing Similar Ideas	Application in Essays
1	Similarly	<u>Similarly,</u> the cost of insurance saw a rising trend, growing from only 2% to 8% by 2001.
2	In the same way	Employers will consider whether those employees can contribute to the companies. <u>In the same way,</u> employees are concerned about what opportunities their superiors may offer to them.
3	By the same token	<u>By the same token,</u> the fall in oil prices has now helped the world economy get back onto its feet.
4	In a like manner	<u>In a like manner,</u> children can also be taught to have a good sleeping habits.
5	Likewise	Children can be forgiven because they do not know any better. <u>Likewise,</u> old people should also be forgiven because they may not be able to keep up with the times.
6	Equally	Learning a foreign language can help improving one's memory. <u>Equally</u> important, it can be regarded as a skill for your future career.
7	Correspondingly	Oil prices increased drastically in 2008. <u>Correspondingly,</u> we saw a similar increase in the share prices of oil and gas companies.
8	In the same manner	Pets are loyal to their masters. <u>In the same manner,</u> people should treat them as their family members.
9	Equally important	It is not enough to merely provide good education for all. <u>Equally important</u> is a good legal environment that is fair and just.

The Academic Writing Section

10	Identically	With enough hard work, we can achieve any goal we set for ourselves. <u>Identically,</u> hard work can cover any weaknesses if the person is not so good at a certain area.
11	In the same fashion	People who have certain talents may gain success more easily than others. But <u>in the same fashion,</u> it may also cause arrogance which can have an adverse impact when they socialize with others.

Writing Move 1.5: Zooming in with Specifications

After making a broad overview of the arguments and viewpoints at hand, you may want to zoom into specific details. For example, if you want to argue that sports is good for health, you may want to zoom in on the effect it has on physical health in particular.

You can also use these transition words to prompt the reader that you are going to dive into closer analysis. For example, instead of highlighting a general trend in the data, let the reader know that you are going to focus on a specific data point that will help you arrive at a more meaningful conclusion.

No.	Writing Move 1.5: Zooming in with Specifications	Application in Essays
1	Specifically	<u>Specifically,</u> people need to join community activities such as teaching children play basketball in order to learn how to adapt to the environment and the people around where you live.
2	By taking (a closer look)	<u>By taking</u> age into consideration, we can see that younger children were able to pick up languages much faster than adults.
3	Close analysis reveals that	<u>Close analysis reveals</u> that doing physical exercise everyday will improve your work efficiency.
4	Close reading tells us that	<u>Close reading tells us that</u> the author was unsure as to why the war occurred.
5	In particular	There seems to be a fundamental belief in China that the best law schools <u>in particular</u> are located in America.

No.		Application in Essays
6	By analyzing (in greater detail)	By analyzing the cost of each service, prices can be set to maximize profits.
7	By paying closer attention to	By paying closer attention to the graph, we can see that the house price in every country was on the upward trend.
8	To explore (this topic further)	To explore why Australia suffered most from the land degradation in this period of time, we can look at the air pollution levels in particular.
9	Deeper analysis shows that	Deeper analysis shows that children can learn a foreign language more quickly in primary schools rather than secondary schools.
10	A more thorough analysis reveals	A more thorough analysis reveals that people will consider brands more than prices of the product.

Writing Move 1.6: Clarifying Points

You may, at times, feel that your earlier sentence is too complex and that you want to break it down once more just to make sure the reader can completely understand your point. To do this, you can use transition words that are specially designed for clarification. Making this move allows you to reword what you just said, hopefully in a manner that is more digestible for the reader.

No.	Writing Move 1.6: Clarifying Points	Application in Essays
1	That is to say	The best way to improve public health is not to increase the number of sports facilities, but rather to improve the public's awareness of the importance of doing physical exercise. That is to say, improving public awareness also has a very significant role to play.
2	To put it another way	To put it another way, unpaid community service will help build up some students' confidence by letting them learn how to communicate with people from different backgrounds.
3	In other words	In other words, with the death of some languages every year, some countries lost irreplaceable cultural heritage.

4	To clarify	<u>To clarify</u> this issue, I still believe fixed punishment is necessary to help the government set a specific standard.
5	To rephrase	<u>To rephrase</u> my earlier point, teaching children their native languages in schools might be a sensible way to protect cultural heritage.
6	To shed more light on the matter	<u>To shed more light on the matter,</u> we can take a closer look at the specific impact that public awareness has on public health.
7	To reframe	<u>To reframe</u> my earlier point, young people should be encouraged to start their own business.
8	As mentioned earlier	<u>As mentioned earlier,</u> doing exercise everyday will help people strengthen their bodies and improve their productivity
9	To repeat	<u>To repeat,</u> it is more essential for students to know how to gain new knowledge by themselves.
10	Once again	<u>Once again,</u> Internet addiction can cause personal, academic and work problems as well as health issues.

Writing Move 2: Introducing Conflict

The IELTS doesn't give you debatable essay topics for no good reason. You are expected to be able to anticipate opposing arguments, and justify why you have chosen the side.

This inevitably leads to the usage of introducing opposing points, or opposing ideas. In your essay, you may want to display your logical prowess by introducing an opposing argument, then explaining why you disagree with it.

But doing so is like changing gears while driving a car. You have to do it smoothly, and that's where the following transition words come in.

Writing Move 2.1: Opposing Points

No.	Writing Move 2.1: Opposing Points	Application in Essays
1	But	Many think that languages are an important part of our heritage. <u>But</u> some people think life will be easier if there are fewer languages in the world.
2	However	Community service is a worthwhile activity. <u>However,</u> not so many students are willing to do unpaid community service because they regard this as a waste of time.
3	In contrast	There are some who believe that education and raising awareness are the two most important steps to improving public health. <u>In contrast,</u> some people say that the best way to improve public health is by increasing the number of sports facilities.
4	By way of contrast	Consuming sugar has, at least, some functional benefits. <u>By way of contrast,</u> consuming recreational drugs has little functional benefit apart from providing the user with temporary pleasure.
5	Yet	When it comes to relationships, there is nothing more important than good listening skills. And <u>yet,</u> developing good listening skills continues to be a challenge for some people.
6	When in fact	People often flock to fast food restaurants just for convenience's sake <u>when in fact,</u> it is not healthy for people to eat too much fast food every week.
7	While	Some people believe that it is better for children to begin learning a foreign language at primary school <u>while</u> others think primary school is still too early to learn complex foreign languages.
8	Whereas	Some people cannot stand the glare of smartphone screens, <u>whereas</u> there are others who are used to staring at smartphones for a long while before they go to sleep.
9	Conversely	Some boarding schools do not impose any restrictions on what students do at night. <u>Conversely,</u> some boarding schools will require their students to sleep before 11 o'clock and turn off the power in all dormitories.

The Academic Writing Section

10	On the other hand	Having a job that pays well is important. <u>On the other hand,</u> you also have to choose the job that makes you happy.
11	Although this may be true	Some believe that you should choose the job that you love. <u>Although this may be true</u> you should also be practical and ensure that the path you choose can at least sustain your daily life.
12	Different from	<u>Different from</u> the normal view, there are some who think that smartphone can cause communication problems.
13	On the contrary	Having fixed legislation will not make trials more complicated. <u>On the contrary,</u> it will help simplify the process of making a judgment.
14	Even so	It is a well-publicized fact that one should both exercise and eat healthily to lose weight. <u>Even so,</u> there are still many people believe that starvation is the best method to lose weight effectively.
15	Though this may be the case	Online shopping is very popular these days. <u>Though this may be the case,</u> online shops can never replace traditional shops because some types of shopping must be done in person.
16	Then again	Various economists have said that the Chinese economy will collapse. <u>Then again,</u> economists have said this for years but the Chinese economy just keeps growing.
17	In spite of	<u>In spite of</u> the global economic slowdown, the Chinese economy has continued to expand at a steady pace.
18	Despite	<u>Despite</u> what is implied by the high unemployment rate, many manufacturers have an urgent need for assembly line workers.
19	In reality	<u>In reality,</u> we have to admit that the quality of life is as important as the length of our lifespan.
20	In actual fact	<u>In actual fact,</u> the most difficult challenge that China will face in 10 years will be environmental pollution.
21	Unlike	<u>Unlike</u> the Western countries, China's economy seems to be steaming ahead.

No.		Application in Essays
22	As much as	As much as some parties may argue that the Chinese economy is on the brink of collapse, there are no signs to show that this is true and the economy is still doing very well.
23	Be that as it may	Online shops often stock many things that people do not really need. Be that as it may, people cannot help paying attention to online shops especially because they offer good discounts.
24	Regardless	Regardless of how you view the issue, good advertising can improve the drawing power of new products.
25	Nonetheless	Steve Jobs, the founder of Apple, passed away last year. Nonetheless, the company is still doing very well under the helm of Tim Cook.
26	Nevertheless	Companies often stipulate that a university degree is a pre-requisite for employment. Nevertheless, companies also appreciate experience especially in relevant fields.

Writing Move 2.2: Making Concessions

Making concessions involves acknowledging that the opposing viewpoint has some truth in it. It doesn't mean that you must completely agree with the opposing viewpoint. Rather, you merely agree that they have some reasonable points as well. This kind of move helps build the perception that you are a mature and reasonable person who is willing to consider both sides of the coin, and willing to pick out the best parts of both viewpoints. It also helps prevent others from thinking that you are overly extreme in making your arguments.

Therefore, don't see making concessions as a sign of weakness. Instead, transform it into a tool to show the reader that you are a reasonable and sensible writer who has considered various possibilities before arriving at a conclusion.

No.	Writing Move 2.2: Making Concessions	Application in Essays
1	Of course	Of course, students will need to set aside a certain amount of time to participate in unpaid community service.

The Academic Writing Section

2	Granted	<u>Granted,</u> some people eat fast food not because they like it, but because they do not have much time during working hours.
3	To be sure	<u>To be sure,</u> smartphone industry has made communication easier and faster.
4	Admittedly	<u>Admittedly,</u> a college education can be very costly and impose a burden on parents.
5	It is undeniable that … however	<u>It is undeniable that</u> having a fixed set of punishments has its merits. <u>However,</u> fixed punishments will not be effective if citizens will regard this as merciless and unfair.
6	Undoubtedly	<u>Undoubtedly,</u> team spirit is a vital element that contributes towards the success of an organization.
7	No doubt	There is <u>no doubt</u> that the celebrities can help boost the sale of a product.
8	Without a doubt	<u>Without a doubt,</u> modern people have become so reliant on computers that they cannot live without them.
9	Naturally	<u>Naturally,</u> women are paid much less than men who have the same positions.
10	While I understand that …	<u>While I understand that</u> a large number of students would not like to take part in social activities because their want to focus more on their study, this is not a wise move to make, as social skills also play an important part in their future careers.
11	I acknowledge that … however	<u>I acknowledge that</u> democracy has its merits. <u>However,</u> it is hard to comprehensively implement this system in China due to the special circumstances.
12	It could be argued that	There are parents who think that sending babies to group lessons is useful for their development. But, <u>it could be argued</u> that babies are much too young to understand anything in these classes.
13	One explanation might be that	There are some who disagree that students should be made to do unpaid community work. <u>One explanation might be that</u> this would be a waste of the students' time.

Writing Move 2.3: Debunking Arguments

If you don't debunk any arguments, it means you haven't written a complete argumentative essay. You may make some concessions along the way, but ultimately you have to prove why you have chosen one viewpoint over another, and that inevitably means that you have to debunk other perspectives as well.

However, you have to do it elegantly. You can't just come out and say "I totally disagree with this statement." It's too rough and uncouth, and you don't want to risk having the reader think that you're not a reasonable person. This is where the transition words come in handy. They send the clear message that you want to debunk other agreements, while avoiding alienating the reader.

No.	Writing Move 2.3: Debunking Arguments	Application in Essays
1	Either way	It is true that students will have to carve time out for community work. But, either way, students will still waste their time regardless by playing games or watching videos in their free time.
2	In either case	In either case, judges who determine punishments should be in a position to do so impartially and objectively.
3	Whichever happens	Whichever happens, fast food will still be an important food industry and will maintain plenty of loyal customers.
4	Whatever happens	Whatever happens, it is definitely beneficial for students to learn a second language.
5	In either event	In either event, employers would consider numerous factors such as working experience, communication skills and learning ability when hiring new staff.
6	All the same	It can be argued that there are some who commit crimes only when they feel that they truly have no other choice. All the same, there are still some people who commit crimes without fearing the law.

7	In any case	There are some who think that college students have a lot of free time to spend. But, <u>in any case,</u> the talents of top college graduates should not be wasted by asking them to spend their time on menial tasks.
8	In any event	<u>In any event,</u> government faces the risk of large protests due to economic instability.
9	At any rate	Economists are divided on the issue of China's economy and whether or not it will slow down in the future. <u>At any rate,</u> China will transform its economy into one that is led by services not manufacturing.
10	Regardless	<u>Regardless</u> of one's position in the company, it is important for everyone to develop their social skills.
11	No matter	<u>No matter</u> how much the cost is, the government should curb pollution and protect the environment for future generations.

Writing Move 2.4: Replacing Ideas

Apart from debunking arguments outright, you may want to go a step further and that is to suggest an alternative solution or idea that is better than the argument you have just debunked. You do this in everyday life — for example, suppose you have just told your friend *not* to buy an iPhone. The next thing you'd probably do is to recommend another smartphone and you would do this by using key transition words like the ones below.

Being able to offer replacement ideas can win you bonus points because it makes your argument all the more convincing, as you prove that there are plausible and realistic alternatives at hand.

No.	Writing Move 2.4 Replacing Ideas	Application in Essays
1	Rather	I prefer to go traveling during holidays <u>rather</u> than to stay at home surrounded by high-tech products.
2	Instead	Universities should not focus on pure academics alone. <u>Instead,</u> universities should add more practical courses in junior and senior year to help improve students' professional skills.

3	By taking another viewpoint	<u>By taking another viewpoint,</u> criminal law should take into account individual circumstances during each trial.
4	In place of	<u>In place of</u> those two views, I would like to propose a third view: a proper diet and exercise are both important for health.
5	An alternative would be	<u>An alternative would be</u> to let the students make their own decisions as to whether or not to join community service once a week.
6	In lieu of	<u>In lieu of</u> the circumstances, my suggestion is that you start with the job you love, then work very hard to make your passion practical enough to support your daily life.

Writing Move 3: Analytics

In both Task 1 and Task 2, you will need to perform a certain degree of analytics. For Task 1, the analytics involve more of data and numbers whereas for Task 2, you will have to do more logical analysis.

Regardless of whether you are dealing with numbers or logic, you will still need to apply appropriate transition words. Imagine, for example, if you merely list out numbers and facts non-stop like this:

> The production of apples has been growing steadily. The production of pears has been in decline. The number of farmers has grown. The amount of rainfall per year has remained stagnant. The average income of each farmer is dropping.

As you can see, it is not only terribly dry, but it's also hard to see how these ideas link together. Sure, if you think hard about it and link the increase in the number of farmers with the stagnant rainfall, you may understand why the average income of each farmer has dropped. But if you don't use analytical words, you won't be able to *show* the reader that you, the writer, have conducted this analysis yourself. And if you don't show that or if the IELTS grader cannot see that, then they won't be able to give you credit.

The Academic Writing Section

Writing Move 3.1: Defining Causes and Reasons

You will almost definitely have to explain causes and reasons in whatever essay you write. You can do this in a very basic way, using a word that you use very often — because — but that won't be enough. If you repeat a word too frequently, it tells the examiner that your command of vocabulary simply isn't solid enough such that you have to keep falling back on old crutches.

While some of the words below may be fairly new to you, try to get used to them and begin employing them in your essays. It makes for a more varied and therefore more elegant piece of writing.

No.	Writing Move 3.1: Defining Causes and Reasons	Application in Essays
1	Because	Advertising on mobile applications is a good way to promote the sale of new products <u>because</u> people will be deeply impressed by the novel introduction on social media platforms such as Weibo and Wechat.
2	Due to	Some smartphone companies had no choice but to close down <u>due to</u> mismanagement.
3	Owing to	<u>Owing to</u> the rapidly changing nature of the smartphone industry, companies have no choice but to innovate or to face bankruptcy.
4	For the reason that	The government decided to allocate more funding to building sports facilities <u>for the reason that</u> it believes this move will help improve public health.
5	Seeing that	<u>Seeing that</u> students can make new friends while doing unpaid community service, schools should encourage them to take part in this kind of meaningful activity.
6	In view of	Many potential buyers have withdrawn from the market <u>in view of</u> the downward trend of house prices.
7	In light of	<u>In light of</u> the company's poor performance, the CEO has been dismissed by the board of directors.
8	Driven by	Ultimately, graduate employment growth is going to be <u>driven by</u> the private sector.

No.		Application in Essays
9	Caused by	Many existing misunderstandings between parents and their children are <u>caused by</u> a lack of interaction and poor communication.
10	Fueled by	The rise in Chinese exports was <u>fueled by</u> increase in sale of electronic products and parts.
11	One of the factors	The quality of materials is <u>one of the important factors</u> that will affect the total performance of this product.
12	One of the reasons	A disproportionate emphasis on academics is <u>one of the reasons</u> that has caused a decline in students' physical fitness levels.
13	One of the causes	Heart attack is <u>one of the most serious causes</u> of death among older people.
14	One of the key drivers	Maintaining honesty and integrity within the company is <u>one of the key drivers</u> to stay ahead in the market.
15	Influenced	The price of oil has always been <u>influenced</u> by politics in addition to supply and demand.
16	Determinant	Technical improvement and innovation is a <u>determinant</u> of economic and social development.

Writing Move 3.2: Consequences and Results

This is another move that you almost certainly have to make. In Task 1, as part of your analysis, you must show the effect of whatever data you are looking at. In Task 2 as well, you will have to show the consequences of the logical argument you are expanding upon. Failure to do so would render your essays incomplete, and there lose marks in terms of structure and logic.

These transition words are here to tell the reader that you are explaining the consequences of a certain action or event. Use them to show the reader how you are linking up ideas in your head, and that you are a clear thinker who can, more importantly, also write in a very lucid manner.

No.	Writing Move 3.2: Consequences and Results	Application in Essays
1	As a result of	<u>As result of</u> increased interest in Chinese law, there have been an increased number of Chinese legal works and legal scholars in recent years.

The Academic Writing Section

2	Because of	<u>Because of</u> over-grazing and deforestation, land degradation has become one of the most serious problems in the world.
3	As a consequence	When doing community service, students will have to learn how to organize activities as well as to work in a team. <u>As a consequence,</u> students can gain more new skills through unpaid community service.
4	Consequently	<u>Consequently,</u> the better way to lose weight often boils down to maintaining a healthy diet and regular exercise.
5	So much so that	Children absorb so much more when they are young, <u>so much so that</u> it would be better for children began learning their second language in primary school.
6	Hence	<u>Hence,</u> vegetarianism is a good idea from an environmental point of view.
7	For this reason	Language is an important part of everyone's identity. <u>For this reason,</u> students should be encouraged to learn their own language in school in order to preserve their own cultural heritage.
8	Accordingly	The graduate unemployment rate has been relatively high in recent years. <u>Accordingly,</u> the government has introduced several measures to make graduates more attractive to employers.
9	In this manner/fashion/way	Some believe that examinations should be abolished. <u>In this manner,</u> students can focus more on class and acquire more knowledge.
10	In effect	Employers tend to value practical and professional skills these days. <u>In effect,</u> students who are able to demonstrate that they possess these skills stand a higher chance of getting their dream job.

Connecting Paragraphs

11	Thus	Gender is not a determinant of one's leadership abilities. <u>Thus,</u> even working women should be encouraged to have strong ambitions and become leaders within their companies or organizations.
12	Therefore	Comparatively, the university graduates lack work experience; <u>therefore,</u> they often find it hard to adapt to working life.
13	Effectively	The number of smartphones sold each years has been increasing at a more rapid pace than the number of laptops. <u>Effectively,</u> this suggests that smartphones may replace laptops one day.

Writing Move 3.3: Defining Purpose

Sometimes, you will have to define the purpose of making a certain point in the essay, so that the reader can understand your logical thought more clearly.

For example, if you want to emphasize why considering the weight of children's backpacks is so important, you must define your purpose in doing so. You can do this by saying something such as, "For the sake of the children's physical health, there should be restrictions placed on how heavy their backpacks can be."

By making this move, you are no longer just stating a point. You are giving a reason why your point is important and valid. Importance and validity are two separate things altogether, and are not to be conflated. This is because a valid point may not be important, such as the statement, "There is dust on the road." That is valid, but why should the reader think it is important? If you alter it slightly by saying, "The local government should perform a clean-up because there is a lot of dust on the road," then it bears more importance because you are giving a solution to a problem.

No.	Writing Move 3.3: Defining Purpose	Application in Essays
1	With this in mind	The technology industry is constantly changing and new products are being launched all the time. <u>With this in mind,</u> it is very important for you to closely research any high-tech products that you are considering purchasing.

The Academic Writing Section

2	For the purpose of	<u>For the purpose</u> of a better future, we have to educate children not only about morality but also about how to live life independently.
3	In the hope that	<u>In the hope</u> that universities could help students find their ideal job, the dean decided to launch a Career Skills Center.
4	To the end that	<u>To the end that</u> a more close-knit community can be built, the government can build more indoor venues for people to spend their free time on group activities such as dancing.
5	In order to	<u>In order to</u> communicate with colleagues better, people should improve their way of socializing and spend more time understanding what their colleagues like and dislike.
6	With this intention	The technology industry focuses on selling products to the everyday consumer. <u>With this intention,</u> electronic gadgets are designed to make the everyday person's life more convenient and must be user-friendly.
7	So that	People should do some simple indoor exercise before going to work <u>so that</u> they can feel more refreshed and concentrate better on work.
8	So as to	Planning ahead is necessary <u>so as to</u> get your dream job.
9	Lest	It is not advisable to publicly criticize the child, <u>lest</u> the child loses confidence or develops insecurities.
10	With the aim to	<u>With the aim of</u> helping law enforcement become more effective, people must make crime reports to the police in a timely manner.
11	With a view to	<u>With a view to</u> improve efficiency, our government should allocate more funds into public transportation especially since so many people rely on it to get from point to point.
12	With the objective of	<u>With the objective of</u> protecting endangered languages, governments should require schools to teach students those languages and organize more activities to raise awareness.
13	In pursuance of	<u>In pursuance of</u> environmental commitments, the Chinese government will reduce carbon emissions.

14	For the sake of	For the sake of social justice, judges should find a balance between dealing out punishments strictly according to the law and according to individual circumstances.
15	In contemplation of	In contemplation of the importance of keeping fit, the government should encourage and promote citizens to do more physical exercise.
16	In consideration of	In consideration of growing environmental pollution, government could encourage companies to develop electric vehicles.
17	In the interest of	In the interest of protecting nature, many governments should cooperate to collectively reduce pollution levels.
18	To the extent of	To the extent of promoting gender equality, women should be given more chances to be promoted into senior management.

Writing Move 3.4: Making Conditions

Making conditions clear can have several purposes. The first purpose is to show what would happen if your recommendation is not accepted. For example, you may say, "If pollution is not reduced immediately, asthma cases are going to keep rising."

The second purpose is to caveat your argument and to show that your argument can only work if certain conditions are fulfilled. This may help you respond to counter-arguments. To illustrate:

> I agree with the statement that a student's learning is highly contingent upon the teacher's abilities and therefore more funds should be directed to the training of better teachers. This is because students often start out without knowing anything. For example, in pre-school or primary school, the student is almost completely dependent on the teacher. However, I also concede that after reaching a certain stage such as high school, students become more independent and less reliant on teachers. Therefore, I still believe that more funds should be spent on teacher training, providing that more emphasis is placed on pre-school and primary school level instructors.

The Academic Writing Section

The above is just an example, but as you can see, you can make certain concessions and still not change your original argument by *placing conditions on the points you make*. Think of it like a father promising to buy his son a PlayStation for Christmas — "I'll buy you that PlayStation, but only if you do well in your examinations." It's not a blanket argument, and that's why it's easier to fend off counter-arguments.

No.	Writing Move 3.4: Making Conditions	Application in Essays
1	On the condition that	Children should only own smartphones <u>on the condition that</u> they use these devices for communication and educational purposes only.
2	In the event that	The death penalty can only be doled out <u>in the event that</u> the convict has committed the most serious crime of all — murder.
3	Granting that	Students should be encouraged to do unpaid community work, <u>granting that</u> they have performed well in their academic studies.
4	Granted that	Tourism should be encouraged since it contributes significantly to the economy, <u>granted that</u> the tourism-related activities do not cause significant harm to the environment.
5	As long as	<u>As long as</u> children do not misuse the smartphone, there seems no good reason to ban them from owning one.
6	So long as	Good employees should be rewarded <u>so long as</u> they have fulfilled the targets that have been set out for them.
7	Providing that	Universities should offer more internship opportunities to students, <u>providing that</u> these opportunities are awarded based on merit.
8	If	<u>If</u> you combine a healthy diet with physical exercise, you will be able to lose weight very easily.
9	Unless	The country cannot progress <u>unless</u> its graduates are better prepared for the workforce.
10	Else	Students must seek out internship or similar opportunities, <u>else</u> they would not be able to adapt to working life since their knowledge is confined only to what can be found in textbooks.

11	Even if	Even if the government abolishes tax on hybrid vehicles, not everyone will buy one as the technology is still new and there are drawbacks to using one.
12	Provided that	Consumers will have confidence in a product provided that the user reviews are consistently good.
13	Given that	Given that there students generally have a significant amount of spare time, it is a good idea to encourage them to do more unpaid community work so as to make better use of their time.
14	Only if	Patients should seek alternative medical treatment only if they have already consulted their medical doctor.
15	In the case of	In the case of countries whereby education funding is limited, we should first allocate funds to core subjects before considering non-critical languages even if these languages are dying out.
16	Until	Until the court can determine beyond reasonable doubt that the suspect has committed the crime, no punishment can be decided upon.
17	Without	Without proper debate and research, we cannot arrive at the best path of action to take.

Writing Move 3.5: Hypothetical Circumstances

Sometimes, you will have to describe and invite the reader to consider a hypothetical situation. Anecdotes and personal examples are not enough, because there is no way that everyone has experienced every single thing in this world.

Inviting the reader to consider a hypothetical situation also indirectly encourages them to see things from your point of view. For the time being, they have to see things from your viewpoint and if the hypothetical situation you have presented is convincing enough, they will slowly begin to support the points you have raised.

Here's an example. Suppose the essay topic is about whether or not the law should consider the individual circumstances of each person and not just the law itself before passing judgment. In your view, the law *should* consider the individual circumstances. To help the reader sympathize with your viewpoint, you may make the following move:

> It is true that following a clear set of rules and laws can help judges work more efficiently. It also allows everyone to be clear about what to expect should they commit certain offences or crimes. However, we should also consider the individual circumstances of each person before passing judgment. Consider a situation whereby a poor man stole some bread to feed his starving family, and did not cause any harm to anyone. If that is the case, can we really give him the same punishment as we would to a robber who stole money from a bank simply because he craved wealth?

The move that you have made is to draw a hypothetical situation. You force the reader into seeing the effect that the opposing viewpoint would have — that is, to give the poor starving man the same punishment as the greedy robber. Is that fair? By doing this, you will convince the reader that it is *not* fair, thereby bolstering your case.

No.	Writing Move 3.5: Hypothetical Circumstances	Application in Essays
1	Under those circumstances	There are cases whereby children have become addicted to smartphone games and videos. <u>Under those circumstances,</u> it is not advisable for parents to allow the children to own a smartphone, as this may worsen the addiction.
2	That being the case	At times, judges may find that the evidence is inconclusive. <u>That being the case,</u> more research must be done before a decision is made.
3	If that is the case	There are some members of the general public who want to exercise, but do not have access to adequate facilities. <u>If that is the case,</u> an initiative to increase the number of sports facilities could improve public health in such areas.
4	If so	High consumption of sugar is said to be one of the key factors driving obesity rates. <u>If so,</u> the government should take action to control the level of sugar especially in soft drinks.

Connecting Paragraphs

5	In that case	Some parents feel that children would be safer if they had a smartphone, which they can use to call for help at any time. <u>In that case,</u> it makes sense to allow even primary school children to own smartphones.
6	Otherwise	Judges should take extra care when dealing with highly complex cases. <u>Otherwise,</u> it could lead to the wrong decision and could ruin innocent lives.
7	If not	The Internet should be regulated to a certain extent. <u>If not,</u> we will witness the proliferation of various illegal activities online.
8	Else	Ex-offenders should be given a chance to reintegrate into society. <u>Else,</u> it would not be fair to them and crime levels could continue to rise.

Writing Move 3.6: Placing Emphasis

In every essay, there will be points that are more important, and points that are less important. As a writer, you want your reader to *especially* notice your important points. It's like doing a project at college. You want your professor to notice the particularly interesting and well-done parts, more so than the less significant ones.

To be able to highlight important points in your essay, you must know how to *place emphasis*. This involves drawing the reader's attention and letting them know that this is where they must pay extra attention.

No.	Writing Move 3.6: Placing Emphasis	Application in Essays
1	Important/crucial/ imperative to realize	<u>It is important to realize</u> that having capital punishment in place not only affects the convict, but also the nation at large.
2	Special attention should be paid to	<u>Special attention should be paid to</u> the way policies are executed, instead of the actual policy itself.
3	Most compelling evidence/point	The <u>most compelling evidence</u> supporting the need for stricter Internet regulation is the rising number of hacking cases that have emerged in recent years.

The Academic Writing Section

4	Must be remembered	It <u>must be remembered</u> that although everyone is entitled to a certain level of freedom, this freedom comes with some responsibilities.
5	Should be noted	It <u>should be noted</u> that competition for admission into the world's top universities is becoming increasingly stiff.
6	A point often overlooked	<u>A point often overlooked</u> is the fact that many students may not even know basic workplace etiquette, such as how to dress and how to interact with professional colleagues.
7	It is crucial to note that	<u>It is crucial to note that</u> if no measures are taken, obesity rates may continue to rise through the roof.
8	To emphasize	<u>To emphasize</u> why this issue is so important, we need to examine sugar consumption figures for the past three years and the correlating rise in the obesity rate.
9	Significant	A <u>significant</u> point to note is how the number of tablet users are beginning to catch up with laptop users, especially in the past two years.
10	Even more (striking/ compelling/ important)	What is <u>even more compelling</u> is how conventional mobile phones have virtually become obsolete since companies started producing affordable and functional smartphones.
11	Above all	<u>Above all,</u> what is most important is that the public is aware of the negative impact that obesity can have on their lives.
12	Indeed	<u>Indeed,</u> university is a defining point in any student's life, and the government should attempt to make the experience as enriching and as educational as possible.
13	More importantly	Academic studies are important. But, <u>more importantly,</u> students should also ensure they are physically and mentally healthy as well.
14	Many do not realize that	<u>Many do not realize that</u> although falling oil prices may seem welcome as petrol is now cheaper as a result, it has an adverse impact on the overall economy especially in oil-exporting nations.
15	What is important to highlight	<u>What is important to highlight</u> is that what employers want in college graduates today is much different from what they wanted a decade ago.

Writing Move 4: Sequencing

This entire section is about learning the key transition words and phrases you can use to sequence from one paragraph to another. Some students stick to stiff and dry techniques, such as "Firstly, Secondly, Thirdly" throughout the entire essay. That's grammatically correct and understandable, but it doesn't display a masterful command of the English language.

Instead of relying on elementary techniques to sequence your essay, try picking up and sharpening the moves below. They will go a long way in helping you transition from one thought to another.

Writing Move 4.1: Numbering

This is the most basic of sequencing moves — numbering. You can use some of these to sequence your points, but it is best to combine it with other writing moves as well. Otherwise, you run the risk of sounding like a robot.

Let's look at an example of a student who relied strictly on the numbering method:

> Essay topic: Some people believe that only those who are born with talent can become accomplished athletes or musicians. Others, however, think that hard work plays a very important role.
>
> Discuss both these views and give your own opinion.

For the first view, talents would be an important key to become successful in a specific area. For example, it is obvious that Michael Jordan has powerful jumping ability and Michael Jackson has unique voice.

For the second view, children should be encouraged to work hard to acquire their own achievements. None of the famous sports persons or musicians succeeded without any efforts. Most of them spent dozens of hours a day to practice and practice again.

In my opinion, I think God helps those who help themselves. If you were born with certain talents, you could gain skills quicker than others. But the more essential thing is to believe after hard work of learning, everyone can be taught to become an expert in different occupations. A person who can play basketball well can also become a famous painter if he endeavors to practice it.

The Academic Writing Section

In the example above, the student adhered to a strict structure of:

1) Here's View 1
2) Here's View 2
3) Here's my view

Notice that the first two paragraphs are very separate. There is no interaction between the two, and no linkage. Transitioning is choppy and if you were to take out any one of those paragraphs and read them on its own, you wouldn't feel like you have missed out on anything.

In addition, when the student describes her opinion, there is absolutely no reference to the points she has made before. How is she going to debunk the counter-arguments that she raised against herself in paragraph 1? And that's precisely the danger of going solely with the numbering method. If you adhere to this strict format, you're less likely to train your brain to become analytical and to keep looking for linkages between ideas.

No.	Writing Move 4.1 Numbering	Application in Essays
1	To start with	To start with, China needs to strengthen scientific and technological cooperation with other countries.
2	First of all	First of all, you should realize that it is unhealthy to lose weight by going on a diet.
3	To begin with	To begin with, most people are not quite familiar with the procedure of a criminal case trial.
4	For a start	For a start, over-exploitation consumes resources, which are likely to be finite.
5	In the (first/second/etc.) place	In the first place, universities should provide far more services to help freshmen to get used to the new environment as soon as possible.
6	Firstly/Secondly/Thirdly etc.	Firstly, public awareness of the importance of environmental protection should be improved.
7	Initially/Initial point	Initially, the number of employees who go to work by car surged while bus riders fluctuated. Bicyclists and those who go by foot were both in low numbers.

Writing Move 4.2: Continuation

After presenting your main point, you may wonder how you are going to introduce your supporting points. Supporting points are often continuations that build upon the main point, hence what you can do is to add some continuation transition words and phrases. These help tell the reader that what you are going to say is connected to the previous point, and that they should bear the prior information in mind while reading the subsequent sentences.

No.	Writing Move 4.2: Continuation	Application in Essays
1	Subsequently	Public awareness about the importance of the environment should be raised. <u>Subsequently</u>, technology to help reduce pollution should be developed and advocated.
2	Following on from the previous point	<u>Following on from the previous point</u>, one needs to exercise in addition to changing one's diet in order to lose weight in a healthy way.
3	Next	<u>Next</u>, it would be better for students to take part in more unpaid community service in order to gain more experience and exposure in society.
4	To elaborate further	<u>To elaborate further</u>, there are several measures that can be taken to prevent children from falling into a life of crime in the future.
5	Following/maintaining/holding this train of thought	<u>Following this train of thought</u>, we can find that children who are isolated from others in contemporary society are also often absorbed in computer games. It may therefore be a good idea to attempt to recapture their attention by using such games as a platform.
6	Moving forward	<u>Moving forward</u>, more public money should be spent on promoting healthy lifestyles rather than treating illnesses.
7	Extending this point/thought	<u>Extending this point</u>, it is much more beneficial to take part in sports instead of just following sports events on television.
8	To develop this idea/thought further	<u>To develop this idea further</u>, part of a growing trend involves more and more people moving to big cities looking for a better life.

The Academic Writing Section

9	As can be seen from the previous example/point	As can be seen from the previous example, criminal law in China has improved with the times.
10	At any rate	At any rate, a number of senior citizens have to work even above the age of 65 to support their families.
11	To return to the point at hand	To return to the point at hand, companies and private tour operators should pay the bill for cleaning up damage caused by pollution.

Writing Move 4.3: Summarizing

After making a few complicated moves or elaborating on a more complex point, you may want to include a brief summary just to ensure the reader understands what your key point really is. It's like a signpost that helps the reader navigate your essay more easily. You can also use summarizing words to help tie your essay together in the conclusive paragraph.

No.	Writing Move 4.3: Summarizing	Application in Essays
1	Essentially	Essentially, in order to improve safety on our roads, more severe punishment should be established for driving offenses.
2	In essence	In essence, art classes are as useful to the development of a child as the other subjects.
3	To summarize	To summarize, university education should not just be about academic subjects alone but also about practical skills.
4	To sum up	To sum up, it will not only boost the profit of a shopping mall by including non-profitable sections, but also improve the shopping environment for consumers.
5	On the whole	On the whole, everyone should be encouraged to spend more time with parents.
6	For the most part	For the most part, the primary successes of global cooperation have been on the business level rather than the environment level.

Connecting Paragraphs

7	In short	<u>In short,</u> the action of national governments is indispensable in tackling environmental problems.
8	To put it briefly	<u>To put it briefly,</u> for a child's development, team activities are more significant and beneficial than individual activities.
9	In a nutshell	<u>In a nutshell,</u> increasing food prices is not a sensible way to tackle the problem of obesity.
10	To put it simply	<u>To put it simply,</u> I believe sports can contribute towards world peace.
11	Simply put	<u>Simply put,</u> death penalty cannot be easily abolished in China due to the culture and historical circumstances.
12	Briefly put	<u>Briefly put,</u> scientists have contributed a great deal to the advancement of the human race.

Writing Move 4.4: Making Conclusions

No.	Writing Move 4.4: Making Conclusions	Application in Essays
1	Ultimately	<u>Ultimately,</u> I believe general education plays a vital role in the future development of a country.
2	In conclusion	<u>In conclusion,</u> I believe rich teaching experience, which corresponds with the competency of an educator, cannot be substituted by mere training alone.
3	To conclude	<u>To conclude,</u> I think despite some negative impacts like air pollution, low-cost airlines are beneficial in allowing more people from various financial backgrounds to travel and in promoting world tourism.
4	As a final point	<u>As a final point,</u> I am surely convinced that working after retirement has negative consequences for both society and the retiree.
5	Lastly	<u>Lastly,</u> I believe the statement that children have too much freedom is flawed.

The Academic Writing Section

6	All things considered	All things considered, I am sure that older people would do a better job in holding important governmental positions.
7	On the whole	On the whole, I am convinced that the benefits brought about by physical museums and galleries cannot be substituted by computers at all.
8	Given these points	Given these points, we can see that a certain gender is more favorable for specific jobs.
9	Overall	Overall, choosing careers carefully is an important decision, as it plays a key role in achieving economic independence.
10	As shown above	As shown above, I would not suggest introducing unpaid community service as a part of compulsory programs in high schools.

IELTS Trainer

Connect each group of sentences by using the "Writing Moves" that are provided in brackets below each question.

1. Would you prefer to wake up early and beat rush hour traffic, or wake up later and spend more time in traffic?
   a. I would prefer to wake up early in order to beat rush hour traffic.
   b. If I get stuck in rush hour traffic, I may end up wasting an hour or two simply sitting in traffic.
   c. If I wake up early, I can make better use of my time.
   d. It is not difficult to go to bed earlier in order to save an hour or two in the morning.
   e. Waking up earlier is the best choice.

   Writing Moves: [To begin with; Conversely; In any case; Therefore]

2. Do you think that top movie stars deserve the exceptionally high income that they earn?
   a. I believe that top movie stars do deserve high income.
   b. It is not easy to become an actor, because the competition is so tough.

Connecting Paragraphs

    c. Those who decide to pursue acting are making a huge sacrifice and taking on a significant amount of risk.
    d. If they succeed, there is no reason why they should not be well compensated for their efforts.
    e. They provide good entertainment and inspiration for many people worldwide.

Writing Moves: [First of all; Effectively; In light of this; Additionally]

3. Should fast food restaurants be allowed to give free toys to children along with their meals?
    a. Fast food restaurants should not be allowed to give free toys to children along with their meals.
    b. Giving free toys to children is similar to "bribing" them to eat unhealthy food.
    c. In the long run, children may prefer unhealthy food just because they receive a free toy along with it.
    d. This will prevent children from adopting healthy eating habits.
    e. Fast food restaurants should focus on improving the quality of their food, rather than giving out merchandise.

Writing Moves: [For a start; In other words; To elaborate further; Ultimately]

4. Should high school students take up part-time jobs?
    a. High school students should take up part-time jobs.
    b. If they have free time (Note: you will need to link this sentence with the preceding sentence)
    c. Part-time jobs can teach students important skills such as teamwork and financial independence.
    d. Students should not take up part-time jobs if they are struggling in their studies.
    e. A part-time job is good to have, but not entirely necessary.

Writing Moves: [On the condition that; Admittedly; However; To sum up]

5. Should the legal drinking age in the United Kingdom be increased from 18 to 21 years of age, in line with the United States?
    a. The legal drinking age in the United Kingdom should not be increased from 18 to 21 years of age.
    b. Each country has their own way of governance.

The Academic Writing Section

    c. Change should not be made on whim.
    d. Increasing the legal drinking age will not necessarily help.
    e. Teenagers will still find ways to gain access to alcohol.

Writing Moves: [It is important to note; Unless; Furthermore; Regardless]

Answers:

1. I would prefer to wake up early in order to beat rush hour traffic. To begin with, if I get stuck in rush hour traffic, I may end up wasting an hour or two simply sitting in traffic. Conversely, if I wake up early, I can make better use of my time. In any case, it is not difficult to go to bed earlier in order to save an hour or two in the morning. Therefore, waking up earlier is the best choice.

2. I believe that top movie stars do deserve high income. First of all, it is not easy to become an actor because the competition is so tough. Effectively, those who decide to pursue acting are making a huge sacrifice and taking on a significant amount of risk. In light of this, if they succeed, there is no reason why they should not be well compensated for their efforts. Additionally, they provide good entertainment and inspiration for many people worldwide.

3. Fast food restaurants should not be allowed to give free toys to children along with their meals. For a start, giving free toys to children is similar to "bribing" them to eat unhealthy food. In other words, in the long run, children may prefer unhealthy food just because they receive a free toy along with it. To elaborate further, this will prevent children from adopting healthy eating habits. Ultimately, fast food restaurants should focus on improving the quality of their food, rather than giving out merchandise.

4. High school students should take up part-time jobs, on the condition that they have free time. Admittedly, part-time jobs can teach students important skills such as teamwork and financial independence. However, students should not take up part-time jobs if they are struggling in their studies. To sum up, a part-time job is good to have, but not entirely necessary.

5. The legal drinking age in the United Kingdom should not be increased from 18 to 21 years of age. It is important to note that each country has their own way of governance. Unless absolutely necessary, change should not be made on whim. Furthermore, increasing the legal drinking age will not necessarily help. Regardless, teenagers will still find ways to gain access to alcohol.

1d Concise Conclusions

As we enter the final unit on structure, let's explore how you can write better and more concise conclusions. You've learnt the transition words for conclusions in the previous chapter, so your job will be made a lot easier in this chapter.

Generally, you should not spend too many sentences on conclusions because the bulk of your essay should be spent on the main body. Write two to three sentences at most, and some people even stick to just one sole sentence.

There's a magic formula that you can use to write concise conclusions, and this is something that you can apply using the three simple steps.

Simple Steps

1. Reiterate your stance in relation to the essay question
2. Generalize a few of your most important points under one umbrella
3. Apply an appropriate transition word, then stitch Steps 1 and 2 together to form a concise and solid conclusion

Elaboration with Examples

Step 1: Reiterate your stance in relation to the essay question

This part is easy. Simply refer to the introduction that you wrote and do a quick sanity check to make sure all your points support the stance that you laid out in the beginning. Then, reiterate your stance. This means that if you said you agreed with the essay question before, repeat that. If you disagreed, just reiterate that you disagree.

Step 2: Generalize a few of your most important points under one umbrella

Next, skim through the main body of your essay and see how you can generalize them under one umbrella. Why? This is because the conclusion is meant to be concise and that means as short as possible without losing the main essence.

Here's an example of how you can generalize your key points under one umbrella. Assuming your key points are as follows:

a) Introduction: It should be mandatory for children to participate in some form of unpaid volunteer work

b) Key point 1: This will help children understand how fortunate they are, and to gain a deeper appreciation of what they have
c) Key point 2: They will learn skills that they cannot learn within the classroom
d) Key point 3: This will also help the society by raising awareness about the need to help the underprivileged

In order to generalize, you must figure out the *common thread* amongst the three points you have mentioned. It can be as general as saying that all these points relate to the benefits that the children and society can gain by making unpaid volunteer work mandatory.

Thus, if you wanted to generalize, you can say something along the lines of:

I agree that students should do compulsory unpaid voluntary work due to the benefits that both the students and society stand to gain.

Step 3: Apply an appropriate transition word, then stitch Steps 1 and 2 together to form a concise and solid conclusion

The last step is simple. Add a transition word to make sure you don't jolt your reader into the conclusive paragraph too suddenly.

To recap, here is the list of transition words that you can apply in your conclusion paragraphs:

Writing Move 4.4: Making Conclusions

No.	Writing Move: 4.4 Making Conclusions
1	Ultimately
2	In conclusion
3	To conclude
4	As a final point
5	Lastly
6	All things considered
7	On the whole
8	Given these points
9	Overall
10	As shown above

Concise Conclusions

In terms of applying it in your essay, an example would be as follows:

All things considered, I agree that students should do compulsory unpaid voluntary work due to the benefits that both the students and society stand to gain.

And there you have a concise yet effective conclusion that can be written within mere minutes if you follow the three simple steps.

IELTS Trainer

Rewrite the following conclusions by using the "Writing Move" that has been included in brackets.
1. It is important for working adults to maintain work–life balance in order to avoid negatively impacting their health. [To conclude]
2. Young children should not be allowed to drink coffee or tea. [All things considered]
3. It should be made illegal to cut down trees that are more than 30 years old. [Ultimately]
4. Social media can be a very powerful tool if it is used wisely. [As shown above]
5. The spread of avian flu can be curbed if everyone takes precautionary measures seriously. [In conclusion]
6. Office workers can and should be encouraged to use public transport. [Overall]
7. Even if the more charitable grants are made available, charity must still come from the heart and people must be willing to do good for others. [As a final point]
8. We should not underestimate the power of students, as they can be a force to drive change. [Lastly]
9. Physical education should not be abolished in favor of "more academic" subjects. [Given these points]
10. Snacking can be healthy if it is done in the right way. [On the whole]

Answers:
1. To conclude, it is important for working adults to maintain work–life balance in order to avoid negatively impacting their health.
2. All things considered, young children should not be allowed to drink coffee or tea.

The Academic Writing Section

3. Ultimately, it should be made illegal to cut down trees that are more than 30 years old.
4. As shown above, social media can be a very powerful tool if it is used wisely.
5. In conclusion, the spread of avian flu can be curbed if everyone takes precautionary measures seriously.
6. Overall, office workers can and should be encouraged to use public transport.
7. As a final point, even if the more charitable grants are made available, charity must still come from the heart and people must be willing to do good for others.
8. Lastly, we should not underestimate the power of students, as they can be a force to drive change.
9. Given these points, physical education should not be abolished in favor of "more academic" subjects.
10. On the whole, snacking can be healthy if it is done in the right way.

2 Tone: Formal Writing

Tone is a bit different. It's not like structure and you can't build it up gradually. Rather, you have to apply it evenly and consistently throughout your entire essay.

The tone that you should use for IELTS work is the formal tone. But what does this mean? For many students, informal and formal may seem the same, since the dictionary won't tell you which is which. What makes things more complicated is the fact that there's no set of hard and fast rules about what constitutes "formal."

For this reason, we've simplified formal writing into three simple steps. We start with examining a common mistake that most students make, and that is to use contractions. Next, we explore how you can use punctuation to make your essay more formal. And lastly, we take a look at some informal words that have commonly been used by students in formal writing.

Simple Steps

1. Avoid using contractions
2. Check your punctuation
3. Make sure that you have not used the common informal words that students often accidentally use in formal writing

Elaboration with Examples

Step 1: Avoid using contractions

Contractions are common. You will see them nearly everywhere and especially in novels or short stories. The word "contract" means to squeeze something together, and in the English language this means making words shorter by combining them together or by placing an apostrophe where certain letters have been omitted. The following are some examples of contractions:

Cannot → can't
I am → I'm
You will → You'll
They are → They're
Is not → Isn't

There is nothing grammatically incorrect about contractions, nor is there anything wrong with them *per se*. The main problem, in the context of the IELTS, is that contractions are informal. Contractions are normally used in the following situations:

a) To establish a more accessible and friendly tone — The use of contractions gives the impression that you are chatting to your reader, as you would to a friend. This creates a warmer and friendlier impression.
b) Reflect how a character speaks — The reason why you will almost definitely see a lot of contractions in novels or short stories is because these types of works almost inevitably involve dialogue. Authors regularly use dialogue as a way to give the character more color. For example, authors can use contractions to give a character a unique way of speaking, or to reflect the character's accent.
c) Save space — In advertisements, contractions are often used not only to give a warm and friendly impression but also to save space. Sometimes, there is limited space on the flyer or billboard and contractions help preserve the message while also allowing it to fit within the limited space.

The IELTS, remember, is a test of how well-prepared you are to face academic life in an English-speaking country. Because academic work is written in the formal tone, it is best to avoid contractions. This will give your reader a much better impression and it is also a tip that you can apply in your future career, whether it be in academia or the corporate world. Just take a look at some top colleges' websites, such as Georgetown Law School — it's explicitly mentioned that students should avoid the use of informal contractions in formal legal writing. The same goes for the IELTS.

Step 2: Check your punctuation

The next element you must check is your punctuation. Let's go through several key do's and don'ts for the IELTS:

a) Do not use exclamation marks (!) — To be on the safe side, don't use exclamation marks at all within your essay. An exclamation mark gives the impression that you are shouting, or that you are over-excited, both of which are not good impressions to give to the reader. It is unusual to find exclamation marks within academic writing simply because it is challenging to pull it off without the risk of sounding too informal.

b) You can use a long dash, or em dash (—), to emphasize important points — Apart from using transition words to place emphasis, you can also use punctuation to highlight certain points. Long dashes are a mark of separation or interruption, and can be used to immediately draw the reader's attention to what you are going to say next. Only use this if you want to introduce a compelling point. For example: Movies often overlook and gloss over one of the most devastating aspects of war — the post-traumatic stress syndromes that it causes in war veterans, and how this can sometimes destroy not just their lives, but their families' lives as well.

c) Connect two independent clauses that are somewhat related (;) — In argumentative writing, this is something that you can use to link two ideas that are related somehow. Using the semicolon helps maintain the flow of the sentence while also building off the first idea. An example would be: There was a sharp increase in the number of household break-ins over Christmas; possibly, this is because many families were away for holidays during this time.

Step 3: Make sure that you have not used the common informal words that students often accidentally use in formal writing

There are many informal words that students accidentally use in formal writing, and this is because rules for formal writing — although strict — are often unwritten.

No.	Informal	Formal	Sample Sentence
1	A lot of Loads of Plenty of	A significant amount of Numerous Several A large amount of	Cancer patients have to take <u>a significant amount of</u> medication
2	A bit	Slight Minimal	It is worthwhile to chase your ideal job even though there is only a <u>slight</u> possibility of success.

The Academic Writing Section

3	Tiny	Minor Less significant Negligible (nearly zero) Inconsequential Paltry (amount)	People who are convicted of minor crimes such as traffic offences and illegal gambling will have to face penalties nonetheless.
4	To start To kick things off	To commence To initiate	It is very costly to initiate a legal proceeding.
5	Big	Major Considerable Large	Economic development is a considerable issue in the new strategy.
6	Thing Stuff	Item Object Device	You must consider several items before making decisions regarding your career.
7	To find out	To ascertain To discover To determine	Sometimes it is difficult to ascertain trends though statistics alone.
8	To do well	To succeed To excel	Young people desire to succeed in the careers that they love.
9	To get rid of	To eliminate	You need to eliminate some bad habits such as staying up late and smoking to maintain a healthy body.
10	To go up and down	To fluctuate Volatile	This chart illustrates figures that were volatile during the period of time.
11	To cut down on	To reduce To minimize	Gambling business can provide jobs and reduce unemployment.
12	To say no to	To refuse To reject To resist	People must maintain calmness to refuse temptations.
13	To take (a statement) back	To retract	Public prosecutors can retract an accusation when the criminal agrees to make a confession.
14	To put up with	To tolerate	These kinds of verbal abuse and cyber crimes should not be tolerated.
15	To come about	To occur To happen To ensue	Some have said that China's real estate industry is going to crash, which is yet to happen.

Tone: Formal Writing

16	To carry out	To conduct To execute To perform To undertake	Each party to the contract party should perform their contractual obligations.
17	To look like	To seem To appear	The death penalty seems to be maintained in China even after a long period of dispute.
18	To stop	To cease	Never cease chasing your ideal job, because it will be worthwhile.
19	To set up	To establish	Establishing more fee-paying schools is the latest trend in the national education system.
20	To go up	To increase	The best way to improve public health is not to increase the number of sports facilities, but rather to improve the public's awareness of the importance of doing physical exercise.
21	To look into	To investigate To explore To analyze To examine To review To scrutinize To delve into	To examine why Australia suffered most from the land degradation in this period of time, we can consider two main factors.
22	To give up (something)	To relinquish	Some mothers will relinquish their careers to care for their children.
23	To make	To produce To manufacture (for products)	Many news organizations now produce news on various media platforms.
24	To eat	To consume	People who want to lose weight must carefully calculate how many calories they consume every day.
25	To shorten (words)	To abbreviate To summarize	Do not abbreviate your words when you are writing a formal essay.
26	To shorten (points or ideas)	To distil To condense To summarize	To summarize, it is better to encourage children to choose their own hobbies.

The Academic Writing Section

27	To want	To wish To desire	The workers <u>desire</u> a better working environment in order to improve their productivity.
28	To show	To demonstrate To display To illustrate	The aim of this speech is to <u>demonstrate</u> that gender inequality still exists.
29	To tell	To inform To let (someone) be aware	It is important to <u>let Internet users be aware</u> of the importance of personal information protection.
30	To keep	To preserve To retain To maintain	It is the duty of the judge to <u>preserve</u> fairness and justice.
31	To free	To release To liberate	Prisoners can be <u>released</u> earlier if they perform well in prison.
32	At once	Immediately Without hesitation	Please call 110 or 120 <u>immediately</u> if you meet an emergency or accident.
33	At the same time	Simultaneously Concurrently	If a food processing company operates illegally, the administrative department in charge will demand a resolution and impose a fine <u>concurrently.</u>
34	On and off	Intermittently	I have worked on this project <u>intermittently.</u>
35	So	Therefore Hence Thus Consequently As a result	The electronic books industry is growing. <u>Therefore,</u> the publishers of physical books regard this as a significant challenge.
36	Understand	Comprehend	Despite the detailed illustration of this point, many students failed to <u>comprehend</u> it.
37	Not enough of	Lack Deficient	In fact, the main reason why the university graduates fine it difficult to find an ideal job is because most of them <u>lack</u> work experience and social skills.
38	Chance	Opportunity	<u>Opportunity</u> is given to the people who are prepared.

39	Wrong	Incorrect Questionable Debatable Can be argued Flawed Incomplete	Please revise the <u>incorrect</u> grammar in your essay.
40	Correct	Plausible Possible Acceptable True	Watching a movie, going shopping and exercising are all <u>acceptable</u> methods to reduce stress.
41	Worse	Inferior to Relatively (+ adjective) Comparatively (+ adjective)	This hotel may be new, but it is still <u>inferior to</u> the older hotel over there.
42	Better	Superior to Relatively (+ adjective) Comparatively (+ adjective)	I am <u>relatively optimistic</u> about my next IELTS score.
43	Enough	Sufficient	The judge has <u>sufficient</u> evidence to convict the guilty man.
44	To ask for	To require To necessitate	Children are <u>required</u> to learn a foreign language in primary schools.
45	More and more	Increasingly Unceasingly	Real estate prices are <u>increasingly</u> high in major cities of China.
46	To get	To obtain To receive To acquire	Students can <u>acquire</u> various social skills such as communication skills in school.
47	Bad Terrible Horrible	Disappointing Did not meet expectations Poor Dismal (extreme) Unacceptable Unsatisfactory	The court case is an <u>unsatisfactory</u> method of deciding an important issue.

The Academic Writing Section

48	Good	Satisfactory Strong (results) Solid performance Robust (for data) Exceeded/met expectations Excellent (for very good results only)	This company displayed <u>solid performance</u> during the financial crisis in 2008.
49	To become worse	To deteriorate To spiral downwards To decline To diminish To weaken To worsen	The environment continues to <u>deteriorate</u> in developing countries.
50	To make/become better	To improve To enhance To advance To boost To elevate	<u>Improving</u> the working environment will definitely <u>enhance</u> employees' job satisfaction.
51	To go down	To decline To dwindle To ebb To wane	The traditional newspaper industry seems to be on a <u>wane</u> due to challenges from online media.
52	To pin down	To identify To determine To establish To distinguish	It takes time for women to <u>determine</u> whether to relinquish their careers in order to raise children or to continue chasing a successful career.
53	To talk about	To discuss To deliberate over (a topic) To dispute (to argue against) To review To contend (To argue against) To exchange views on	The judge <u>deliberated over</u> this case for a relatively long time.

54	There are two sides to a coin	There are advantages and disadvantages to … There are pros and cons to …	There are pros and cons to both electronic books and physical books.
55	By chance	Incidentally	Incidentally, I met professor Wang at the opening ceremony of a basketball game.
56	To try	To endeavor To attempt To strive (for something)	The government promulgated a law and attempted to crack down on illegal gambling.
57	To think of	To conceive of To imagine	As you can imagine, the final exam is very difficult.
58	To skip	To omit To leave out To set aside	Do not omit any steps when you practice your writing skills.
59	To sort out	To resolve To find a solution to To clarify To disentangle (a problem) To reason out	The two countries are endeavoring to resolve the conflicts between them though negotiations.
60	Hard	Challenging Difficult Problematic Complicated Complex	It is challenging for children to have a good command of two languages.
61	The same as	Equivalent to	The consumption of fish in 2008 was equivalent to the consumption of beef.
62	Drink	Beverage	Soda is one of the unhealthiest beverages that children love.
63	Old people	Senior citizens Retirees Elders	The children in our family are always respectful to their elders.

64	Kids	Children	To help develop a child's creative skills, parents may enroll their <u>children</u> in painting classes.
65	To think (that)	To assume (that)	I <u>assume</u> that passion for the job is much more important because you can realize your dream more whole-heartedly.
66	I think that	It could be argued that It is possible that	<u>It could be argued that</u> it is fine for primary school children to own smartphones, as long as they use it for communicating with their parents and for educational purposes, as opposed to playing games.
67	About	Regarding With regard to As to With reference to Concerning In relation to With respect to	<u>With regards to</u> learning a foreign language, I would suggest children begin learning at primary school rather than secondary school.
68	To make sure	To ensure To confirm	Though some websites <u>ensure</u> they will protect your personal details, hackers can find other ways to steal all the information and sell it to others, or even use it for their personal gain.
69	To check	To verify To validate	Before we let children have smartphones, we need to <u>verify</u> that they will not misuse them.
70	Careful	Prudent	You must make a <u>prudent</u> decision about what occupation you would like to take up in the future.
71	To take away	To withdraw To revoke To rescind	Many potential buyers have <u>withdrawn</u> from the market in view of the downward trend of house prices.

Tone: Formal Writing

72	One after the other	At regular intervals	Children who exercise <u>at regular intervals</u> can grow up into positive and healthy adults.
73	vs	As opposed to Versus	Go for a salad or lighter meal <u>as opposed to</u> a burger and fries if you want to control your weight.
74	e.g. i.e.	For example For instance Namely	<u>For example,</u> most people would not hurt or kill someone just for fun because they know that will also risk their own life.
75	Nice Cute	Attractive	Some people who are keen on physical exercise believe it would make them more <u>attractive.</u>
76	Smart Clever	Intelligent Sharp	It is hard to decide whether a candidate is <u>intelligent</u> or not simply based on the application.
77	Really Super	Extremely (for more extreme cases) Very Significantly	Growth in the country's GDP decelerated <u>significantly,</u> from 10.5 percent in real terms in 2000 to a mere 0.1 percent in 2005.
78	To do away with	To abolish To eradicate To suppress To negate To obliterate To cancel To ban	If a state decides to <u>abolish</u> the death penalty, that means it needs to build more prisons to hold prisoners.
79	Quarrel	Debate Dispute Contend	The Chinese government is going to levy an inheritance tax. If that is the case, I suppose it can decrease family <u>disputes</u> about inheritance.
80	New	Novel	Advertising on mobile applications is a good solution to promote the sale of new products because people will be deep impressed by this <u>novel</u> method.

267

The Academic Writing Section

81	Way	Manner Solution Course of action Approach Means Measure Mode Process Procedure Style	To elaborate further, there are several <u>measures</u> that can be taken to prevent children from falling into a life of crime in the future.
82	To imagine	To conceive of To envision To conceptualize To picture To visualize	I cannot even <u>conceive of</u> what life would be like without the smartphone.
83	Money	Funds Monies Capital	To young people, <u>capital</u> is probably the item they need most if they want to establish their own business.
84	Place	Location Venue	The original game of basketball had no strict requirement on the number of players, size of <u>venue</u> and game time.
85	Fast Quickly	Rapidly Promptly To expedite (to make something go faster)	Real estate prices have been increasing very <u>rapidly</u>; soon, many will not even be able to buy a decent home.
86	To follow (rules)	To adhere to To abide by To comply with To observe (the rules)	<u>Complying with</u> the traffic rules can avoid many road accidents.
87	Boss	Superior Head	Employees are concerned about what opportunities their <u>superior</u> may offer to them.
88	Shop	Retail outlet	One advantage of Xiaomi is that it does not need to build many <u>retail outlets,</u> which saves a significant amount of cost.

Tone: Formal Writing

89	To not do something	To refrain from To avoid To resist To curb (someone or something)	Many of these disasters could have been <u>avoided</u> if we humans hadn't abused natural resources.
90	To tell you about something in detail	To describe To depict To elaborate To detail To outline To illustrate To present	Please <u>describe</u> this chart based on the three different categories presented.
91	Maybe	Perhaps Possibly Probable Likely Perchance	It is <u>probable</u> that these disasters tell us exactly why we need to protect the environment.
92	10 years	Decade	Though the price of rubber decreased generally for several <u>decades,</u> it rebounded in 2000 and reached the peak in just 5 years.
93	Every year	Annually	Employees and general managers will take part in an <u>annual</u> development program.
94	Every month	Monthly	The company produces some assessments such as the <u>monthly</u> Star Manager project.
95	Every two months	Bi-monthly	The website visitors who register will have the chance to receive the <u>bi-monthly</u> magazine for free.
96	Every three months	Quarterly	Companies should publish regular reports that include annual reports, half-yearly reports and <u>quarterly</u> reports.
97	Job	Occupation	Everyone can be taught to become an expert in different <u>occupations.</u>

The Academic Writing Section

98	To give (in order to help)	To contribute To reinforce To support To strengthen To supplement	China is ready to become a leader in <u>contributing</u> to international development cooperation.
99	To help	To assist To support To facilitate	It is better for parents to <u>support</u> their children's decisions on their careers.
100	Cool Hot Hip	Advanced Latest Modern Popular Fashionable Trendy	Nowadays, it has become <u>fashionable</u> for children to learn hip-hop dancing.

IELTS Trainer

Use the *Simple Steps* to apply a more formal tone to the following paragraphs:

1. Kids these days are really spoilt! Even those who are still in primary school get to have cool smartphones from their parents. It really doesn't make sense because they cannot stop themselves from playing all sorts of games. Before we let kids have these gadgets, we need to check that they will not misuse them.

2. Recently, there have been a lot of disasters. First, there was a hot dry spell, and we had to ration water for days! Second, there were loads of floods which caused a great deal of pain to many families. I think that these disasters tell us exactly why we need to protect the environment. Many of these disasters could have been avoided if we humans hadn't abused natural resources.

3. Music lessons are really important and all kids should take at least one music class at school. This can help develop their creative abilities. Maybe, it could even help them discover a new hobby that can be a form of stress release.

4. Real estate prices have been increasing very quickly. Soon, many will not even be able to afford a decent home. The government must help the lower-income groups own their own properties.

Tone: Formal Writing

5. The government must do away with allowing drivers to speak on phones while driving. It is really very dangerous, as it can lead to more and more accidents on the road.
6. Old people need enough support from the government and society to live through their golden years happily. We need to stop viewing old people as members of society who do not contribute much. Instead, we should show and remind everyone of how grateful we are to the previous generation for helping to give us all that we have today.
7. To kick things off, I think that we must first think of why the examination results this year were very bad. About the science results in particular, there was a huge plunge in performance from an average of 78 percent down to a mere 60 percent.
8. Various types of electronic gadgets have been arriving in local market one after another. However, the same can't be said for traditional toys such as toy trains and toy cars!
9. It is hard to tell whether a candidate is smart or not simply based on the application. To sort out this problem, we should redesign the application and make it more holistic.
10. The suggested approach is wrong. In the process of finding a solution, we cannot skip the most basic step of first doing a survey to see what people really think.

Answers:

1. Children these days are very spoilt, even those who are still in primary school receive the latest smartphones from their parents. It truly does not make sense because they cannot prevent themselves from playing all sorts of games. Before we let children have these gadgets, we need to verify that they will not misuse them.
2. Recently, there have been a significant amount of disasters. First, there was a hot dry spell, and we had to ration water for days. Second, there were numerous floods which caused a great deal of pain to many families. It is possible that these disasters tell us exactly why we need to protect the environment. Many of these disasters could have been avoided if we humans had not abused natural resources.
3. Music lessons are very important and all children should take at least one music class at school. This can help develop their creative abilities. Perhaps,

it could even help them discover a new hobby that can be a form of stress release.
4. Real estate prices have been increasing very rapidly; soon, many will not even be able to afford a decent home. The government must assist the lower-income groups to own their own properties.
5. The government must abolish the policy of allowing drivers to speak on phones while driving. It is extremely dangerous, as it can lead to an increasing number of accidents on the road.
6. Elders need sufficient support from the government and society to live through their golden years happily. We need to cease viewing elders as members of society who do not contribute much. Instead, we should display and remind everyone of how grateful we are to the previous generation for helping to give us all that we have today.
7. To commence with, it is possible that we must first conceive of why the examination results this year were very poor. Regarding the science results in particular, there was a considerable plunge in performance from an average of 78 percent down to a mere 60 percent.
8. Various types of electronic gadgets have been arriving in local market at regular intervals. However, the same cannot be said for traditional toys such as toy trains and toy cars.
9. It is challenging to decide whether a candidate is intelligent or not simply based on the application. To solve this problem, we should redesign the application and improve it more holistically.
10. The suggested approach is incorrect. In the process of finding a solution, we cannot leave out the most basic step of first doing a survey to see what people truly assume.

Data Analysis Skills: Analytic Vocabulary

In this section, let's delve deeper into the specific skills that you need to hone in order to excel at Task 1. The best part about Task 1 is that you have plenty of support that you can draw upon from the prompts and data given. Even if it is just a pie chart or graph, there is a lot for you to work on. For example, the y-axis and x-axis labels and the title of the graph itself can go a long way. In the IELTS, you have a very limited amount of time, so use this time wisely and efficiently by leveraging on the information that is already given to you.

The first thing that you must know is the relevant analytic vocabulary needed to describe the data at hand. If you don't even have the tools to convey the message given in the data, then your essay will remain very weak.

More importantly, on top of teaching you analytical vocabulary, we will also show concrete examples where you can see how these words are used in action. These will help you understand the bigger picture and how to use these words in different contexts, which is as important as knowing the vocabulary itself.

Here's an example of how a student, who had memorized the analytical vocabulary but did not know how to apply it in an essay. As a result, she accidentally wrote a paragraph that conveyed a very different meaning from what she intended:

In short, chicken became the <u>largest consumption</u> of meat and fish was consumed with the <u>meager figure.</u>

In the example above, the student tried hard to apply vocabulary such as "largest consumption" and "meager figure." But, these were applied wrongly, which resulted in the following interpretations:

Chicken became the largest consumption of meat = Chickens were the largest consumers of meat (this means that the student believes chickens go around eating meat)

Fish was consumed with the meagre figure = Fish ate something called the "meagre figure"

The Academic Writing Section

In actual fact, she probably meant to say that:

Consumption of chicken was the highest among the different types of meat, whereas the corresponding figures for fish were very low.

All things considered, yes, the student did know the vocabulary. She managed to pump a few advanced-sounding words out. But did she use it correctly? Not at all. On the contrary, as a result of the wrong application of words, she ended up giving the reader a very bizarre impression of what she was trying to say.

In this chapter, you will learn the basic analytic vocabulary needed to describe charts and graphs. It will prepare you for the next chapter, which focuses on how to generate analytical insights.

Simple Steps

1. Identify the type of chart or table presented within the question
2. Based on Step 1, ask yourself key questions
3. Write a brief description of the data based on these key questions, and also by applying analytical vocabulary

Elaboration with Examples

Step 1: Identify the type of chart or table presented within the question

There are four main ways in which data will be presented in the IELTS:

1) Bar charts
2) Pie charts
3) Line charts
4) Tables

The next step will elaborate on each type in detail.

Step 2: Based on (1), ask yourself key questions

The IELTS uses four main methods to present data in Task 1. In this step, we will guide you through each type of presentation method and the key questions that you can ask about each one to get your thought process going.

1) Bar charts

Data Analysis Skills: Analytic Vocabulary

Bar charts can come in many shapes and sizes, but they are all the same. They can come in vertical or even horizontal bars and yet bear the same meaning. Some, like the example below, may even come in a clustered format — meaning that numbers for different items are grouped together according to year. You should welcome clustered bar charts, in fact, because they make it easier for you to compare and contrast.

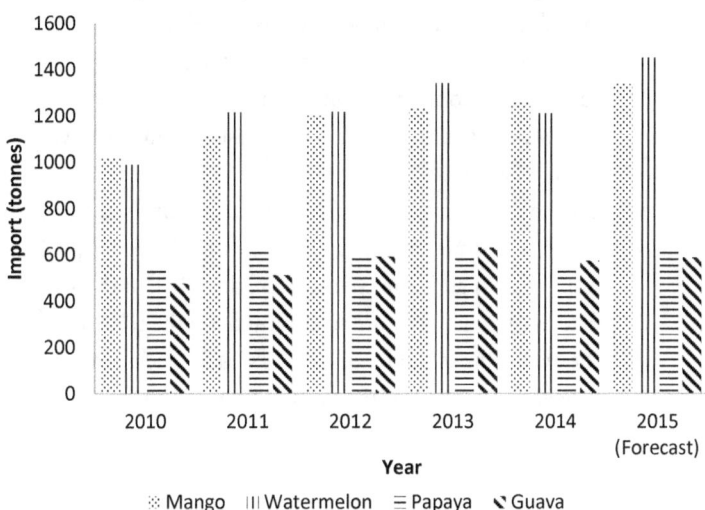

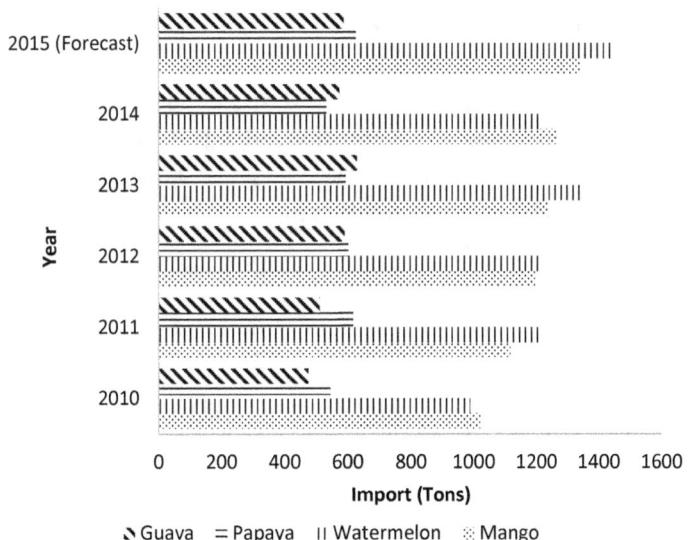

When analyzing bar charts, you can ask yourself the following questions if you find it hard to get your mind moving:

a) Which bar is the tallest/longest?
b) Which bar is the shortest?
c) Have the bars changed over time, and, if so, how?
   - Which bars have had the greatest volatility?
   - Which bars have been stagnant?
   - Which bars have been on a steady increase?
   - Which bars have been on a steady decline?
d) How do the bars compare to one another?
   - It may be useful to compare the most extreme bars with the more stagnant ones.
e) What is the difference between historical and projected trends?
   - There are times when the bar chart will show projections or estimates, in addition to historical data. When these two types of data exist, you may want to comment on the relationship between the two. For example, are oil prices projected to recover? Will property prices come down in five years' time?

2) Pie charts

Pie charts are very straightforward. There is not much variation except in terms of design, and its purpose is to show data in a segmented form. One pie chart represents 100 percent of the data recorded, hence each segment constitutes a percentage of that 100 percent.

Unlike bar charts, which can have two variables (for example the year and tons of fruit imported), pie charts are static and only show you the segmented data at one point in time. At times, the IELTS may show you more than one pie chart but for different time periods to display how segments have changed over time.

Data Analysis Skills: Analytic Vocabulary

A typical pie chart looks like this:

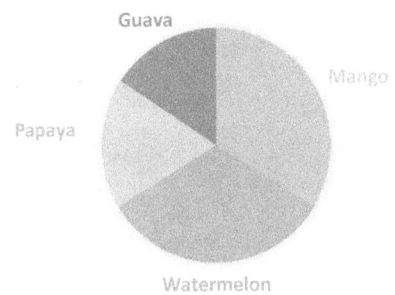

Import of Tropical Fruits into the United Kingdom 2010

You can ask yourself questions similar to the ones that were asked for bar charts, but note that the range of questions is more limited due to the nature of pie charts:

a) Which segment is the biggest?
b) Which segment is the smallest?
c) How do the segments compare against each other?

- For example, is the difference between the largest and smallest segment significant, or not?

3) Line charts

Line charts are similar to bar charts in the sense that there are two variables. A line chart can also display information about several items simultaneously. However, there is an additional feature in line charts — you can comment on a continuous data trend over time. Unlike bar charts, which show data in separate blocks, line graphs are continuous lines that display the overall trend more clearly. Refer to the following example:

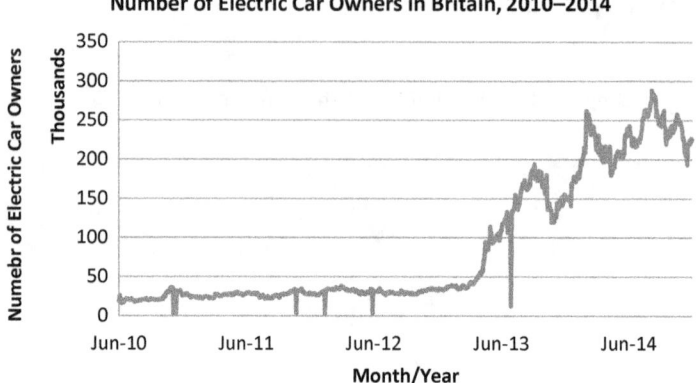

You can start by asking yourself:

a) What is the overall trend that you see based on the line graph itself?

- If there's a clear trend upward or downward, you could state that the trend is steadily increasing or decreasing.
- If the line is flat, you could say that the growth is stagnant.
- If there is a lot of volatility, you could simply state that the numbers are volatile or you could count the number of times the line peaked.

b) At what point in time did the changes in the data trend occur?

- If there was a sharp rise or fall, you can state the point at which this change occurred.
- If there were several spikes, you could state the time period during which those spikes happened. For instance, you could state that there were several spikes between 2010 and 2012, but that the trend eventually flattened out between 2013 and 2014.

c) At what rate did the changes occur?

- If a change did occur, it either happened at a steady rate or at a sudden sharp rate.

4) Tables

Tables are perhaps the most challenging because you do not have a pictorial or graphical help to assist you in spotting the overall trend quickly. It can be even more challenging if the numbers seem very large, but are in fact very close, for example:

Table: Annual Number of Manchester United Football Club Fans

Year	London	Manchester
2009	421,394	422,232
2010	455,938	459,384
2011	521,233	521,457
2012	602,348	602,009
2013	601,920	602,892

You can see the problem that this kind of table poses. It's not easy to immediately see the trend in the data because each cell contains a six-digit figure, and these figures are often very close.

If you are fortunate, you may receive a table that has very clear-cut trends. But if you're not, we would strongly suggest you draw a bar chat as you read the table. This can help you see the overall trend in a shorter amount of time, and also reduce the margin for error.

For example:

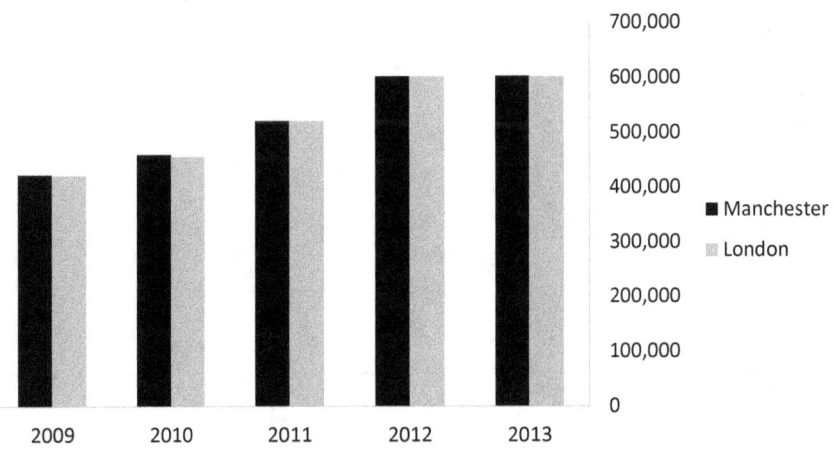

After you have turned it into a bar chart, you can then apply the same types of questions as you did previously in order to interpret the data.

The Academic Writing Section

Step 3: Write a brief description of the data based on these key questions, and also by applying analytical vocabulary

In this section, we will teach you analytical vocabulary by providing a list of words that you can use depending on the data trends.

How to Use the Table Below:

1) First, select the degree at which the trend has occurred. Is it slight, moderate or extreme?
2) Next, depending on whether the trend is showing an increase or decrease, select one of the words from the second or the third column and pair it up with the relevant word from the first column
3) Examples:

There was a slight increase in the number of teachers in Birmingham.
The number of teachers in Birmingham has grown rapidly.
The economy of Birmingham has seen steady growth.
The price of petrol has fallen even though the price of diesel has risen.

Degree	Increase	Decrease
Slight		
Slight	Climb	Decline
Slow	Accelerate	Decrease
Gentle	Increase	Decelerate
Limited	Gain	Diminish
Mild	Expand	Less
Minimal	Rise	Lost
Small	Went up	Reduce
Minor	Grow	Compress
Negligible	Strengthen	Fell
Weak		Shrink
Slim		Slide
		Weaken
Moderate		
Moderate		
Gradual		
Progressive		
Steady		
Continuous		
Even		

Data Analysis Skills: Analytic Vocabulary

Extreme			
Extreme			
Sudden			
Decisive			
Sharp			
Dramatic			
Overwhelming			
Significant			
Steep			
Rapid			
Quick			
Swift			
Swing			

However, there are also words that can describe data quite aptly on their own. Here are other situations that you may face, if the previous table has not answered what you seek. Some of the words are more specialized words, for which we have brief descriptions in brackets.

Increase	Decrease	No Change	Many Changes
Improve	Fade (gradual)	Constant (neutral)	Fluctuate
Augment	Dwindle (gradual)	Even out (neutral)	Volatile
Advance	Wane (gradual)	Hold (neutral)	Oscillate
Appreciate	Peter out (gradual)	Level-off (neutral)	Erratic
Boost	Subside (gradual)	Level-out (neutral)	
Upward trend (general)	Taper off (gradual)	Persist (neutral)	
Exceed (passed a certain mark)	Deteriorate (extreme)	Plateau (neutral)	
Leap (extreme)	Dip (extreme, short-term)	Remain (neutral)	
Skyrocketed (extreme)	Plummet (extreme)	Stay (neutral)	
Surge (extreme)	Sink (extreme)	Stagnate (negative)	
Peak (highest)	Slump (extreme)	Stall (negative)	
All-time high (highest)	All-time low (lowest)	Stable (positive)	
Rebound (increase after poor results)	Trough (lowest)	Maintain (positive)	
Recover (increase after poor results)	Hit the bottom (lowest)	Sustain (positive)	
Pick up (increase after poor results)		Consistent (positive)	

The Academic Writing Section

Next, we show examples of selected graphs that you may encounter in the examination. Key analytical vocabulary will be underlined, and its meaning will be intuitive based on the accompanying graph or chart.

Example 1:

The numbers made a <u>rebound</u> in 2010, and projections show that the company has good <u>growth prospects.</u>

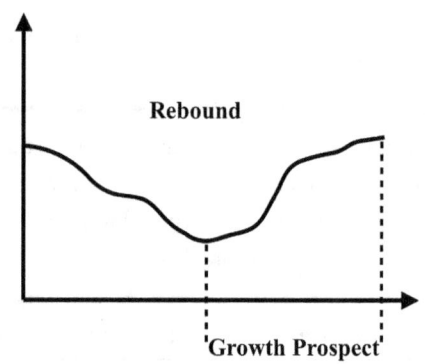

Example 2:

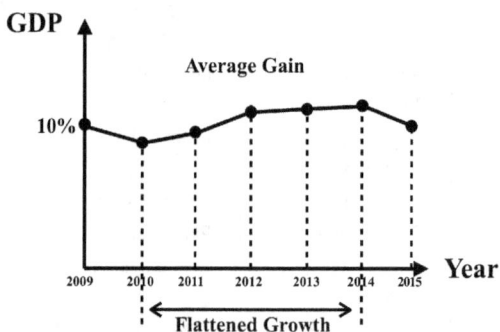

China's economy, in terms of Gross Domestic Product (GDP), had an <u>average gain</u> of about 10 percent.

OR

Between the years 2010 and 2014, China's economy showed <u>flattened growth,</u> albeit at the relatively high <u>average gain</u> of approximately 10 percent.

282

Example 3:

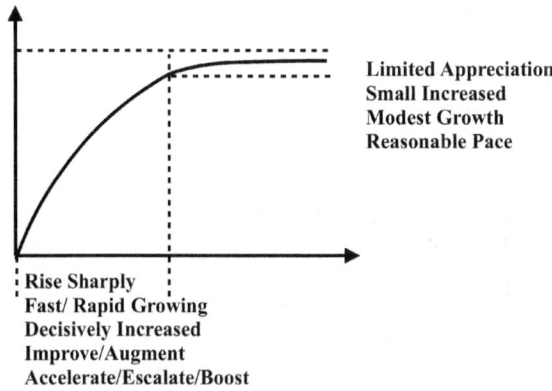

The sale of cosmetics in London <u>rose sharply/ grew rapidly/ was fast-growing/ improved significantly/ decisively increased/ accelerated sharply/ received a significant boost/ escalated rapidly/ augmented significantly</u> between 2009 and 2011. However, after 2011, sales of the same product had <u>limited appreciation/ began to slow down to a more reasonable pace/ only increased in relatively small increments/ only had modest growth.</u>

Example 4:

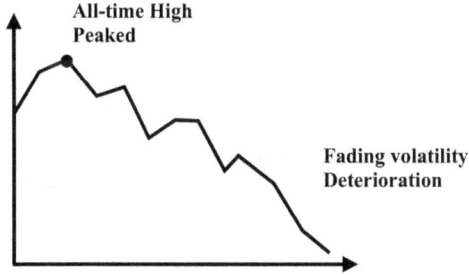

The company's share price reached an <u>all-time high</u> in May 2010.

The company's share price <u>peaked</u> in May 2010.

After hitting an all-time high in May 2010, the company faced fading volatility for a few months. Thereafter, the company's share price began deteriorating and lost more than half of its value.

Example 5:

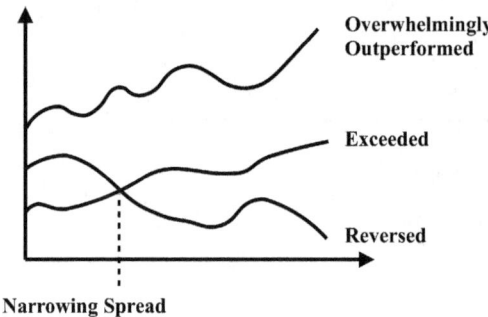

The spread between the Japanese Yen and Chinese Renminbi began to narrow between 2010 and 2012. Subsequently, the value of the Chinese Renminbi exceeded that of the Japanese Yen. In fact, the Japanese Yen's upward trend reversed towards the end of 2013, until it hit a three-year low.

Meanwhile, the American Dollar outperformed the Japanese Yen and Chinese Renminbi, with overwhelmingly strong growth.

Example 6:

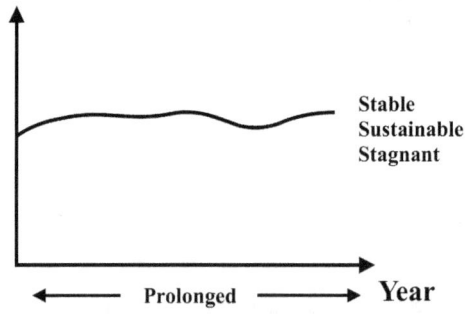

Positive wording:

The country had stable/sustained economic growth over a prolonged period.

The country had prolonged economic growth.

Negative wording:

The country's economic growth stagnated over a prolonged period.

The country's economic growth was stagnant over a prolonged period.

Example 7:

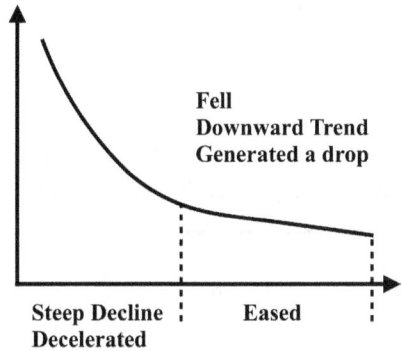

There was a steep decline in handbag sales between 2009 and 2010. However, subsequently, the downward trend began to ease and stabilize.

Handbag sales decelerated/ fell sharply between 2009 and 2010.

IELTS Trainer

Use the new vocabulary from this chapter to describe the data in each chart or table below.

1.

The following chart shows the number of new banking card applications in Scotland, which is divided between debit cards and credit cards.

The Academic Writing Section

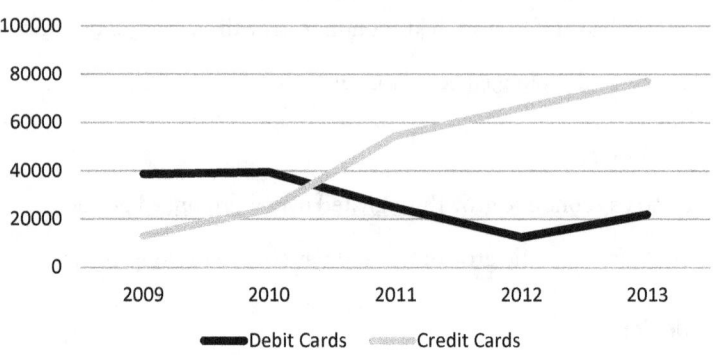

2.

The following table shows the number of employees and their respective lunch choices from Monday to Friday at the Brigadier Health Company Limited.

	Monday	Tuesday	Wednesday	Thursday	Friday
Sandwich	500	650	400	300	150
Salad	200	300	450	200	350
Pie	550	400	500	600	550
Soup	150	300	200	300	250
Hot meal	600	350	350	600	700

3.

The following pie chart shows the number of patients based on the ailments they reported while visiting a doctor's office in Oxford.

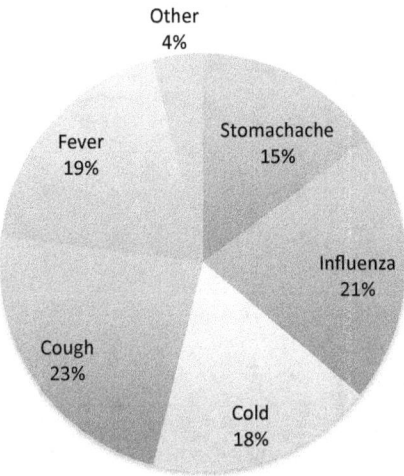

4.

The following chart shows the major causes of road accidents in the United Kingdom in 2014.

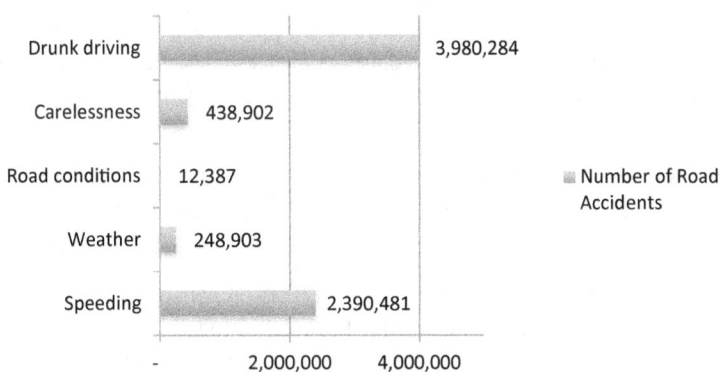

5.

The following chart shows a comparison of coffee prices across three main stores.

The Academic Writing Section

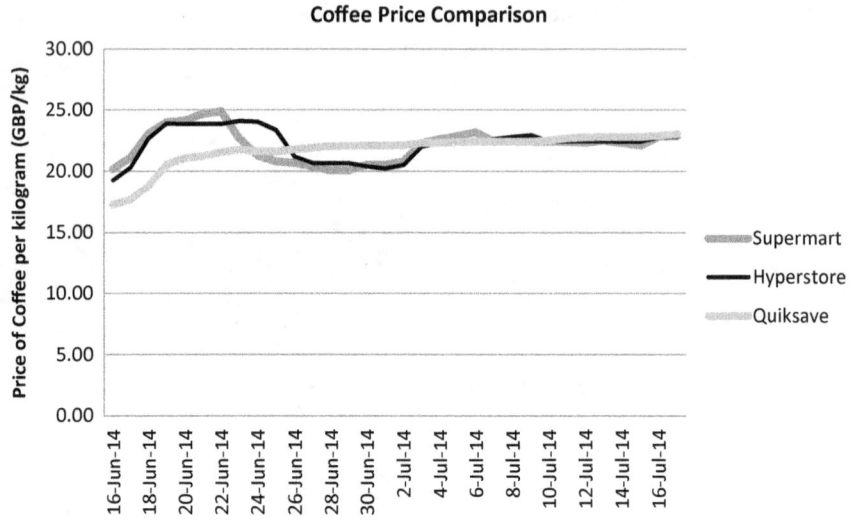

Answers:

1. The number of new credit card applications was lower than debit cards at the beginning. Credit card applications later <u>rebounded</u> and <u>climbed steadily,</u> while debit card applications <u>declined</u> between 2010 and 2012 only to <u>pick up slightly</u> thereafter.
2. Hot meals are the most popular lunch choice. Apart from a <u>slight dip</u> on Tuesdays and Wednesdays, the number of hot meal buyers is <u>consistently</u> around 600–700. Pie comes in as a close second, with <u>stable</u> purchases at around 400–600. Sandwiches are much more <u>volatile,</u> reaching <u>peaks</u> as high as 650 but later <u>plummeting</u> to as low as 150.
3. The <u>majority</u> of patients who visited the doctor did so due to a cough. This is <u>followed closely</u> by influenza, colds and fevers. Stomachaches were the <u>least</u> frequently reported out of the five major illnesses, while a small <u>minority</u> had ailments that could not be categorized.
4. An <u>overwhelmingly</u> large proportion of road accidents were caused by drunk driving, which is approximately a <u>dramatic</u> 400 times more than the number of accidents caused by road conditions.
5. In mid-June, coffee at Quiksave was <u>significantly</u> cheaper than Supermart and Hyperstore. Coffee prices reached an <u>all-time high</u> of about GBP25 at Supermart, and began <u>weakening</u> thereafter. The prices at all three stores eventually <u>plateaued</u> after around July 4, 2014 onwards.

Data Analysis Skills: Generating Insights

Now that you know the vocabulary and how to apply your newfound words, it's time to move to the next level and to learn how to generate insights. In other words, this means that you have to learn how to conduct some meaningful analysis. Recall the basic blueprint needed for Task 1:

1) Introduction — Describe the data presented in general terms
2) Main Point 1 — Describe the first chart or table
3) Main Point 2 — Describe the second chart or table
4) **Conclusive Point — Analyze both charts or tables side by side, and generate some insights**

You need to be able to generate insights to give your essay some depth. You don't have to do too much, but just enough so that your essay doesn't end up sounding like this:

In the line graph, in 2008, consumption of beetroot went up whereas carrots went down. The same trend was observed in 2009. However, in 2010, the consumption of carrots surpassed beetroot by about two tons. Then, in 2011, the consumption of carrots and beetroot was about the same.

In the pie chart, in 2008, only 32 percent of farmers planted beetroot. 47 percent planted carrots while the remaining 21 percent planted tomatoes.

The statements above are all grammatically correct and valid. But, if the IELTS had wanted to test you on data description alone, they would not have included two data sources for you. The reason why two are provided is because you do need to demonstrate some level of analysis. For example, you do need to know how to express inconsistencies or linkages in English:

Despite the higher consumption of beetroot as compared to carrots in 2008, there were surprisingly only 32 percent of farmers who planted beetroot in that same year — significantly less than the 47 percent who planted carrots.

You don't have to speculate on the reasons behind why there was higher consumption of beetroot despite the comparatively lower number of farmers who planted beetroot. By highlighting this inconsistency through the usage of the word "despite" and via stacking the numbers together in a single sentence, you have already demonstrated to the examiner that you can describe data in a more advanced manner. This type of analysis is what will get you the extra points needed for a Band 8 or 9.

Unfortunately, analysis is a big word that gets thrown around a lot. The only problem is that not everyone has done analysis (even if they say they have). Let's take a look at an example of how a student did some decent analysis, but also made some mistakes in the process:

The number of people who sat for the IELTS between 2010 and 2014 has been steadily increasing. Based on the line graph, the IELTS is most popular in China with the number of test-takers fast approaching one million in 2014. As someone who is from China, this is likely because many Chinese university students want to study abroad and an increasing number of students are able to do so because of growing income levels.

There are good and bad parts here:

The good part is that the student made some analysis (albeit just based on a single graph) by stating that China has the highest number of test-takers, which has touched the one-million milestone.

The bad part is that the student includes his own speculation about the reasons behind this trend. Even though he attempts to lend credibility to this statement by saying he is from China, this kind of claim is not entirely relevant as it is not based on the data. It is more of the sort of thing you would include in a Task 2 argumentative-type essay.

This brings us to the next point — be careful not to mistake generating insights with giving your own interpretation. The IELTS does not require you to give your own interpretation. Rather, the focus should be on describing the relationships between the data and on giving comments about the data trends. What is the difference between the two?

Here's another example of giving your own interpretation:

> I believe that while car ownership has been on an upward trend according to the data shown, this will not continue in the future because public transport is improving. As environmental pollution becomes a growing concern, more emphasis will certainly be paid on reducing the number of cars on the road.

As you can see, the portion that is underlined is not found within the data. Therefore, these are your own conjectures and hypotheses about what might happen in the future — effectively your *interpretation* of events. This is not what Task 2 requires of you. On the contrary, what Task 2 requires is for you to be able to use analytical vocabulary to describe trends and relationships within the data. Refer to the following example:

> Car ownership has been on an upward trend despite a similar upward trend in petrol prices. In fact, between the years 2008–2010, car ownership continued increasing at an even faster rate even though oil price spiked from $70 to $85 per barrel.

In this new iteration of analysis, notice how it is very much focused on two specific data trends: car ownership numbers and oil prices. There is no personal interpretation at all, thus ensuring you stick closely to what the IELTS asks of you. This will help you gain more points.

Simple Steps

There are several ways to generate insights, and these are techniques anyone can use under any situation.

The Academic Writing Section

1. Compare and contrast the available data
2. Identify correlations, and highlight inconsistencies between data trends (if any)
3. Suggest reasons for data movement, or lessons we are able to learn from the data

Elaboration with Examples

Step 1: Compare and contrast the available data

This is the most basic of all analysis and is definitely something you will be able to do in 99 percent of data presented to you.

Step 2: Identify correlations, and highlight inconsistencies between data trends (if any)

After you have compared and contrasted the data, you may be able to notice some connections between the trends. Usually, these connections tend to be one of the following:

a) Both moving in the same direction — possible correlation or causal link

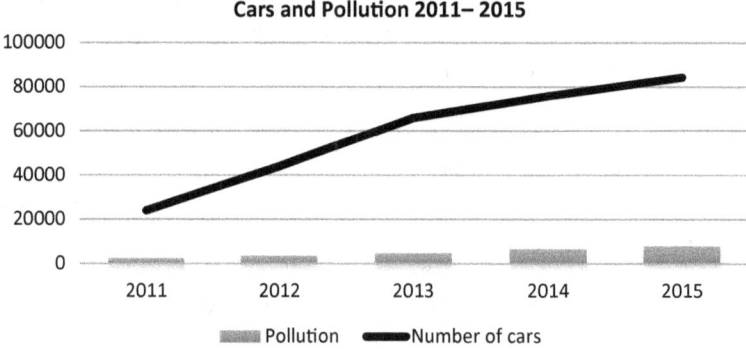

Data Analysis Skills: Generating Insights

b) Trends moving in the opposite direction — also a possible correlation or causal link

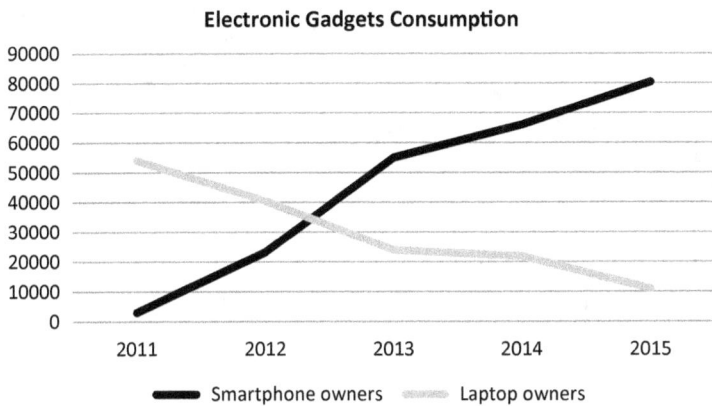

c) Simple comparison — where there are more than one items measured on the same scale, you can arrive at conclusions by making relative comparisons

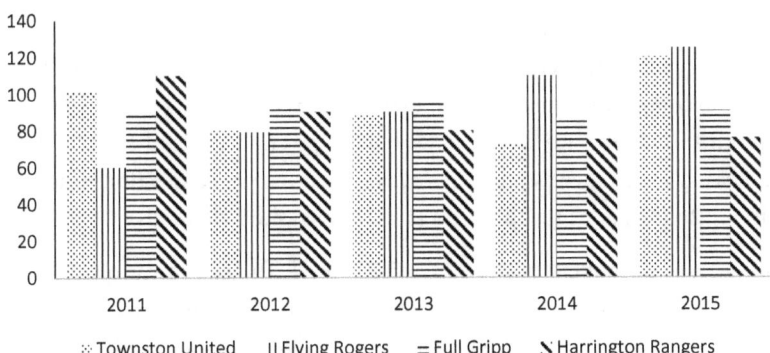

The Academic Writing Section

d) Volatility — where the numbers moves up and down rapidly

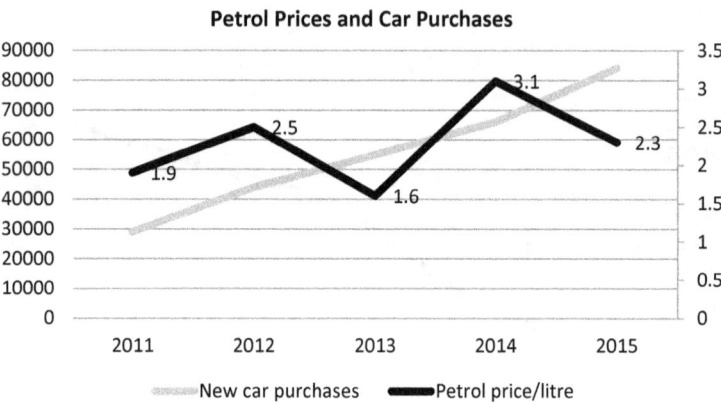

Step 3: Suggest reasons for data movement, or lessons we are able to learn from the data

Let's build on some examples from the previous step. One important aspect to bear in mind when completing this third step is to apply some common sense or do some "sanity testing." If you see obesity rates increasing as sugar consumption increases, you could say that the two are linked. Logically, it makes sense since higher consumption of sugar can result in increased weight gain.

But, you may also encounter data that are moving in the same direction but have no connection at all. For example, the number of crows in a neighborhood and the number of ice cream cones bought by children aged 10–12 may have increased simultaneously, but there is no clear logical connection. Under such circumstances, don't try to force a link between the two trends.

    a) Both moving in the same direction — The rise in car ownership has been accompanied by a similar rise in pollution, which suggests that cars may be contributing to increased pollution levels.

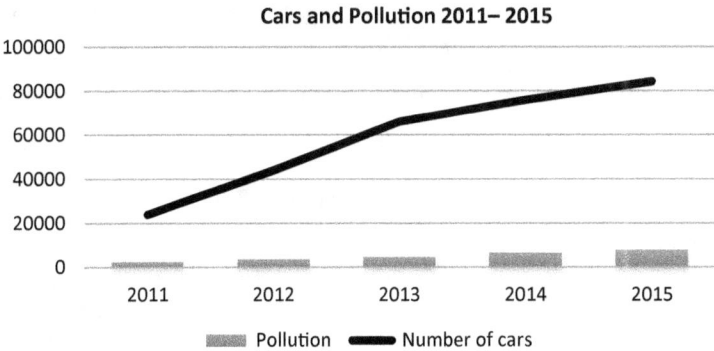

b) Trends moving in the opposite direction — The number of smartphone owners have been on the rise while laptop owners have been on the decline, suggesting that smartphones are beginning to replace laptops in terms of electronic gadgets.

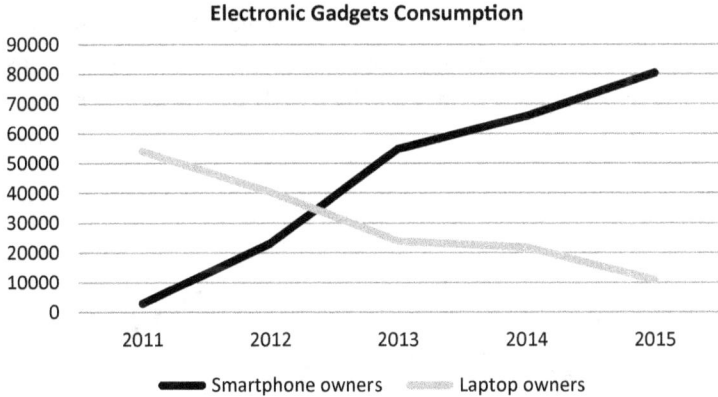

c) Simple comparison — The Flying Rogers started out with the lowest number of goals in 2011 but ended up with the highest number in 2015, showing the greatest improvement amongst all four football teams.

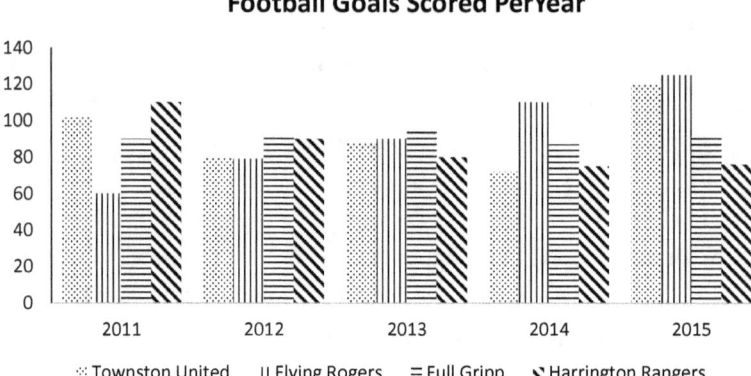

Football Goals Scored PerYear

d) Volatility versus stability — despite volatile petrol prices, the number of new car purchases has increased since 2011, suggesting that consumers view cars as important enough to justify the higher expense associated with petrol prices.

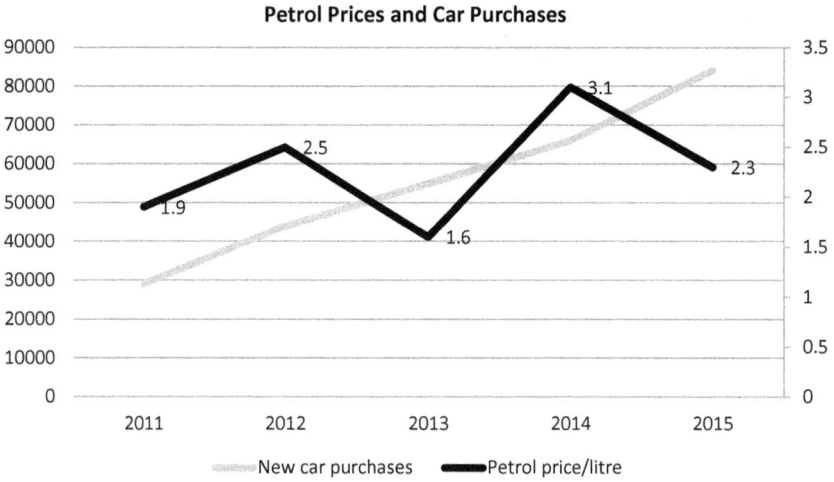

Petrol Prices and Car Purchases

Data Analysis Skills: Generating Insights

IELTS Trainer

Use the *Simple Steps* to write one or two analytical sentences about the data provided.

1.

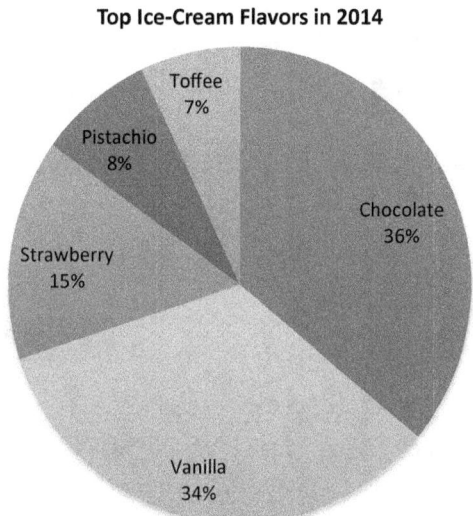

2.

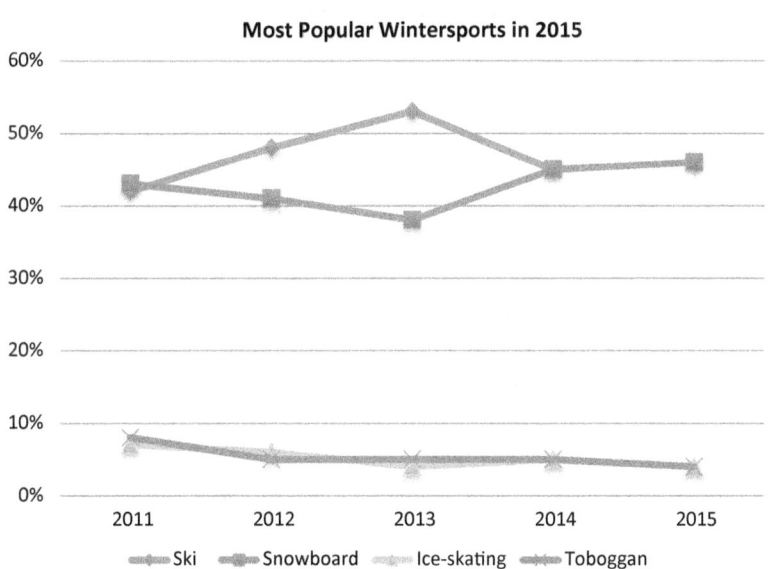

The Academic Writing Section

3.

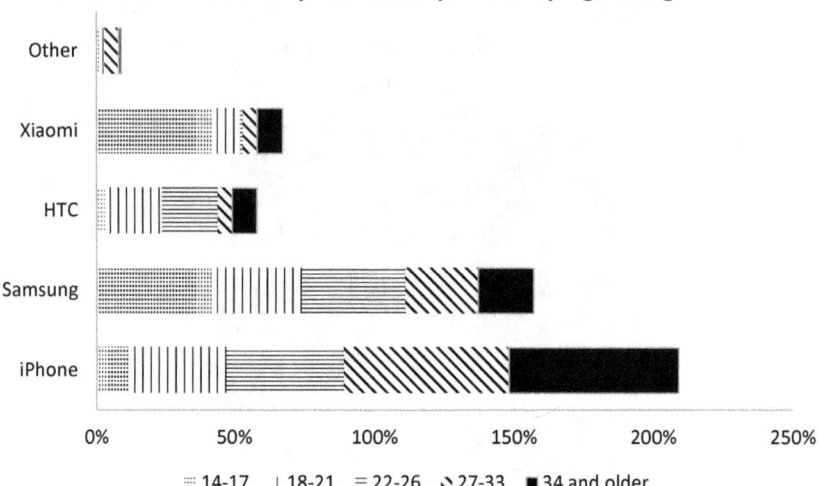

4.

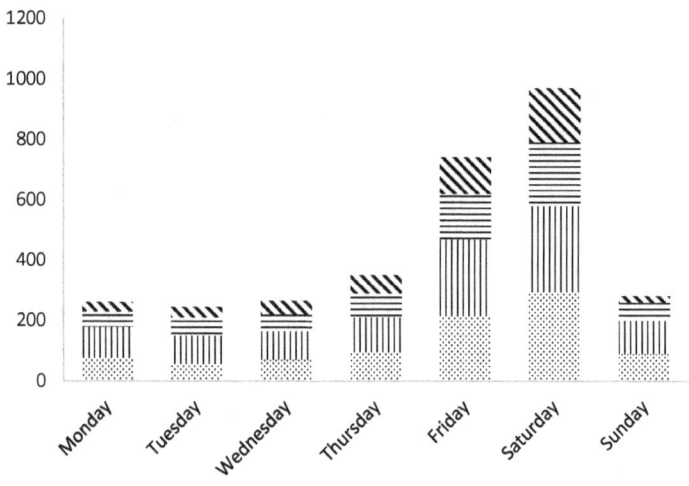

5.

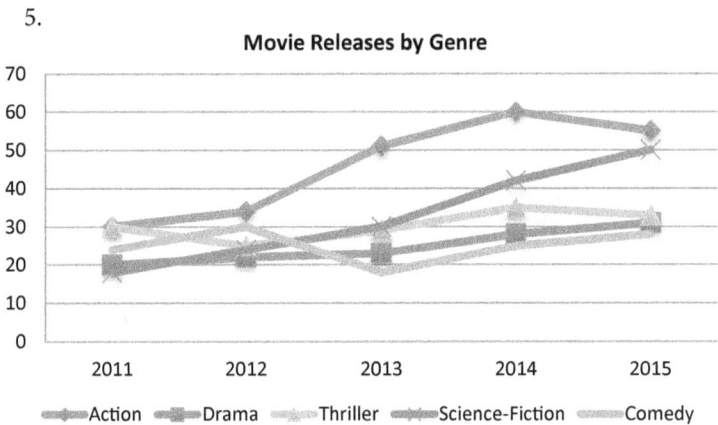

Answers:

1. Chocolate and vanilla were by far the most popular ice-cream choices in 2014. Conversely, pistachio and toffee were the least popular.
2. The number of people who chose skiing increased between 2011 and 2013 while ice-skating and tobogganing remained constant, implying that skiing gradually replaced snowboarding as the most popular winter sport activity during this time.
3. iPhone is the most popular smartphone overall with the exception of among the 14–17 age group, which is dominated by Samsung and Xiaomi users. Samsung comes second, but has a more even distribution over each age group, which suggests that Samsung is the more generally preferred brand.
4. Saturdays and Sundays are the days that the bar receives the most business, with sales across all drinks peaking over these two days. This suggests that the bar's clientele frequent the bar mostly on the weekends.
5. Movie releases of every genre have increased, except for comedy, which dipped slightly in 2012 and only just recovered by 2015. This implies that the market for movies is growing as a whole, and consumers in particular have a preference for action and science-fiction movies.

Argumentative Skills: Forming a Viewpoint

Forming a viewpoint may seem easy. But, many students often unknowingly underperform in this regard. When something as fundamental as a viewpoint is not established clearly throughout the essay, the reader will start to seriously call into question the quality of the essay and that's when you will begin to lose points.

Let's take a look at an example of student writing, where the viewpoint was not established clearly. We will ignore the grammatical mistakes and language errors so that we can focus solely on how important the *viewpoint* is to the entire essay.

To do this, we will refer to the earlier essay topic regarding unpaid voluntary work:

Essay topic: Some people argue that <u>unpaid voluntary work</u> should be made <u>mandatory</u> for <u>high school students</u>. This could be in the form of working for a charitable organisation or giving free tuition to younger children from underprivileged backgrounds.

To what extent do you agree or disagree?

Give reasons for your answer and include any relevant examples from your own knowledge or experience.

Write at least 250 words.

There is an argument that whether unpaid voluntary work should be a mandatory part of high school. For instance, students can work for a charity or teach underprivileged children. Concerning about the study mission, my suggestion is that school can encourage its students to take part in unpaid community service instead of constraining them.

Comment: In an earlier chapter, we have already explained how the student misinterpreted the question by assuming the school had "constrained" students from participating in unpaid community service. However, this aside, the introduction is still not clear. The student does not explicitly say that unpaid community service should be made compulsory. Instead, she uses the word "encourage," which seems to suggest that community work should be optional.

The Academic Writing Section

What she could have done to make this better would be to clarify her stance. If she thinks that community work has value, but should not be forced upon students, then she should say so. Alternatively, if she believes that unpaid community work should be mandatory for all students, she should also make that clear.

High school students who were involved in community service are usually responsible and skilled. These important features may help them adapt the society more quickly than others. Indeed, it is important to cultivate your own abilities in young age.

Additionally, doing unpaid community service will also improve students' mental capacity. People who attend charitable activity such as improving the neighborhood or helping donations are optimistic. Considering a lot of news reported the upward trend of suicide cases in high school and according to some psychological experts suggestions, school could hold some community service to help reduce the study stress.

Comment: Based on paragraphs 2 and 3, the student seems to support unpaid community work. But there is still no clarification as to whether she thinks it should merely be encouraged, or absolutely mandatory. The reader is still left wondering about what the viewpoint really is.

However, some people think that high school students should pay much more attention on their study instead of doing compulsory unpaid community service because it wastes time and has no help for being enrolled by an university. It might be more sensible to let the students make their own decisions whether to join the unpaid community service.

Comment: In paragraph 4, however, the student takes a turn and seems to lean towards making community work optional. But because she says "it _might_ be more sensible to let the students make their own decision," we **still** don't know her exact viewpoint since "might" reflects doubt.

In short, I strongly feel the advantages far outweigh its disadvantages in participating unpaid community service. At the same time, schools play an important role in encouraging students rather than regarding the service as a compulsory part.

Comment: The last paragraph is of no use either. She states that she feels the advantages outnumber the disadvantages. She also states that the schools play an important role in encouraging students. But there is still no conclusion on the original essay question, which is whether unpaid community service should be made compulsory or not.

As you can see from the above example, it is a pity the student did not establish her viewpoint clearly because the points she made were fairly logical. The only problem was because she did not have a clear viewpoint, she had difficulty linking her main points to the original argument and therefore veered off track in the main body of the essay. By doing so, she confused the reader and lost valuable points.

To form a solid viewpoint and to ensure that you maintain this viewpoint throughout the essay, follow the three simple steps.

Simple Steps

1. Make a decision
2. Ensure each paragraph supports the decision
3. Conclude by reiterating your decision

Elaboration with Examples

Step 1: Make a decision

Many students spend far too much time making a decision. Be rational and efficient by going with whichever viewpoint you can generate the most justifications for. It doesn't matter whether you genuinely believe in that particular viewpoint or not. This is an English examination, not a personal statement.

Once you decide, stick with it. Don't start looking back halfway through your essay, as poor time management can be as detrimental to your score as poor English.

The Academic Writing Section

Step 2: Ensure each paragraph supports the decision

You will have already built an outline for your essay. Now, the key is to do a "sanity check" to ensure that each paragraph does truly support the decision you have made. Many students may accidentally confuse supporting an opposing viewpoint with the art of counter-arguments. Here's the difference:

> **Opposing viewpoint:** I believe that wearing glasses is better than wearing contact lens. This is because glasses are less expensive in the long run. However, contact lens are more convenient. Those who play sports will find it cumbersome to wear glasses. Therefore, contact lens have many benefits too.

> **Counter-argument:** Although glasses are less expensive in the long run, contact lens are still the better choice because they are more convenient and are necessary for those who play sports.

As illustrated above, supporting the opposing viewpoint halfway involves bringing up justifications for the opposing view and then declaring that you agree with those justifications. There is no response whatsoever to explain why the opposing view's justifications are not as convincing as the view you have declared support for.

On the contrary, countering an argument effectively involves explaining why the opposing view's justifications are not sound enough. This usually involves putting some "Writing Moves" into action.

Step 3: Conclude by reiterating your decision

Always make sure that your conclusion rephrases what you have declared in the introduction. A quick two-second sanity check could make all the difference.

IELTS Trainer

Identify the paragraphs that have conflicting viewpoints. If applicable, turn these conflicting viewpoints into counter-arguments.

1. Comic books can be educational because they convey messages in an entertaining and memorable way. They may not be as intellectual as works of literature, but we should respect all forms of creative expression and focus on seeing the benefits that they can bring.
2. Letting children do housework from a young age is a good idea as it teaches them the value of being organized and clean. Doing so from a young age is

especially important because these values will be carried onto adulthood. Then again, perhaps it may be better for parents to employ part-time help to complete housework so that children can focus on other activities such as learning. This will help them prepare for university.
3. I prefer water to fruit juice because water is the most essential liquid for our body. However, it does not contain the vitamins, minerals and fiber that can be found in fruit juice. Fruit juice can also serve as a meal especially when it is blended into a smoothie.
4. Terminally ill patients should be allowed to choose when to stop life support. Even though family members may disagree, as they would be devastated about losing a loved one, the patient ultimately has the right to his or her own life.
5. While I agree with the concept of equality, some jobs should be done by men instead of women simply due to physical differences. For example, work that involves a great deal of manual labor would be better suited for men. Granted, there are some women who are physically stronger than men, but what I would like to emphasize is that I am not suggesting that women stay away from strenuous jobs altogether. I am merely suggesting that men are more suitable for certain roles.

Answers:
1. No conflicting viewpoints.
2. Letting children do housework from a young age is a good idea as it teaches them the value of being organized and clean. Doing so from a young age is especially important because these values will be carried onto adulthood. While some may argue that the children's time is better spent studying, the self-discipline that they will learn will actually equip them to study more effectively in the future. In the long run, letting children do housework is still the better choice.
3. I prefer water to fruit juice because water is the most essential liquid for our body. It may not contain all the vitamins, minerals and fiber that fruit juice contains, but at least it also does not contain the high levels of sugar. Water is what our body is meant to consume, and it is the best form of rehydration.
4. No conflicting viewpoints.
5. No conflicting viewpoints.

Argumentative Skills: Countering Arguments

It's not enough to just highlight within your essay that you are aware of other counter-arguments. You need to counter them, and doing so requires a specific set of skills. Many students often do the first part (raising counter-arguments) without completing the second part (*countering* these counter-arguments). Why is this important? Take a step back and imagine you were asking your friend about which laptop to buy. The dialogue may go as follows:

> Friend: Adam, you should get a Lenovo laptop. They are relatively cheap and you can get good specifications too. [Your friend raises a good main point]
>
> You: I know, but Apple Macbooks are just designed so well and are so appealing to look at. I don't mind paying a bit more for something that looks good. [You raise a counter-argument]
>
> Friend: Yes, that's true. Apple Macbooks are nice. [Acknowledges counter-argument]

Now, imagine if the conversation were to stop there. Would you be convinced and go for the Lenovo? Probably not. Why? Because you raised a counter-argument, and your friend was unable to respond to it. It makes you doubt whether his original argument could hold any weight at all.

On the flip side, if your friend were able to respond to your counter-argument, the situation would look very different:

> Friend: Adam, you should get a Lenovo laptop. They are relatively cheap and you can get one with good specifications too. [Your friend raises a good main point]
>
> You: I know, but Apple Macbooks are just designed so well and are so appealing to look at. I don't mind paying a bit more for something that looks good. [You raise a counter-argument]
>
> Friend: Yes, that's true. Apple Macbooks are nice. [Acknowledges counter-argument] But, I don't think you realize that Lenovo has also come a long way in terms of design.

The Academic Writing Section

You: Really?

Friend: Absolutely. Have you seen their latest laptop? It's ultra-thin and at the same time so flexible that you can transform the laptop into a tablet in no time. And, did I mention? It's touchscreen. Macbooks can't do this kind of thing. [Your friend gives a response to the counter-argument that you raised earlier]

Let's take a look at this in the IELTS context, and back to the example of last chapter:

High school students who were involved in community service are usually responsible and skilled. These important features may help them adapt the society more quickly than others. Indeed, it is important to cultivate your own abilities in young age.

Additionally, doing unpaid community service will also improve students' mental capacity. People who attend charitable activity such as improving the neighborhood or helping donations are optimistic. Considering a lot of news reported the upward trend of suicide cases in high school and according to some psychological experts suggestions, school could hold some community service to help reduce the study stress.

However, some people think that high school students should pay much more attention on their study instead of doing compulsory unpaid community service because it wastes time and has no help for being enrolled by an university. It might be more sensible to let the students make their own decisions whether to join the unpaid community service.

In the previous chapter on forming viewpoints, we highlighted that the student had thrown the reader off by initially appearing to be an advocate of unpaid community service but later on conceding that it might be more sensible to let students make their own decisions. To prevent this, the student could have raised the counter-argument nonetheless, but more importantly also responded to it.

For example, she could have added one more line saying that:

Be that as it may, making community service mandatory is no different from making education compulsory for students. After all, the experience gained as part of doing community service is a crucial component of every student's journey and should not be seen as merely a waste of time.

By doing this, you are letting the reader know that you understand the counter-arguments and more importantly you can refute them. Now, the more pertinent question is, how do you execute this effectively?

Simple Steps

1. List out possible counter-arguments that others could make against your points; be selective
2. Formulate a justified response to the counter-argument
3. Apply the appropriate transition words to ensure your response is written in an elegant manner

Elaboration with Examples

Let's use a sample IELTS essay question for Task 2 to illustrate how the *Simple Steps* will work in practice:

> Essay Question: Some people believe that public speaking and presentation skills should be a mandatory component of the education syllabus, even starting from primary school. Others believe that public speaking and presentation skills are not essential for everyone, and should not be mandatory as it may place the more introverted students at a disadvantage.
> To what extent do you agree or disagree with this opinion?
> Give reasons for your answer and include any relevant examples from your own knowledge or experience.
> Write at least 250 words.

Step 1: List out possible counter-arguments that others could make against your points; be selective

Suppose you have already written at least a basic structure for your essay, with the main points listed out neatly like this:

1) Introduction — Agree that public speaking and presentation skills should be a mandatory part of the education syllabus even starting from primary school

2) Main Point 1 — Public speaking and presentations are skills that everyone has to pick up, regardless of the career path they choose. Just as the syllabus dictates that all students should learn how to read and write, it should also make it compulsory for students to learn how to speak and present well
3) Main Point 2 — Starting from primary school is a good idea, as children absorb more at a young age
4) Main Point 3 — This move will also be good for the child's personal development and mental health, as they can learn how to express themselves
5) Conclusion — Reiterate that public speaking and presentation skills should be made mandatory even at the primary school level

Now, you only have a limited amount of time and words. No one is expecting you to write an entire thesis in just 20 minutes or so. Thus, you've got to be selective about which points you want to raise counter-arguments against. Choose the ones that have obvious counter-arguments and for which you feel fairly confident of giving a justified response.

Let's take Main Point 2 as an example. You may want to concede that there are some who may say that starting public speaking and presentation classes from the primary school level is not a good idea, as this could cause undue stress.

Step 2: Formulate a justified response to the counter-argument

Now you have a Main Point and a possible counter-argument against your Main Point. The next step that you must do is to formulate a justified response to the counter-argument. This means explaining why you are still right *despite* the counter-argument that was raised.

Main Point 2 — Starting from primary school is a good idea, as children absorb more at a young age
- Counter-Argument: There are some who may say that starting public speaking and presentation classes from the primary school level is not a good idea, as this could <u>cause undue stress</u>

Focus on responding only to core of the counter argument, which explicitly states that introducing public speaking and presentations can cause undue stress to the student. You can underline the keywords within the counter-argument if that helps you channel your thoughts better.

Since the counter argument is concerned about the stress that could be caused to the students, you have two choices:

a) Argue that the stress, to a certain extent, can be good for the student
b) Argue that it will not be as stressful as portrayed. For example, public speaking and presentations can be taught in a manner that is fun for the student. It also provides a break from the routine of reading, writing and memorizing

Step 3: Apply the appropriate transition words to ensure your response is written in an elegant manner

Now that you have two possible justified responses to the counter-argument, all that is left for you to do is to stitch everything together. To do this, you will need to use some transition words.

There are some "formulas" that you can use when it comes to integrating the transition words:

Introduce the counter-argument by

[Inserting "Writing Move 2.1: Opposing Points"]

OR

[Inserting "Writing Move 2.2: Making Concession"]

+

Respond to the counter-argument by

[Inserting "Writing Move 2.3: Debunking Arguments"]

OR

[Inserting "Writing Move 2.4: Replacing Ideas"]

To refresh your memory, the relevant writing moves are copied as follows. It is a good idea to memorize at least a few from each category, so that you have enough tools to help you make your case.

The Academic Writing Section

Writing Move 2.1: Opposing Points

No.	Writing Move 2.1: Opposing Points
1	But
2	However
3	In contrast
4	By way of contrast
5	Yet
6	When in fact
7	While
8	Whereas
9	Conversely
10	On the other hand
11	Although this may be true
12	Different from
13	On the contrary
14	Even so
15	Though this may be the case
16	Then again
17	In spite of
18	Despite
19	In reality
20	In actual fact
21	Unlike
22	As much as
23	Be that as it may
24	Regardless
25	Nonetheless
26	Nevertheless

Writing Move 2.2: Making Concessions

No.	Writing Move 2.2: Making Concessions
1	Of course
2	Granted
3	To be sure
4	Admittedly
5	It is undeniable that … however
6	Undoubtedly
7	No doubt
8	Without a doubt
9	Naturally
10	While I understand that …
11	I acknowledge that … however
12	It could be argued that
13	One explanation might be that

Writing Move 2.3: Debunking Arguments

No.	Writing Move 2.3: Debunking Arguments
1	Either way
2	In either case
3	Whichever happens
4	Whatever happens
5	In either event
6	All the same
7	In any case
8	In any event
9	At any rate
10	Regardless
11	No matter

Writing Move 2.4: Replacing Ideas

No.	Writing Move 2.4 Replacing Ideas
1	Rather
2	Instead
3	By taking another viewpoint
4	In place of
5	An alternative would be
6	In lieu of

In practice, how would you stitch the paragraph together? Let's use the formula and see how it works.

Introducing public speaking and presentation classes at the primary school level is a good idea, as that is the age when children can absorb lessons most easily. **However** [Writing Move 2.1: Opposing Points], there are some who believe that this could cause undue stress to the young students. This concern is not valid, because **regardless** [Writing Move 2.3: Debunking Arguments] of whichever subject a student takes, there will always be a certain degree of stress. **Rather**, [Writing Move 2.4: Replacing Ideas] public speaking could even help to reduce stress by breaking the daily routine of simply reading, writing and memorizing, as students will have the opportunity to learn how to express themselves better in front of larger audiences.

As you can see from the example above, we haven't changed the original points much except to use some writing moves here and there, which help smoothen the transition process.

IELTS Trainer

Think of a counter-argument for each point given below. Then, use "Writing Moves" to write a one-line counter-argument.
1. Children who are overweight should be put on a diet.
2. The legal drinking age should be increased from 18 to 21 years of age.
3. Schoolchildren should not be allowed to dye their hair.

Argumentative Skills: Countering Arguments

4. Everyone should pay for private health insurance.
5. An inevitable part of leadership involves instilling fear in those under your care.

Suggested answers:

1. Being overweight is <u>undoubtedly</u> bad for health. <u>However,</u> regular exercise must be included in any weight-loss program, as relying on dieting alone may not be good for health.
2. Alcohol education is more important than raising the legal drinking age because without addressing the root cause of the issue, people will still abuse alcohol <u>in any event.</u>
3. Banning all schoolchildren from dyeing their hair would restrict their liberty. <u>Instead</u> of an outright ban, schools can consider allowing schoolchildren to dye their hair if there is written consent from parents.
4. Although private health insurance would be nice to have, paying for it can be very costly. It should not be mandatory for everyone to pay for private health insurance, as many lower-income earners may not be able to afford it.
5. <u>While</u> some leaders resort to fear to maintain control, this is not the only way. <u>On the contrary,</u> leaders can also exert the same influence by caring for and showing concern for those whom they lead.

Academic Writing Practice Examinations

Practice Examination 1

Writing Task 1

You should spend about 20 minutes on this task.

> The table below gives information about college graduates between 2006 and 2012, and the chart shows post-graduation employment for the years 2006 and 2012.
>
> Summarize the information by selecting and reporting the main features, and make comparisons where relevant.

Write at least 150 words.

Year	Number of college graduates
2006	200,304
2007	232,049
2008	299,300
2009	301,329
2010	323,937
2011	301,232
2012	342,393

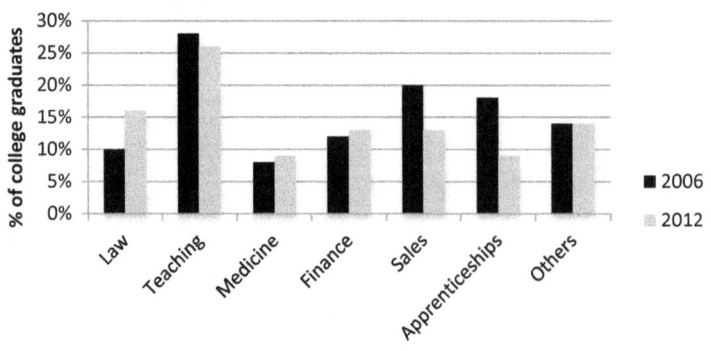

Writing Task 2

You should spend about 40 minutes on this task.
Write about the following topic:

> Deciding on a career is often a challenging process because many are torn between chasing a passion that may not pay much and stable jobs that may not be their passion.
> Which do you think is more important?

Give reasons for your answer and include any relevant examples from your own knowledge or experience.
Write at least 250 words.

Model Essays for Practice Examination 1
Writing Task 1

The table illustrates the number of college graduates from 2006 to 2012, while the chart displays figures for post-graduate employment with a further classification by type of job in 2006 and 2012.

The number of college graduates increased rapidly during this period of time, rising from 220,304 in 2006 to 342,393 in 2012. Though the number declined slightly in 2011, it rebounded in the next year.

As we can see in the chart, teaching was the most popular job in both 2006 and 2012, accounting for 28% and 26% respectively. Post-graduate employment for law, medicine and finance was on the upward trend and the increase for those who joined the law profession was the largest, leaping from 10% to 16%. On the contrary, the percentage of college graduates working in sales and apprenticeships dropped by 7% and 9% between 2006 and 2012. Meanwhile, post-graduate employment in other types of jobs remained at 14%.

As shown above, the number of college graduates increased year on year. Close analysis reveals that teaching remains the most popular job, with more than 25% of post-graduates joining the teaching workforce in both 2006 and 2012.

Writing Task 2

People often find it difficult to decide on a career because they feel confused as to whether to chase a passion that may not come with a high salary, or choose a stable job which is not their passion. I believe that having passion for the job is much more important because only then can you realize your dream wholeheartedly.

To begin with, you will excel at your career if you have a passion for it. For instance, the reason why most celebrities such as singers, basketball players and painters became successful is because of their passions for their career. Recall that these kinds of careers are precisely the ones that are idealistic and do not pay much at the beginning. However, even though you may not be paid much at first, you will be more likely to work harder, achieve more and be promoted.

Some might argue that receiving a decent salary is important in order to make ends meet. However, this viewpoint is shortsighted. Building on the previous point, one needs passion in order to work wholeheartedly. If you have a job that you dislike, you will not put all your effort into the job and it will be challenging for you to receive a promotion. In the short run, you may earn more. But, in the long run, your salary may remain stagnant.

Furthermore, forcing yourself to pursue a career solely for the sake of financial compensation can be detrimental to your health. There are some who have pursued such a path, only to fall into depression or face nervous breakdowns because they are unhappy with their jobs. Once you reach this point, even money cannot buy you happiness.

Ultimately, many aspects should be considered when choosing a career and passion is certainly one of them. While many tend to value money, choosing a job simply based on its pay is not wise and may backfire in the long run.

Practice Examination 2

Writing Task 1

You should spend about 20 minutes on this task.

> The charts below give information about annual expenditure on online shopping between 2011 and 2014, which is further categorized into the transaction method used. Information about the breakdown of products bought online in 2014 is also provided.
>
> Summarize the information by selecting and reporting the main features, and make comparisons where relevant.

Write at least 150 words.

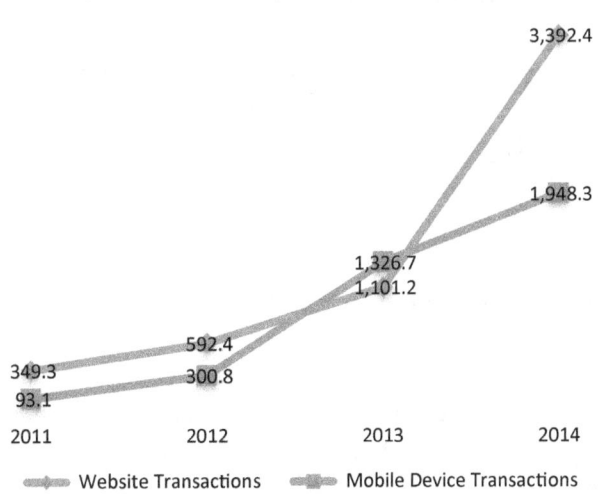

Expenditure on Online Shopping (GBP, Millions)

Academic Writing Practice Examinations

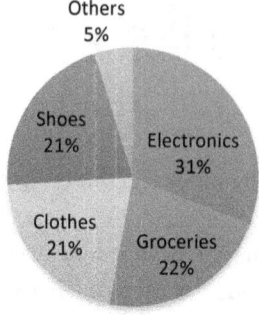

Type of Products Bought Online in 2014

Writing Task 2

You should spend about 40 minutes on this task.
Write about the following topic:

> *Electronic books are far better than physical books, as they are cheaper and more environmentally friendly. Some, however, believe that physical books have benefits that cannot be replaced by electronics.*
> *To what extent do you agree or disagree with this opinion?*

Give reasons for your answer and include any relevant examples from your own knowledge or experience.
Write at least 250 words.

Model Essays for Practice Examination 2

Writing Task 1

The charts show annual expenditure on online shopping from 2011 to 2014 and the type of products bought online in 2014. Moreover, the expenditure is classified by website transactions and mobile device transactions.

    According to the line chart, the sum of expenditure on website transactions and mobile device transactions rose at the same pace between 2011 and 2012. However, the expenditure on mobile device transactions in 2013 exceeded website transactions by 225.5. It is easy to see that the expenditure on website transactions rose steeply in 2014 from 1101.2 to 3392.4, which overtook expenditure on mobile device transactions.

Additionally, we can observe that electronic products occupied the first place (31%) in terms of products bought online. Furthermore, the percentages of groceries, clothes and shoes bought online were almost the same, accounting for 22%, 21% and 21% respectively. The remaining 5% included other various products.

In short, an increasing number of people shopped online from 2011 to 2014, and the most popular type of goods they bought was electronics.

Writing Task 2

The question raises the issue of whether physical books will be replaced by electronic versions due to the latter's cheaper price and lower impact on the environment. Both electronic books and physical books have their advantages and disadvantages, but it is my belief that electronic books should and will replace physical books one day.

First of all, it is more convenient to choose and purchase electronic books. As we know, people can buy electronic books and physical books online. However, it will take only a few seconds to receive the electronic books while you will only receive the physical books after several days, or even a couple of weeks if you buy imported books. In fact, people are more likely to buy physical books in book stores, but sometimes they cannot find what they want. On the contrary, you can search for any electronic books on the Internet by using only a few keywords. Furthermore, the cost of buying electronic books is far lower than physical books.

Extending this point, electronic books are more environmentally friendly. No trees are required to manufacture paper for the pages of electronic books. In addition, improving the electronic books industry can help reduce environmental pollution that is caused by recycling and transporting physical books. Some may argue that you need to purchase an expensive electronic book reader before being able to read electronic books, and that this may consume a significant amount of resources as well. However, I believe that if one reads enough books, the cost incurred for the electronic book reader will be worthwhile. Furthermore, most people possess smartphones, tablets or laptops that can also be used to read electronic books.

Even though there are some people who love physical books, they cannot deny the fact that electronic books have several useful and convenient functions that physical books do not have. For example, it is easy to change the font size of electronic books depending on the reader's requirements. You can also search through the whole book to find the information that you want. In terms of storage, physical books definitely occupy much more space than electronic books, and its paper form can be difficult to maintain in good condition.

In short, electronic books are cheap, portable and environmental friendly. They are far better than physical books, and I am confident that they will replace physical books eventually.

Practice Examination 3

Writing Task 1

You should spend about 20 minutes on this task.

> The graph below provides information about the number of road accidents between 2002 and 2006, which is further categorized according to the type of vehicle involved. Information about the top ten reasons behind these road accidents is also provided.
>
> Summarize the information by selecting and reporting the main features, and make comparisons where relevant.

Write at least 150 words.

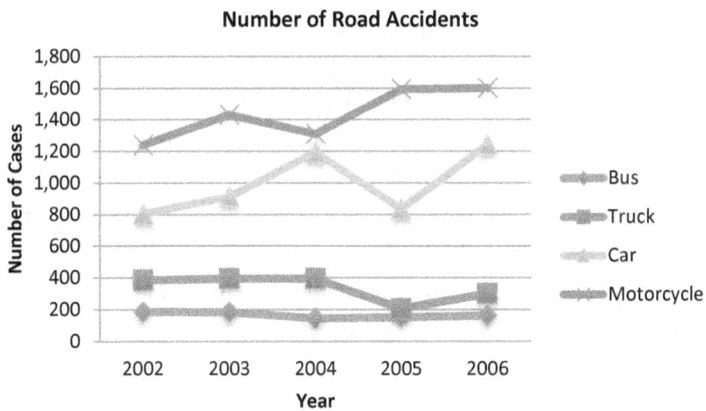

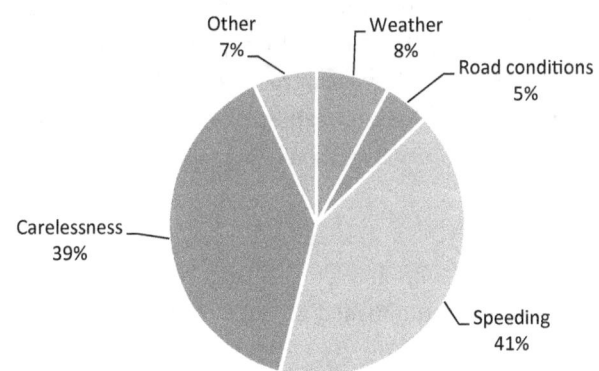

Academic Writing Practice Examinations

Writing Task 2

You should spend about 40 minutes on this task.
Write about the following topic:

> Mothers who give up their careers to care for their children are as accomplished as any other successful woman leader or businesswoman there is.
> To what extent do you agree or disagree with this opinion?

Give reasons for your answer and include any relevant examples from your own knowledge or experience.
Write at least 250 words.

Model Essays for Practice Examination 3

Writing Task 1

The graphs show data about the number of road accidents between 2002 and 2006, which is further categorized according to vehicle type. Furthermore, the top 10 reasons behind these road accidents are also provided.

Generally, the number of road accidents involving motorcycles was the highest during this period of time. It rose sharply from 1,200 in 2002 to 1,600 in 2005 and remained flat the next year. The number of accidents involving cars fluctuated, between 800 and 1,200. On the other hand, truck accidents remained at around 400 between 2002 and 2004, and then dropped by about half in 2005. It rebounded slowly from 200 to 300 in 2006. Buses were involved in the least number of accidents, with numbers remaining anchored near the lowest levels between 2002 and 2006, with an average of 200.

According to the pie chart, speeding was the top reason as to why accidents happened during this period of time, accounting for 41% of all incidents. It was followed by carelessness (39%) and weather (8%). As shown in this chart, poor road conditions were least likely factor to cause road accidents.

In conclusion, the highest number of road accidents was caused by motorcycle, with the most likely reason being speeding.

Writing Task 2

I believe that mothers who give up their careers in order to care for their children are just as accomplished as other successful women leaders or businesswomen, especially because taking care of children is a very challenging job.

The accomplishment of housewives is no less than the accomplishment of professional women. Just because there is no salary involved in caring for children does not mean that this act is not valuable. On the contrary, it is invaluable and priceless, because nothing can replace a mother's love. Without a caring home environment, there could be an increase in the number of social issues, as children may veer off track.

In addition, giving up their careers to care for children temporarily does not mean that women lack ambition. Some mothers may still do part-time work while taking care of their children. They may have plans to return to work right after their children grow older or become more independent. Making a choice to care for their children halfway through their careers should not be seen as a sign of weakness or of giving up.

Women often make have to make difficult choices when it comes to their families and careers. Whatever they choose, they should be encouraged and respected. For example, quite a number of women would like to put more effort into managing families and raising children, especially new mothers. Instead, women who give up their careers are not resting on their laurels. They are even braver then other professional women. Some children can be challenging to raise, and taking care of them can be far more difficult than working.

In conclusion, mothers who quit work to care for their children are definitely as accomplished as successful women leaders or businesswomen.

Practice Examination 4

Writing Task 1

You should spend about 20 minutes on this task.

> The charts below provides information about customer ratings for three different online retailers in 2014, which is further categorized according to the metrics measured. Information about number of users for each online retailer between 2012 and 2014 is also provided.
>
> Summarize the information by selecting and reporting the main features, and make comparisons where relevant.

Write at least 150 words.

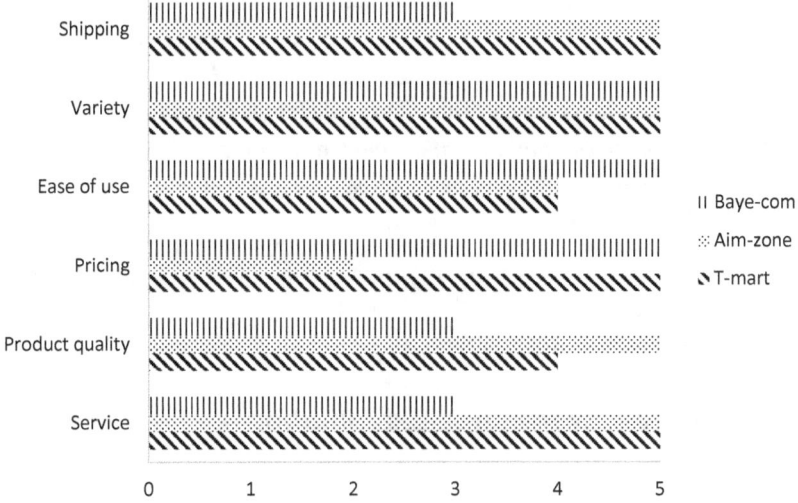

Academic Writing Practice Examinations

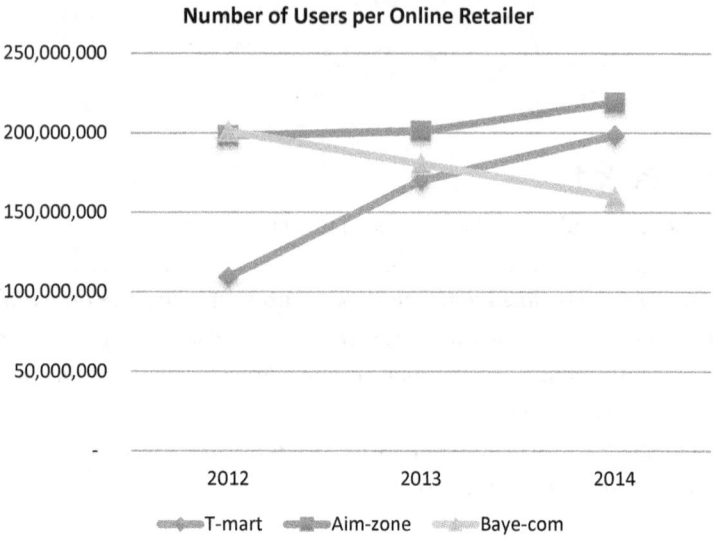

Writing Task 2

You should spend about 40 minutes on this task.
Write about the following topic:

> *Primary and secondary schools should provide laptops or computers for each student, as doing so can make learning and teaching more efficient.*
> *To what extent do you agree or disagree with this opinion?*

Give reasons for your answer and include any relevant examples from your own knowledge or experience.
Write at least 250 words.

Model Essays for Practice Examination 4

Writing Task 1

The bar chart shows the customer ratings for three online retailers in 2014, while the line chart shows the number of users that each online retailer possessed between 2012 and 2014.

T-mart received the best customer ratings across the board. The only areas where it did not score a "5" were "product quality" and "ease of use." Aim-zone comes in a close second, with pricing emerging as a key weak area. Baye-com had the poorest customer ratings overall but beat both Aim-zone and T-mart in the "ease of use" category.

The line chart shows that Aim-zone has the highest number of users. However, growth in the number of users has plateaued whereas T-mart's numbers are still rocketing upwards. To draw an example, T-mart's figures jumped from about 100 million to 175 million between 2012 and 2013. During this same time period, Aim-zone's user numbers remained stagnant at 200 million. Baye-com's users have been falling over the years, despite starting out with the relatively high number of 200 million users in 2012.

Closer analysis therefore reveals that there is some correlation between customer ratings and the number of users.

Writing Task 2

In this modern digital age, there has been debate as to whether schools should provide laptops or computers for each student to make learning and teaching more efficient. In my opinion, students should be given exposure to computers but they need not be completely dependent on them because traditional methods of teaching still has its merits.

To begin with, it is important to recognize that computers can also be a distraction instead of a learning tool. Since the advent of smartphones, for example, people constantly check their phones even at face-to-face mealtimes or meetings. This is because there is such a wide range of distractions available on such gadgets that it is nearly impossible to completely disconnect. The danger of providing computers to every student is that these computers may be misused and detract the students from learning.

Furthermore, staring at a computer screen for too long can cause vision problems. This is because our eyes are not used to staring at bright computer screens all day. Moreover, using a computer for prolonged periods of time can also cause back and shoulder problems. If children are extensively exposed to computers since young, the effect may be even more pronounced in years to come. It is already becoming commonplace to see youngsters wearing glasses or contact lens, which was not the norm before.

Additionally, traditional methods of teaching also has many merits that should not be easily overlooked in favor of technology. For example, teachers play an important role in facilitating interactive learning. Students are not only supposed to absorb textual knowledge; they should also develop their speaking and listening skills, which can only be honed effectively if it is learnt in person. Otherwise, there would be no need for a teacher in the classroom as students could rely solely on the Internet for their education.

As a final point, providing computers and laptops for each student would also be a significantly expensive exercise. The funds could be used for other purposes, such as upgrading facilities or better teacher training especially when it is not clear that computers and laptops are absolutely essential to a child's learning.

Practice Examination 5

Writing Task 1

You should spend about 20 minutes on this task.

> *The table below provides information on the number of wine bottles sold between 2012 and 2014, which is further categorized according to the country the wine originated from. Information about wine buyers' nationality in 2014 is also provided.*
>
> *Summarize the information by selecting and reporting the main features, and make comparisons where relevant.*

Write at least 150 words.

Table: Number of Wine Bottles Sold (by the Wine's Country of Origin)

Origin of Wine	2012	2013	2014
French	9,230,843	10,938,904	14,908,349
Italian	10,983,492	13,948,033	16,908,453
Australian	8,903,489	9,834,902	12,908,343
Chilean	2,093,843	3,490,832	4,390,824
American	4,908,342	3,948,024	3,746,293

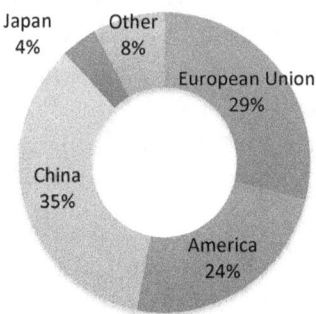

Wine Buyers by Country, 2014

- Japan 4%
- Other 8%
- European Union 29%
- China 35%
- America 24%

Writing Task 2

You should spend about 40 minutes on this task.
Write about the following topic:

> Many young adults and teenagers nowadays have shopped online at least once in their life. However, there are still some who prefer frequenting traditional brick-and-mortar stores when it comes to making purchases.
> Which type of shopping do you prefer, and why?

Give reasons for your answer and include any relevant examples from your own knowledge or experience.
Write at least 250 words.

Model Essays for Practice Examination 5

Writing Task 1

The table shows the number of wine bottles sold according to the wine's country of origin from 2012 to 2014, while the pie chart illustrates the wine buyers according to nationality in 2014.

Overall, purchases of wine have increased over the years, with the most popular wine being Italian, followed by French and Australian wine. There was a significant leap in purchases between 2013 and 2014, except for American wine which declined slightly from approximately 3.9 million to 3.7 million bottles sold.

As we can see in the pie chart, the largest percentage of wine buyers come from China, followed by the European Union and America. However, once you take into account the fact that the European Union consists of many different countries, the majority that Chinese buyers hold over American buyers becomes much more pronounced. There are also a small percentage of Japanese buyers, whereas the remaining four percent come from other countries.

Closer analysis of the table and chart would suggest that Chinese buyers have an appetite for French, Italian and Australian wine.

Writing Task 2

Online shopping used to be a far-fetched dream. However, today, it has become almost a daily routine. In my opinion, online shopping is very convenient especially for staple goods but I would still prefer to visit brick-and-mortar stores when it comes to more specific purchases such as clothing.

It is easy to see why online shopping is a great option when it comes to staples. With free or very cheap food deliveries, I no longer have to lug sacks of rice or bottles of detergent back from the supermarket to my home. Instead, the supermarket delivers right to my doorstep. Because the type of items I order rarely fluctuate from week to week, I can even place a recurring order to save time.

Furthermore, ordering online tends to be cheaper for two reasons. First, I can easily make a comparison across all supermarkets within minutes, from the comfort of my home. Second, many supermarkets would actually prefer selling goods online because they do not have to incur extra cost of renting a space. For this reason, there are often many online promotions or discounts to encourage more online spending.

Admittedly, online shopping has many benefits. But I still prefer visiting brick-and-mortar stores when it comes to more specific purchases such as clothing or even buying fruit and vegetables. For clothing, this is because images online can be misleading and also because I need to physically try on clothes in order to determine whether it fits me or not. For other items like fruit and vegetables, I still prefer being able to pick out my own produce to determine freshness and quantity.

To conclude, online shopping is very convenient for certain purchases, as it can save both time and cost. To an extent, it is also a fun and relaxing activity. However, I would still prefer brick-and-mortar stores for certain other purchases.

Appendix — References for Reading Passages

Books, Journal Articles, Newspaper Articles, Reports

Aaby, P (1998). Are Men Weaker or Do Their Sisters Talk Too Much? Sex Differences in Childhood Mortality and the Construction of Biological Differences. In AM Basu and P Aaby, eds., *Methods and Uses of Anthropological Demography*. Oxford: Clarendon Press, 223–245.

Alvar, J, Aparicio, P, Aseffa, A, Den Boer, M, Canavate, C, Dedet, J, Gradoni, L, Ter Horst, R, Lopez-Velez, R, and Moreno, J (2008). The Relationship between Leishmaniasis and AIDS: The Second 10 Years. *Clinical Microbiology Reviews* 21(2): 334–359.

Badaró, R, Carvalho, EM, Rocha, H, Queiroz, AC, and Jones, TC (1986). Leishmania Donovani: An Opportunistic Microbe Associated with Progressive Disease in Three Immunocompromised Patients. *The Lancet* 327(8482): 647–649.

Banks, SC, Lindenmayer, DB, McBurney, L, Blair, D, Knight, EJ, Blyton, MDJ (2011a). Kin Selection in Den Sharing Develops Under Limited Availability of Tree Hollows for a Forest Marsupial. *Proceedings of the Royal Society B*, 278(1791): 2768–2776.

Banks, SC, Blyton, MDJ, Blair, D, McBurney, L, and Lindenmayer, DB (2011b). Adaptive Responses and Disruptive Effects: How Major Wildfire Influences Kinship-Based Social Interactions in a Forest Marsupial. *Molecular Ecology* 21(3): 673–684.

Basile, Joseph and Joukowsky, Martha (2001). More Pieces in the Petra Great Temple Puzzle. *Bulletin of the American Schools of Oriental Research, No. 324. Nabataean Petra*, 43–58.

Basu, AM (1997). Underinvestment in Children: A Reorganization of the Evidence on the Determinants of Child Mortality. In GW Jones, ed., *The Continuing Demographic Transition*. Oxford: Clarendon Press, 307–331.

Berman JD (1988). Chemotherapy for Leishmaniasis: Biochemical Mechanisms, Clinical Efficacy, and Future Strategies. *Reviews in Infectious Diseases* 10(3): 560–586.

Blanche, KR (1992). Preliminary Observations on the Distribution and Abundance of Seaweed Flies (Diptera: Coelopidae) on Beaches in the Gosford District of New South Wales, Australia. *Australian Journal of Ecology* 17(1): 27–34.

Appendix — References for Reading Passages

Boyne, George (2002). Public and Private Management: What's the Difference?. *Journal of Management Studies* 39(1): 97–122.

Bronson, B (1977). Exchange at the Upstream and Downstream Ends. In Karl Hutterer, ed., *Economic Exchange and Social Interaction in Southeast Asia*. Ann Arbor: University of Michigan, 39–51.

Bryceson, A (2001). A Policy for Leishmaniasis with Respect to the Prevention and Control of Drug Resistance. *Tropical Medicine and International Health* 6(2): 928–934.

Bureau of Meteorology, Australia (2012). Latest Weather Observations for Garden Island. Available at http://www.bom.gov.au/products/IDW60901/IDW60901.95607.shtml (accessed 16 February 2012).

Cassidy, CM (1987). World View Conflict and Toddler Malnutrition: Change Agent Dilemma. In: Nancy Scheper-Hughes, ed., *Child Survival: Anthropological Perspectives on the Treatment and Maltreatment of Children*, 293–324.

Coale, Ansley J and Watkins, Susan Cotts (eds.) (1986). The Decline of Fertility in Europe: The Revised Proceedings of a Conference on the Princeton European Fertility Project.

Daley, Suzanne and Castle, Stephen (2012). "As European Union Beckons, Allude Fades for Wary Croatia." *The New York Times*.

Department of Transport, Western Australia (2009). Shoreline Movement Study, Point Peron, Rockingham. Department of Transport, Government of Western Australia, Fremantle.

Deringil, Selim (2011). *The Well-Protected Domains: Ideology and the Legitimation of Power in the Ottoman Empire 1876–1909*. London; New York: I.B. Tauris & Co Ltd.

Douglas, AE (2003). Coral Bleaching — How and Why?. *Marine Pollution Bulletin* 46(4): 385–392.

Effros RB, Boucher N, Porter V, Zhu X, Spaulding C, Walford RL, Kronenberg M, Cohen D, and Schächter F (1994). Decline in CD28+ T Cells in Centenarians and in Long-Term T Cell Cultures: A Possible Cause for both *in vivo* and *in vitro* Immunosenescence. *Experimental Gerontology* 29(6): 601–609.

Evered, Emine (2012). *Empire and Education under the Ottomans: Politics, Reform, and Resistance from the Tanzimat to the Young Turks*. London; New York: I.B. Tauris & Co Ltd.

Fortna, Bejamin C (2000). Islamic Morality in Late Ottoman "Secular" Schools. *International Journal of Middle East Studies* 32(3): 369–393.

Fortna, Bejanmin C (2002). Imperial Classroom: Islam, the State, and Education in the Late Ottoman Empire. Oxford: Oxford University Press.

Geertz, Clifford (1993). Deep Play: Notes on the Balinese Cockfight. In Clifford Geertz, *The Interpretation of Cultures: Selected Essays*. London: Fontana Press (Harper Collins), 412–453.

Gordon, DM (1986). Marine Communities of the Cape Peron, Shoalwater Bay and Warnbro Sound Region, Western Australia. Department of Conservation and Environment, Marine Impacts Branch, *Bulletin No. 264*, Perth.

Gottfried, H and O'Reilly, J (2002). Reregulating Breadwinner Models in Socially Conservative Welfare Systems: Comparing Germany and Japan. *Social Politics: International Studies in Gender, State & Society 9*, no. 1.

Grear, D, Samuel, M, Scribner, K, Weckworth, B, and Langenberg J (2010). Influence of Genetic Relatedness and Spatial Proximity on Chronic Wasting Disease Infection among Female White-Tailed Deer. *Journal of Applied Ecology* 47(3): 532–540.

Guerin, PJ, Olliaro, P, Sundar, S, Boelaert, M, Croft, SL, Desjeux, P, Wasunna, MK, and Bryceson, AD (2002). Visceral Leishmaniasis: Current Status of Control, Diagnosis, and Treatment, and a Proposed Research and Development Agenda. *The Lancet Infectious Disease* 2(8): 494–501.

Hall, HR, Kenyon, Frederick, and Alois, Musil (1924). The Rocks and Monuments of Petra: Discussion. *The Geographical Journal*, 63(4): 295–301.

Hammond, Philip C Jr (1960). Petra. *The Biblical Archaeologist* 23(1): 29–32.

Hoegh-Guldberg, Ove (1999). Climate Change, Coral Bleaching and the Future of the World's Coral Reefs. *Marine and Freshwater Research* 50(8): 839–866.

Hyndes, GA and Lavery, PS (2005). Does Transported Seagrass Provide an Important Trophic Link in Unvegetated, Nearshore Areas?. *Estuarine, Coastal and Shelf Science 63*: 633–643.

Jeronimo, SMB, de Queiroz Sousa, A, Pearson, RD, Guerrant, RL, Walker, DH, and Weller, PF, eds. (2006). *Tropical Infectious Diseases: Principles, Pathogens and Practice*. Edinburgh, Scotland: Elsevier, 1095–1113.

Joukowsky, Martha (2002). The Petra Great Temple: A Nabataean Architectural Miracle. *Near Eastern Archaeology* 65(4): 235–248.

Kahn, Louis I, and Twombly, Robert C (2003). *Louis Kahn: Essential Texts*. New York: W.W. Norton.

Kennedy, Alexander (1926). New Light on Petra. *The Geographical Journal* 67(4): 358–361.

Appendix — References for Reading Passages

Kennedy, Alexander (1924). The Rocks and Monuments of Petra. *The Geographical Journal* 63(4): 273–295.

Kirkman, H, and Kendrick, GA (1997). Ecological Significance and Commercial Harvesting of Drifting And Beachcast Macroalgae and Seagrasses in Australia: A Review. *Journal of Applied Phycology* 9(4): 311–326.

Kux, Stephan, and Ulf Sverdrup (2000). Fuzzy Borders and Adaptive Outsiders: Norway, Switzerland and the EU. *Journal of European Integration* 22(3): 237–270.

Lenanton, RCJ, Robertson, AI, and Hansen, JA (1982). Nearshore Accumulations of Detached Macrophytes as Nursery Areas for Fish. *Marine Ecology Progress Series* 9: 51–57.

Leruth, Benjamin (2013). Differentiated Integration and the Nordic States: The Case of Norway. ISL Working Paper 2013:2, University of Agder.

Levine, Neil (2009). *Modern Architecture: Representation and Reality*. New Haven, Connecticut: Yale University Press.

Levi-Strauss, C (1969). Nature and Culture. In C Levi-Strauss, *The Elementary Structures of Kinship*. Boston: Beacon Press, 3–10.

Lewis, Jane (1992). Gender and the Development of Welfare Regimes. *Journal of European Social Policy* 2(3): 165.

Lord, DA and Associates Pty Ltd (2001). The State of Cockburn Sound: A Pressure-State-Response Report. Cockburn Sound Management Council, Report No. 01/187/1.

Maltezou, HC (2010). Drug Resistance in Visceral Leishmaniasis. *Journal of Biomedicine and Biotechnology* Volume 2010: Article ID 617521.

Manning, Martha (2002). *The Common Thread*. New York: HarperCollins.

Marx, Karl (1887). *Capital: A Critique of Political Economy, Volume 1*. Available at: https://www.marxists.org/archive/marx/works/download/pdf/Capital-Volume-I.pdf (accessed November 14, 2014).

Merrill, Michael, and Kahn, Louis I (2010). *Louis Kahn: Drawing to Find Out: The Dominican Motherhouse and the Patient Search for Architecture*. Baden: Lars Muller.

Mosley, WH and Chen, LC (1984). An Analytical Framework for the Study of Child Survival in Developing Countries. *Population and Development Review* 10 (Supplement: Child Survival: Strategies for Research): 25–45.

Murray, Michael (1975). Comparing Public and Private Management: An Exploratory Essay. *Public Administration Review* 35(4): 364–371.

Pettersen, Per Arnt, Todal Jenssen, Anders, and Listhaug, Ola (1996). The 1994 EU Referendum in Norway: Continuity and Change. *Scandinavian Political Studies* 19(3): 257–281.

Pollard, AH, Yusuf, F, and Pollard GN (1990). *Demographics Techniques*. Oxford, UK: Pergamon Press.

Potter, S, Goldblatt, D, Kiloh, M, and Lewis, P (1997). *Democratization*. Milton Keynes: Polity Press.

Robertson, AL, and Lenanton, RCJ (1984). Fish Community Structure and Food Chain Dynamics in the Surfzone of Sandy Beaches: The Role of Detached Macrophyte Detritus. *Journal of Experimental Marine Biology and Ecology* 84: 265–283.

Rodrik, D (2005). Growth Strategies. In Philippe Aghion and Steven Durlauf, eds., *Handbook of Economic Growth*, Volume 1, First Edition, 967–1014. Amsterdam: Elsevier.

Rolland-Berger, Laurence, Rolland, Xavier, Griever, Caroline W, Monjour, Loic (1991). Immunoblot Analysis of the Humoral Immune Response to Leishmania Donovani Infantum Polypeptides in Human Visceral Leishmaniasis. *Journal of Clinical Microbiology* 29(7): 1429–1435.

Roy, Delphine (2012). Unpaid Domestic Work: 60 Billion Hours in 2010. *INSEE Premier* 2012(1423).

Saad-Filho, A (2005). From Washington to Post-Washington Consensus: Neoliberal Agendas for Economic Development. In A Saad-Filho and D Johnston, eds., *Neoliberalism: A Critical Reader*. London: Pluto Press.

Sciarini, Pascal, and Listhaug, Ola (1997). Single Cases or a Unique Pair? The Swiss and Norwegian "No" to Europe. *Journal of Common Market Studies* 35(3): 407–438.

Sidel, John T (1998). Macet Total: Logics of Circulation and Accumulation in the Demise of Indonesia's New Order Indonesia, Vol. 66, Oct., 1998 (Oct., 1998), pp. 158-195

Singh N (2006). Drug Resistance Mechanisms in Clinical Isolates of Leishmania Donovani. Indian Journal of Medical Research 123(3): 411–422.

Somel, Selcuk Aksin (2001). The Modernization of Public Education in the Ottoman Empire 1839-1908 — Islamization, Autocracy and Discipline. Leidin: Brill.

Steedman, RK and PD Craig. (1983). Wind-driven circulation of Cockburn Sound. Australian Journal of Freshwater Research 34: 187–212

Appendix — References for Reading Passages

Strathern M (1980). 'No Nature, no Culture: The Hagen Case'. In: P. MacCormack & M. Strathern, Nature, Culture and Gender. Cambridge: Cambridge University Press, pp. 174-222.
Tilly, C (1985). "War Making and State Making as Organized Crime", in Evans, P., D. Rueschemeyer and T. Skocpol (eds.), *Bringing the State Back in*. New York: Cambridge University Press.
Waldron, I (1998). "Sex Differences in Infant and Early Childhood Mortality: Major Causes of Death and Possible Biological Causes." In: *Too Young to Die: Gender or Genes?*. UN Dept of Economic and Social Affairs, Population Division, pp. 64–83.
World Economic Forum, 2012 Global Gender Gap Report 23.
Zeitler, John P (1993). Excavations and Surveys in Petra, 1989–90. Syria, T. 70, Fasc. 1/2, pp. 255–261.

Multimedia

Dir. Tony Britten (2010). *Gilbert and Sullivan: A Motley Pair*. DVD. Capriol Films Ltd.

Webpages

http://ec.europa.eu/enlargement/policy/conditions-membership/index_en.htm.
http://english.cntv.cn/special/moutaiprice/homepage/
http://info.worldbank.org/governance/wgi/index.aspx#home
http://inventors.about.com/od/cstartinventions/a/credit_cards.htm
http://motherboard.vice.com/blog/dr-robert-white-transplanted-first-monkey-head
http://news.discovery.com/history/us-history/earliest-french-wine-making-discovered-130603.htm
http://news.nationalgeographic.com/news/2004/07/0721_040721_ancientwine.html
http://purecircle.com/products/stevia-leaf/
http://vosdroits.service-public.fr/F15292.xhtml
http://www.ambafrance-us.org/spip.php?article555
http://www.bbc.com/news/science-environment-22758119
http://www.cancer.gov/about-cancer/causes-prevention/risk/diet/artificial-sweeteners-fact-sheet
http://www.cdc.gov/parasites/leishmaniasis/

Appendix — References for Reading Passages

http://www.coca-cola.co.uk/stories/health/choice-and-information/the-sweet-news-about-stevia-extract-our-zero-calorie-sweetener/
http://www.coralwatch.org/web/guest/coral-bleaching
http://www.creditcards.com/credit-card-news/credit-cards-history-1264.php
http://www.europa.admin.ch/themen/00499/index.html?lang=en
http://www.ft.com/intl/cms/s/0/a89532b4-9bc2-11e4-b6cc-00144feabdc0.html?siteedition=intl
http://www.gbrmpa.gov.au/managing-the-reef/threats-to-the-reef/climate-change/what-does-this-mean-for-species/corals/what-is-coral-bleaching
http://www.independent.co.uk/news/science/man-undergoing-head-transplant-could-experience-something-a-lot-worse-than-death-says-neurological-expert-10164423.html
http://www.japantimes.co.jp/text/nn20120512a1.html
http://www.languagetrainers.co.uk/blog/2007/09/24/top-10-hand-gestures/comment-page-2/
http://www.lsuagcenter.com/en/communications/publications/agmag/Archive/2002/Fall/Sugarcane+History.htm
http://www.mda.org/disease/spinal-muscular-atrophy/signs-and-symptoms
http://www.mof.go.jp/budget/fiscal_condition/related_data/sy014/sy014f_a.htm
http://www.nature.org/ourinitiatives/urgentissues/coralreefs/coral-reefs-coral-bleaching-what-you-need-to-know.xml
http://www.news.com.au/technology/science/terminally-ill-man-set-to-be-first-to-undergo-the-worlds-first-full-head-transplant/story-fn5fsgyc-1227301771920
http://www.nytimes.com/2010/10/12/world/europe/12iht-fffrance.html?pagewanted=all&_r=1&
http://www.oecd-ilibrary.org/economics/oecd-factbook-2013/total-fertility-rates_factbook-2013-table9-en
http://www.sucden.com/statistics/1_world-sugar-production
http://www.sugarnutrition.org.uk/history-of-sugar.aspx
http://www.sugarnutrition.org.uk/Worldwide-sugar-production-and-consumption-data.aspx
http://www.telegraph.co.uk/expat/expatnews/6406138/Bordeauxs-winemakers-reconstruct-the-past-to-charm-tourists.html?mobile=basic
http://www.telegraph.co.uk/finance/newsbysector/retailandconsumer/10414807/Five-things-to-know-about-the-global-wine-industry.html
http://www.thewinecellarinsider.com/wine-topics/wine-educational-questions/wine-grapes-vineyard-france-classifications-appellation-law/

Appendix — References for Reading Passages

http://www.who.int/leishmaniasis/about_disease/en/
http://www.who.int/leishmaniasis/visceral_leishmaniasis/en/
http://www.winegeeks.com/articles/139
http://www.wsj.com/articles/credit-card-issuers-are-charging-higher-1413156229
https://pepsinext.ca/
https://www.wto.org/english/thewto_e/whatis_e/tif_e/agrm7_e.htm

www.ingramcontent.com/pod-product-compliance
Lightning Source LLC
Chambersburg PA
CBHW061931220426
43662CB00012B/1866